PC MAGAZINE
C

LAB NOTES

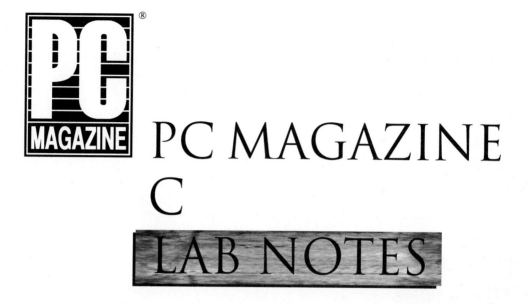

PC MAGAZINE C

LAB NOTES

BOB FLANDERS AND
MICHAEL HOLMES

ZIFF-DAVIS PRESS
EMERYVILLE, CALIFORNIA

Series Editor	Robert L. Hummel
Editor	Carol Henry
Technical Reviewer	Robert L. Hummel
Project Coordinator	Sheila McGill
Proofreader	Pat Mannion
Cover Design	Tom Morgan/Blue Design, San Francisco
Book Design	Tom Morgan/Blue Design, San Francisco
Technical Illustration	Cherie Plumlee Computer Graphics & Illustration
Word Processing	Howard Blechman and Cat Haglund
Page Layout	Sidney Davenport and M.D. Barrera
Indexer	Mark Kmetzko

This book was produced on a Macintosh IIfx, with the following applications: FrameMaker®, Microsoft® Word, MacLink®*Plus*, Aldus® FreeHand™, Adobe Photoshop™, and Collage Plus™.

Ziff-Davis Press
5903 Christie Avenue
Emeryville, CA 94608

ISBN 1-56276-063-7
Manufactured in the United States of America
⊕ The paper used in this book exceeds the EPA requirements for post-consumer recycled paper.
10 9 8 7 6 5 4 3 2

CONTENTS AT A GLANCE

TABLE OF CONTENTS

FOREWORD

PC Magazine C Lab Notes is the most recent addition to Ziff-Davis Press's unique new Lab Notes series. What exactly is the Lab Notes series? Simply put, it is a new breed of programming book that embodies one of the oldest and most effective teaching principles: The best way to learn is by doing. But a Lab Notes book doesn't teach just programming—it teaches the problem-solving approach to programming. Each book in the Lab Notes series is a collection of utility programs, written in the author's native programming language, that address real-world problems that you're likely to encounter as you work. For example, in this book the NETRUN utility helps alleviate a problem experienced by most LAN users: the inability to submit commands on one network node for execution on another computer. As you work through the process of creating NETRUN, you not only solve the problem, but you also learn one of the fundamentals of network programming: passing messages between network nodes.

A typical discussion begins by examining why the problem exists, including shortcomings in the existing solutions. Next, a clear outline of the problem is developed. This done, the author proposes an approach to solving the problem using the resources available. Finally, the program is developed step by step, with clear explanations presented along the way. The author explains not only why certain choices were made, but also points out alternatives and areas where the program could be expanded and improved. The complete source code listing for each utility appears with each explanation. Annotated liberally with comments and explanations, the source code used in the programs is contained on a disk that accompanies each book, saving hours of input and debugging time.

Each utility in a Lab Notes book is completely independent. You'll find that you can examine each utility in the order it's presented, or skip around to select a program that deals with your specific topic of interest.

The Lab Notes series is well suited to some unique programming situations. Experienced programmers, for example, who wish to come up to speed quickly in a second language will find that the Lab Notes' blend of theory and practical code can reduce transition time. Lab Notes books are also ideal as textbooks for small or large programming classes, such as those sponsored by user groups. These groups can study the examples together and stimulate personal development by encouraging individuals to modify the programs and present them to the group.

The emphasis of the Lab Notes series is squarely on bringing practical program techniques to bear on everyday programming problems. Programs are not presented as a take it or leave it proposition. Instead, you'll find yourself a participant in every step of the process from the recognition of the problem right through to the creation and implementation of the solution.

Robert L. Hummel
Series Editor

ACKNOWLEDGMENTS

There are a great number of people who deserve recognition and thanks for the help and support they have provided. First, had it not been for *PC Magazine*, this book would have had a different author, so I thank Trudy Neuhaus for letting me contribute to the "Productivity" section of the magazine.

While writing the book, several individuals have unselfishly shared their insight, offered their support, and waited patiently as I muddled through the first chapters and found my footing. I offer hearty thanks to Cindy Hudson, Cheryl Holzaepfel, Sheila McGill, Carol Henry, and Dan Brodnitz. Also, thanks to Karen Swim of the Halifax city government and Dr. Peter L. Petrakis of Life Sciences Editorial Services for his help with ZCLOCK. (Dr. Petrakis' TIMESET utility is what ZCLOCK could be with a few years more work.)

On a more personal note, there are those who have stood by me through thick and thin. I appreciate and thank my Mom and Dad for urging me to pursue a career in computers. I also thank my friends Harry Selfe, Judy Selfe, and Shelley Matthews, who offered me guidance when I needed it. Sincere thanks to Claudette Moore of Moore Literary Agency, who didn't let the false starts dissuade her. And thanks to my coauthor, Michael Holmes, whose attention to detail turned good ideas into excellent utilities.

Special thanks to a man who gave me a start at *PC Magazine*, who was the technical editor for this book, and who has been a good friend—Rob Hummel. Thanks, Rob.

Finally, saving the best for last, thanks to my wife Carol and my kids Elise (Hi Sweetie!), Jonathan (Hey Bud!), and Ian (How are ya doing, Little Guy?)—thank you, and I love you!

Bob Flanders

A project of this size is not just the work of the authors. Long days and even longer nights do not allow us to take the glory which should be shared. I would like to acknowledge the work of those whose efforts were behind the scenes. First, thanks to Rob Hummel for his technical editing and perseverance to see Bob and me over the early speed bumps and through to completion; to Cindy Hudson at Ziff-Davis Press and Claudette Moore at Moore Literary Agency for their faith that we could do this; and to Carol Henry and Sheila McGill for their help in copy preparation. And I would like to give special thanks to Trudy Neuhaus at *PC Magazine* for all her help over the years.

I also would like to thank Bob Flanders for taking the leadership and for taking on a project like this, and also for having the persistence in working with me to complete it. Bob, thanks for being a good friend.

I would also like to recognize Harry and Judy Selfe, whose counsel has helped me in more than just the technical areas, and my Mom and Dad for encouraging me in all my endeavors. Last but certainly not least, I thank my wife, Roxane, and my three boys, Matthew, Jeremy, and Zachary for supporting me through the whole book process.

Michael Holmes

INTRODUCTION

Visit any bookstore and you'll find no lack of books on C and C programming. Volumes on the language, program structure, and algorithmic theory line the shelves. Yet nowhere will you find, in our experience, a book that successfully marries all three of these concepts. In a nutshell, that was the goal for this book. *PC Magazine C Lab Notes* is a collection of real-world programming problems and solutions, written in C for real C programmers.

Each of the programs presented fulfills a specific utility function and provides an example of how to use certain programming techniques in solving problems. Many of these techniques are encapsulated in C routines, which you can extract from the utility, modify for your purposes, and insert into programs of your choice. Although the programs are not the smallest or fastest, they are clear and easy to modify. In fact, modifications are encouraged by suggestions at the end of each chapter.

■ WHO THIS BOOK IS FOR

Programmers of all levels will benefit from this book's problem-solving approach. Experienced programmers learning a second language will appreciate the clear documentation of advanced utilities. Intermediate programmers will gain the skills to begin developing programs of their own. The hands-on approach of this book allows novices to learn programming techniques and gain practical experience.

■ WHAT YOU'LL FIND IN THIS BOOK

Each of the nine chapters in this book examines a useful program, such as ZCLOCK, which sets the internal clock of your PC to match a cesium clock located at the United States Naval Observatory in Washington, D.C. The program in Chapter 2, INFORMER, simplifies the task of analyzing programs by collecting and reporting statistics about a program that you specify. CHKSTRUC, in Chapter 8, helps you pinpoint problems in the logical structure of a DOS drive. Feel free to skip to the chapters about the utilities that interest you most.

Chapters are broken into three sections. The first section introduces the program and explains its function and use. When appropriate, this section also discusses setting up the DOS environment to run the utility.

The second section discusses the program's internal structure. In this section, we also examine why certain algorithms were used and others were disqualified.

The last section of each chapter contains the listing of the utility's source code. The source code listing is compatible with Borland C++ 3.0.

In some cases, additional information is presented at the end of the chapter in the form of an "Endnote." An endnote discusses a particular algorithm, method, procedure, or condition that you should be aware of, or that you may be interested in, when exploring the inner workings of the utility.

■ THE COMPANION DISK

At the back of the book, you will find a disk containing the source code and executable files for the utilities. The instructions for installing the disk are presented in the appendix.

■ CONVENTIONS

As you examine the source code for each of the programs, you will notice that they share certain common traits. First, the printed source (and associated discussions) refer to features and functions of Borland C++ 3.0. (Just before going to press, we also compiled and tested the programs under Borland C++ 3.1.) Although the Microsoft C/C++ 7.0-compatible source code is provided on the disk, the programs were written and debugged with Borland's compiler.

Where possible, we compiled the utilities in small or tiny model. Only when a utility needed access to more memory did we compile in compact model. (In no case was either large or huge model used.) Of course, we designed the programs to work in the MS-DOS environment, and tested them in a DOS box under Windows 3.1. Aside from timing considerations, they should also work in DOS under OS/2 or Desqview.

Since the programs are small, limited-function utilities, the source code for each is presented as a single file with all of the support routines enclosed within that file. Each of the programs also contain a significant number of global variables referenced by several routines within each program. The use of global variables is not a recommended programming practice when writing large, complex programs (or systems). However, the judicious use of global variables in small programs can decrease the number of arguments passed when calling a routine, significantly reducing the complexity of the code.

In keeping with the Lab Notes series philosophy, the programs are implemented in a single language, C, and all functions are implemented in C, even when another language, such as assembler, would be more appropriate. When using this book, there is no assembly required.

As you work with the utilities, you'll notice that in all of the programs, some obvious function is left out, or not completely implemented (such as insert mode in CAL.) This is intended to encourage you to try your hand at modifying the utility to add the missing function or feature.

We hope you will find the utilities, source code, and book as interesting and informative when using them as we did when writing them.

1

SETTING THE CLOCK WITH ZCLOCK

ZCLOCK sets the date and time in the internal clock of your PC to match the reading from the cesium clock at the United States Naval Observatory in Washington, D.C.

One of the most basic functions performed by today's personal computers is keeping track of the date and time. Unfortunately, even the cheapest wrist watch generally keeps time better than most PCs. On occasion you will find a machine whose clock actually reflects the true time, but most are fast or slow by several seconds a day. And after a few days, the accumulated deviation can be several minutes. If your machine is used for time-critical or time-sensitive projects, this can mean the difference between success and failure.

ZCLOCK helps you alleviate this problem by setting your computer's clock to the time reported by a cesium clock located at the United States Naval Observatory in Washington, D.C. Using a modem, ZCLOCK dials the observatory's number, receives a one-line message containing the date and time, and sets the computer's clock to that date and time.

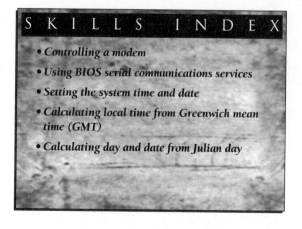

S K I L L S   I N D E X

- *Controlling a modem*
- *Using BIOS serial communications services*
- *Setting the system time and date*
- *Calculating local time from Greenwich mean time (GMT)*
- *Calculating day and date from Julian day*

■ USING ZCLOCK

ZCLOCK allows you to specify your own time zone. The program has easy-to-use default settings for the serial port where your modem is located, and the telephone number to dial; if your settings don't match the defaults, you can change them. The syntax for the ZCLOCK command is

```
ZCLOCK zone [port [phone-number]]
```

You must supply the *zone* argument so that ZCLOCK can correctly set the time on your computer. The serial *port* and *phone-number* arguments default to COM1 and 1-202-653-0351, respectively. If you enter the command ZCLOCK with no arguments, ZCLOCK displays a brief message describing its options, and returns to DOS.

The *zone* argument tells ZCLOCK the time zone in which you are located. For example, most of the East Coast of the United States uses eastern standard time (EST) or eastern daylight time (EDT), depending on the time of year. Table 1.1 shows the time zones recognized by ZCLOCK.

TABLE 1.1
List of Time Zones Recognized by ZCLOCK

Time Zone	Standard	Daylight
Atlantic	**AST**	**ADT**
Eastern	**EST**	**EDT**
Central	**CST**	**CDT**
Mountain	**MST**	**MDT**
Pacific	**PST**	**PDT**
Alaskan	**KST**	**KDT**
Hawaii-Aleutian	**HST**	**HDT**
Samoan	**SST**	**SDT**
Yukon (now Alaskan)	**YST**	**YDT**
Universal coordinated time (Greenwich mean time)	**UTC or GMT**	**Not used**

You may specify to which serial port the modem is connected, via the *port* argument. The format for *port* is COM*n*, where *n* may be 1 through 4. If you specify a serial port that does not exist, ZCLOCK issues an appropriate error message and returns to the DOS prompt. ZCLOCK requires that you have a modem that uses the standard Hayes AT command set and is capable of communicating at 1200 bits per second (bps).

The *phone-number* argument tells ZCLOCK the telephone number to use to call the Naval Observatory. If you need to specify *phone-number,* you must specify the serial port, even if your modem is connected via COM1. There are only three circumstances in which the *phone-number* argument is required: when you must use a telephone number that differs from the default, when you must use a different dialing pattern, or when you must use specific pulse or tone dialing.

The default value for *phone-number* used by ZCLOCK is in standard long-distance number format (1-202-653-0351), and should work from most locations; however, when you run ZCLOCK in your location, you may need to use a different telephone number. For example, if you run ZCLOCK on a local telephone line within Washington, D.C., you do not need the 1-202- portion of the telephone number. Let's assume you are in Washington, D.C., your modem is connected via COM2, and it is midsummer (eastern daylight time). You would use the following command:

```
ZCLOCK EDT COM2 653-0351
```

In some situations, you may require a dialing pattern different from the default used by ZCLOCK. For example, if your modem is on COM1, and you call from an office in Colorado Springs during the winter (mountain standard time) via telephone equipment that requires you to dial 9 to get an outside line, you would issue this command:

```
ZCLOCK MST COM1 9,1-202-653-0351
```

Although most modern telephone equipment accepts tone or pulse dialing, some older equipment only accepts pulse dialing. You can specify tone or pulse dialing by preceding the *phone-number* argument with a *T* for *tone* or a *P* for *pulse*. For example, to pulse dial via the modem connected to COM3 when calling from Richardson, Texas, during the summer (central daylight time), you would enter this command:

```
ZCLOCK CDT COM3 P1-202-653-0351
```

The modem's AT command to dial a number is ATD*n*, where *n* is the telephone number to dial. ZCLOCK always supplies the ATD portion of this command. If you do not specify the *phone-number* argument, ZCLOCK replaces *n* in the ATD*n* command with 1-202-653-0351. Otherwise, ZCLOCK replaces *n* with the string specified by *phone-number*.

As ZCLOCK runs, it displays a series of messages indicating its progress. If at any point ZCLOCK is unable to continue, it displays an appropriate error message and returns to DOS. Otherwise, the final message displayed by ZCLOCK shows the time and date set into the computer's clock. Figure 1.1 shows the typical output from a successful execution of the ZCLOCK utility.

<table>
<tr><td>FIGURE 1.1</td></tr>
<tr><td>Sample output</td></tr>
<tr><td>from ZCLOCK</td></tr>
</table>

```
C:\ZCLOCK>ZCLOCK EDT COM1 9,202-653-0351
ZCLOCK 1.00 • Copyright (c) 1992, Bob Flanders and Michael Holmes
PC Magazine C Lab Notes • Set CMOS clock from the National Observatory

Initializing modem
Dialing observatory
Connected to host system
Setting clock to: Wednesday, 04/29/1992 at 16:54:44, the 120th day of the year

C:\ZCLOCK>
```

■ INSIDE ZCLOCK

ZCLOCK is implemented as a simple, four-step procedure, with each step reflected as a call from main(). The steps are initialization, serial port setup, calling and connecting to the Naval Observatory, and processing the messages received from the observatory.

■ Initialization

Program initialization is carried out by the initialization() routine. During the initialization step, ZCLOCK installs a control break handler and checks the command line arguments. The control break handler lets you halt ZCLOCK's execution by pressing the Ctrl-Break or Ctrl-C key-combination, thereby allowing ZCLOCK the opportunity to disconnect the line should you cancel the program after it has connected to the observatory.

ZCLOCK's main() routine calls parse_parms() to perform an initial check of the command line arguments. Specifically, parse_parms() scans each command line argument, looking for any option starting with a forward slash (/). (ZCLOCK accepts only the /? option.) If parse_parms() finds the /? option, it displays the help message and exits to DOS. If parse_parms() finds any other / option, it displays a message indicating the incorrect option and returns to DOS.

In the course of searching for options, parse_parms() also initializes the parms_array. Each entry in the parms_array points at the start of one command line argument that does not start with a forward slash (/). Also, if an argument contains a forward slash, the slash and all subsequent characters are stripped from that argument. The starting address of the argument is then placed in the next entry of parms_array.

After all command line arguments have been checked, parse_parms() returns the number of non-option arguments found (that is, arguments that do not start with a forward slash).

The initialization() routine checks the value returned by parse_parms() to ensure that you included at least one argument on the command line. The first argument (*zone*) is not optional.

■ **VALIDATING THE TIME ZONE**

The validate_timezone() routine ensures that the first command line argument identifies a valid time zone. Initially, validate_timezone() sets all the characters in the argument to uppercase, and then checks if the argument specifies Yukon time zone (YST/YDT). If so, the argument is changed to Alaskan time zone (KST/KDT).

Next, validate_timezone() checks to ensure that the argument contains exactly three characters and matches an entry in either the time_zones string or GMT_zones string. If validate_timezone() finds no matching entry, it displays an error message and returns to DOS. Otherwise, if the entry is not GMT or UTC, it calculates the index of the matching entry by using the offset from the beginning of time_zones, and uses the index to calculate the zone_offset variable. ZCLOCK uses zone_offset to determine local time from the information sent by the Naval Observatory.

ZCLOCK uses the strstr() library function to validate the time zone argument. Since validate_timezone() ensures that the argument is exactly three characters long, and the entries in the time_zones and GMT_zones strings are separated by blanks, there is no way to enter an invalid argument that will be mistaken for a valid one.

Unfortunately, however, this implementation also has a disadvantage. Because the index is used to calculate the zone_offset value, the position within the table of the entry matching the argument is of paramount importance. Should the entries become rearranged, an invalid time would be generated for any entries in an incorrect position. Also, adding new entries requires significantly more work unless the entries can be added to the end of the table.

This is clearly seen in the code used to implement support for the Yukon time zones (YST/YDT) and Universal coordinated time (UTC/GMT). The validate_timezone() routine checks for these entries right after setting the argument to uppercase. If the argument requests Yukon time, the argument's first character is changed to a K, effectively changing it to Alaskan time zone. If Universal coordinated time (or Greenwich mean time) is requested, validate_timezone() leaves zone_offset at zero, and the date and time of your computer is set to the date and time reported by the Naval Observatory clock.

Although the algorithm does have these shortcomings, it is unlikely that ZCLOCK would be used outside of the United States due to the cost of calling the observatory. Nevertheless, an alternative implementation is to use an array of structures containing the time zone names, and an absolute offset from the time reported by the observatory.

■ **VALIDATING THE SERIAL PORT**

The initialization() routine next calls validate_port() to validate the serial port argument. The *port* argument may be omitted, or specified as COM*n* or COM*n*:. If specified, the *n* must be replaced with a number in the range 1 to 4.

The validate_port() routine first looks for a serial port argument specified on the command line, and if there is one, checks to make sure the argument is formatted properly. Next, validate_port() checks the BIOS data area in low memory to ensure that the specified serial port is valid. The BIOS data area resides at the fixed address, 0x40:0. The first four words of this area make up the communications port table. When the computer is initialized, the BIOS fills in this table with the base I/O addresses of the serial communications controllers. If an entry contains zero, the hardware corresponding to the serial port is not installed. The validate_port() routine retrieves the entry from the BIOS data area, and saves it for future use.

■ **What's an MCR?**

Standard PC serial communications ports are based on a device known as a UART (Universal Asynchronous Receiver/Transmitter). The PC communicates with the UART by exchanging data through a range of I/O ports. (In the UART documentation, the I/O ports are called registers, which should not be confused with the CPU registers.) Some of the UART registers are read-only, providing information about the current state of the UART. Others are read-write, and are used to send data, receive data, or change the operating state of the UART.

Of particular interest to ZCLOCK is the MCR, or *modem control register*. The MCR is a read/write register on the UART, and the values in this register allow the program to control certain signals sent to the modem. ZCLOCK must control two of these signals: DTR (Data Terminal Ready) and RTS (Request to Send).

> ■ The DTR signal tells the modem that the PC is on line and ready to communicate. If you properly configure the modem, it will only maintain connection to the observatory's modem while ZCLOCK leaves the DTR signal on. During program termination, ZCLOCK always clears DTR. See the Endnote "Setting Up the Modem" for more information.

- In many modems, RTS tells the modem whether it can send data to the PC. Although this function varies from modem to modem, ZCLOCK accommodates modems that honor the signal by always setting RTS on.

ZCLOCK controls DTR and RTS by direct I/O to the MCR, because BIOS provides no support for controlling the MCR. The last function that validate_port() performs is calculating the address of the MCR, and saving it for future use.

- **PREPARING THE SERIAL PORT**
After completing initialization(), main() sets up the serial port by calling set_up_comm(). The set_up_comm() routine clears the DTR (and thereby ensures that the modem disconnects from any existing connection); uses the BIOS to initialize the serial port to 1200 bps, no parity, 8 data bits, and 1 stop bit; and raises the DTR and RTS signals.

The set_up_comm() routine clears DTR by reading the contents of the MCR, clearing the appropriate bit using a bitwise AND, and writing the new value back to the MCR. Because set_up_comm() uses the #define value DTR, and because this value includes both DTR and RTS, set_up_comm() also clears RTS.

- **POLLING VERSUS INTERRUPTS**
There are two general methodologies used when writing programs that perform serial communications: *polling software* and *interrupt-driven software*. Polling software checks the serial port at regular intervals to determine if a character has arrived. Interrupt-driven software sets up the UART so it generates a hardware interrupt each time a character arrives, allowing the interrupt handler to retrieve the character from the UART.

Although most general-purpose communications programs use the more efficient interrupt-driven method, ZCLOCK uses the polling method. ZCLOCK uses polling because it is a single-purpose program that has no other function except to retrieve the required information from the observatory and process the response. Also, the communications line runs at a relatively slow speed (1200 bps). Implementing the interrupt-driven methodology would simply be overkill in this situation.

At the very end of set_up_comm(), there is a call to the wait() routine, which accepts the number of timer ticks as an argument. A PC clock generates a timer tick approximately 18.2 times per second. The call to wait(9) in set_up_comm() causes a delay of approximately one-half second, allowing both the modem and UART time to "settle" after changing DTR and RTS.

■ **Calling the Observatory**

Having set up the serial port, ZCLOCK is ready to make the call to the observatory, by invoking the place_call() routine. The place_call() routine first builds the AT command string used to dial the observatory. The command string starts with ATD, followed by 12026530351 if you entered no *phone-number* argument on the command line. Otherwise, place_call() inserts the exact contents of the *phone-number* argument after the ATD to form the dial command. For example, in Figure 1.1, the third argument shown is 9,202-653-0351, causing place_call() to build the command ATD9,202-653-0351.

After building the dial command, place_call() sends the command ATE0V1X1 to the modem. This command tells the modem not to echo the commands sent to it, and to use verbose responses such as OK and CONNECT. ZCLOCK then waits for one second, giving the modem ample time to process the command.

ZCLOCK uses the send_string() routine to send commands to the modem. Since the UART can only accept one character at a time, send_string() enters a while loop, sending the command string to the modem character by character as the UART becomes ready to process each character.

While the serial port is sending a character, send_string() calls kbhit(), which checks if any key has been pressed. ZCLOCK does not care if a key has been pressed, but the kbhit() routine allows DOS to gain control momentarily, to see if a control break has been entered. If you do not enter a control break, and the serial port completes sending a character, send_string() sends the next character from the string. The loop continues until all characters in the string have been sent, or a control break has been entered, or an error comes back from the serial port. If an error occurs, send_string() returns the error value to the calling routine.

At this point, ZCLOCK sends the command that causes the modem to dial the observatory. Using send_string(), place_call() sends the dial command that was built earlier. Unlike the previous modem command, place_call() takes an active interest in the modem's response to the dial command. Using get_line(), place_call() waits for a response from the modem. After dialing, the modem will respond with either a CONNECT message indicating that the observatory has answered, or another message (such as NO CARRIER) indicating that the connection was not successful. If any other message except a CONNECT is received, ZCLOCK displays a message indicating that it could not connect with the observatory, and returns to DOS.

■ READING THE DATA

The get_line() routine uses a for loop to retrieve the characters from the serial port. Note, however, that between characters, get_line() restores the value of the modem control register (MCR). It seems that certain versions of the BIOS clear the RTS signal after receiving a character, causing occasional lost characters with some modems. Restoring the MCR between characters forces the RTS signal to remain high. If get_line() has not received a carriage return-terminated line from the modem within 45 seconds, it displays an error message and returns to DOS.

The Naval Observatory continuously sends out time messages. As soon as a connection with the observatory is established, messages start arriving at the rate of one per second. See the Endnote "The Observatory Messages" for more information on the format and content of the message. ZCLOCK's main() routine calls process_message() to receive and process a message from the observatory. As shown in the above-referenced Endnote, the message has a very strict format. The process_message() routine calls get_line() to receive a message from the observatory. It then uses several tests to ensure that the message meets the required format. If the message fails the format check, it is rejected, and process_message() calls get_line() again to retrieve the next message. ZCLOCK will make a maximum of 30 attempts to get a valid message from the observatory; under most circumstances, the program correctly receives and processes the first message.

After receiving a valid message, process_message() uses sscanf() to translate the ASCII characters in the message into binary values. Of these values, the most interesting is the first one, the Julian day. The Julian day is a five-digit number representing the current date as a number of days since the beginning of recorded time (or, January 1, 4713 B.C.). Actually, the five-digit number, when added to the value 2,400,000, represents the current day, and will do so for approximately 140 years. Note that the value 1,721,118 represents the date March 1, 1 B.C.

The process_message() routine invokes jul2greg() to translate the Julian day into today's date. First, jul2greg() subtracts out the March 1, 1 B.C. base date from today's Julian day value, and then calculates the day of the week for today. Next, jul2greg() calculates the century in which the day occurs. In 1992, the resulting century value is 19. Knowing the century, jul2greg() removes the appropriate number of days from March 1, 1 B.C., to the start of the century represented, and runs through a series of calculations to determine the year within the century, the month, and the day. Finally, jul2greg() adjusts the month, because the base date falls in March, 1 B.C.

When process_message() calls jul2greg(), it passes a series of pointers as arguments. Then jul2greg() fills in the variables referenced by these pointers with the calculated information, and in the process, actually fills in the structure needed to set the DOS date.

The structure representing the time is filled in by process_message() itself. As this happens, process_message() applies the offset derived from the time zone argument supplied on the command line, as calculated by validate_timezone().

■ **ON MY MARK**
In many movies, you will see two or more people synchronize their watches with a line such as, "Okay... on my mark, it's 11:53... MARK!" This is the approach the Naval Observatory takes, too. When the observatory sends the time message, it is an announcement of the *approaching* time and date: "In a moment it is going to be such-and-such a time and date." But the time and date do not actually occur until the observatory says, "Mark!"—and in this case, "Mark!" is a line consisting of a single asterisk.

After placing all of the essential data in the appropriate variable, process_message() issues a get_line() to retrieve the "Mark!" message. If the next message does not start with an asterisk, process_message() attempts to receive and process another observatory time and date message. When it does receive the "Mark!" message, process_message() calls the _dos_setdate() and _dos_settime() functions to set the current date and time into your system clock, displays a message telling you what time it is, and returns to DOS. And you can set your watch by that!

■ ## SUMMARY
ZCLOCK demonstrates a methodology for interfacing with external devices via a serial port. ZCLOCK also overcomes some of the limitations imposed by the BIOS when dealing with serial ports (such as directly setting and clearing RTS and DTR via the modem control register).

Two upgrades you may wish to make in this program are as follows:

- Perform all I/O directly to the serial port, cutting the BIOS out of the process.

- Change from a polling method to an interrupt method.

ENDNOTE

SETTING UP THE MODEM

ZCLOCK relies on certain modem settings to operate properly: Data Terminal Ready (DTR), Carrier Detect (CD), and Data Set Ready (DSR). The modem must be programmed to honor DTR, and to disconnect should the computer lower the DTR signal. This allows ZCLOCK to hang up the modem when required.

The modem must be programmed also to accurately reflect the current condition of the CD line to the computer. ZCLOCK uses CD as a secondary indicator that the connection to the observatory succeeded.

Finally, the BIOS may require that the modem send the DSR signal. If the BIOS does not detect DSR, it will not send data to the modem. The modem must be set so DSR is sent to the computer at all times. ■

ENDNOTE

THE OBSERVATORY MESSAGE

Once your modem is connected to the United States Naval Observatory, the clock at the observatory will start transmitting two alternating messages. The first message, the time message, is an announcement of the date and time coming up. The second message, a synchronizing message, coincides with the actual occurence of the date and time announced by the first message. This alternating message technique allows ZCLOCK to receive and validate the time message before the synchronizing message is received.

The format for the time message transmitted by the Naval Observatory is as follows:

```
jjjjj ddd hhmmss UTC<cr><lf>
where: jjjjj  is the last five digits of the Julian day
       ddd    is the day of the current year (001 = January 1)
       hhmmss is the current time (UTC)
```

When 2,400,000 is added to the *jjjjj* portion of the message, the number becomes a Julian day number. For example, the Julian day number 2,448,743 is equivalent to May 1, 1992 A.D. (Note that a Julian day does not recognize B.C. or A.D.)

The *ddd* portion of the message is the day of the year, with January 1 being 001. Having the numbers for both Julian day and day of the year allows ZCLOCK to cross-check the two and determine if the observatory's message was received properly.

The *hhmmss* portion of the message is the time in 24-hour format. The last data on the line, UTC, stands for Universal coordinated time (Universel Temps Coordiné in French, hence, UTC) and generally concurs with Greenwich mean time (GMT), the current time in Greenwich, England. See the Endnote "Time Trivia" for more information about time zones and related topics.   ∎

ENDNOTE

TIME TRIVIA

While writing the ZCLOCK utility, we came across some fascinating information. We present it here for you to peruse; though not crucial to programming technique, you may find it helpful and interesting.

ZCLOCK owes its existence to the United States Naval Observatory. The observatory houses an extremely accurate clock known as the Master Clock of the observatory. This clock is a system of 24 cesium clocks and five to eight hydrogen MASER atomic clocks. The system is accurate to approximately one nanosecond per day; that is, in a billion days, the clock's time would be off by one second.

ZCLOCK's hardware interface to the Master Clock is a 1200-bps modem, and ZCLOCK receives a message via that modem indicating the current date, and the time in Universal coordinated time (UTC). UTC is a time scale based on measurements of both the Master Clock and astronomical observations. For all practical purposes, UTC is the same as Greenwich mean time (GMT).

When you execute ZCLOCK, you must know your time zone. The time zone argument describes to ZCLOCK the offset of your local time from UTC. But time zones have not always been used to establish geographical time differences. Prior to the establishment of standard time zones, localities set their time by the sun, and time from place to place would vary by as little as a few minutes. For example, the time difference between New York and Boston was about ten minutes. Differences in local time made it difficult for railroads to schedule trains, so in 1883, the railroads established four standard time zones across the continental United States. Later, in 1884, worldwide time zones were created. Greenwich, England was chosen as the "starting point" for all of the time zones, and that time zone was named Greenwich mean time (GMT).

During the 1940s, it was discovered that astronomical measurement of time was not as accurate as previously thought, since the earth speeds up and slows down as it moves through space. Ultimately, this resulted in one second being redefined in terms of a cesium atom's natural rate of vibration. Because of a conflict between the new length of the second and the astronomical observance of a year, the new Universal coordinated time scale was created, and this is the time reported by the Naval Observatory.

The date provided in the Naval Observatory message is a Julian day, which is the last five digits of the number of days that have passed since January 1, 4713 B.C. Adding 2,400,000 to the number sent by the observatory results in the value for the current Julian day. ■

LISTING

ZCLOCK 1.00

```
/* ********************************************************************* *

    ZCLOCK 1.00, Copyright (c) 1992, Bob Flanders and Michael Holmes
    PC Magazine C Lab Notes, Set CMOS clock from the National Observatory

 * ********************************************************************* *

    This code for Borland C++ version 3.0. (MSC version on diskette)

        Compile with: BCC -02 -ms zclock.c

    To compile for Microsoft C, you need to change the following:

        - handle MK_FP() macro differences
        - change control break handling for ctrlbrk() and control_break()

 * ********************************************************************* *

    Special note for usage under Windows

        This program makes heavy usage of the _bios_serialcom()
        function.  This function in turn calls the BIOS serial support
        (int 14h).  Because interrupt 14h works as a non-interrupt
        mode device driver, this program may miss characters during
        its receive operations.  To work around this problem, a PIF file
        can be set up with the following options:

            Display Usage: Full Screen
            Foreground Priority: 10000
            Detect Idle Time: Off

 * ********************************************************************* */


#pragma   pack(1)                          /* pack to byte alignment   */
#pragma   warn -eff                        /* remove erroneous msgs    */
#include <stdio.h>                         /* standard i/o library     */
#include <stdlib.h>                        /* commonly used routines   */
#include <dos.h>                           /* DOS rtn definitions      */
#include <string.h>                        /* string functions         */
#include <stdarg.h>                        /* argument functions       */
#include <bios.h>                          /* bios manifest constants  */
#include <math.h>                          /* math functions           */
#include <ctype.h>                         /* character classifications*/
#include <conio.h>                         /* console i/o routines      */

#define NOT !                              /* logical not              */
#define UINT  unsigned int                 /* unsigned integer type    */
#define UCHAR unsigned char                /* unsigned character type  */
#define SEND_READY  0x2000                 /* UART ready for next char */
#define COMM_ERROR  0x9e00                 /* int 14h error flags      */
#define DATA_READY  0x0100                 /* int 14h data ready       */
#define CARRIER_DET 0x0080                 /* int 14h carrier detected */
#define DTR         0x03                   /* DTR and RTS bits in mcr  */
```

```
#define MSG_ATTEMPTS 30                    /* attempts to get good msg */
#define BCD(x) ((x) / 10 << 4) + ((x) % 10) /* integer to BCD format    */

/* ***************************************************************** *
 *        routine definitions                                        *
 * ***************************************************************** */

void    quit_with(char *, ...),            /* quit with error message  */
        initialization(int, char **),      /* init and parse cmd line  */
        validate_port(void),               /* validate comm port parm  */
        validate_timezone(void),           /* validate time zone parm  */
        set_up_comm(void),                 /* set up port and modem    */
        get_line(void),                    /* receive a comm line      */
        place_call(void),                  /* call Naval Observatory   */
        process_message(void),             /* process time message     */
        touppers(char *),                  /* string to uppercase      */
        wait(UINT);                        /* wait n timer ticks       */
int     parse_parms(int, char **, char ***),/* parse command line      */
        control_break(void),               /* control break handler    */
        send_string(char *),               /* send string out comm port*/
        jul2greg(long n,                   /* base date                */
            UCHAR *, UCHAR *, UINT *, UCHAR *);


/* ***************************************************************** *
 *        globals                                                    *
 * ***************************************************************** */

int     pos_found,                         /* number positionals found */
        rc = 1,                            /* errorlevel return code   */
        zone_offset,                       /* time zone offset in hours*/
        port,                              /* int 14h port number      */
        hw_port,                           /* hardware port address    */
        mcr_port,                          /* modem control reg port   */
        mcr_val;                           /* mcr value w/o DTR & RTS   */

char    **pos_parms,                       /* positional parms array   */
        i_buf[80],                         /* input comm buffer        */
        *i_ptr;                            /* input pointer            */

union   REGS  r;                           /* other registers          */


/* ***************************************************************** *
 *        messages and strings                                       *
 * ***************************************************************** */

char    copyright[]     = "ZCLOCK 1.00 \xfe Copyright (c) 1992, "
                          "Bob Flanders and Michael Holmes\n"
                          "PC Magazine C Lab Notes \xfe "
                          "Set CMOS clock from the "
                          "Naval Observatory\n\n",
        too_many[]      = "Too many parameters\n",
        bad_op[]        = "Invalid parameter %s\n",
        stop_here[]     = "\nStopping at user's request\n",
        no_mem[]        = "Not enough memory for processing\n",
        no_port[]       = "System does not have a COM%d:\n",
        bad_port[]      = "Bad port name %s\n",
        bad_tz[]        = "Bad time zone %s\n",
        bad_date[]      = "DOS would not set date to %d/%2d/%d\n",
        bad_time[]      = "DOS would not set time to %d:%2d:%2d\n",
        rtc_error[]     = "Real time clock might not be set\n",
        not_ready[]     = "Modem not ready\n",
```

```c
    no_good[]       = "No useable responses from observatory\n",
    no_connect[]    = "Could not connect with observatory\n",
    timed_out[]     = "Time out waiting for a response\n",
    modem_init[]    = "Initializing modem\n",
    modem_dial[]    = "Dialing observatory\n",
    connected[]     = "Connected to host system\n",
    time_out[]      = "Time out sending to comm port\n",
    *yukon[2]       = { "YST", "YDT" },      /* Yukon              */
    GMT_zones[]     = "UTC " "GMT ",         /* Greenwich          */
    time_zones[]    = "AST " "ADT "          /* Atlantic           */
                      "EST " "EDT "          /* Eastern            */
                      "CST " "CDT "          /* Central            */
                      "MST " "MDT "          /* Mountain           */
                      "PST " "PDT "          /* Pacific            */
                      "KST " "KDT "          /* Alaskan            */
                      "HST " "HDT "          /* Hawaii-Aleutian    */
                      "SST " "SDT ",         /* Samoan             */
    *days[7]        = { "Sunday", "Monday", "Tuesday", "Wednesday",
                      "Thursday", "Friday", "Saturday" },
    setting[]       = "Setting clock to: %s, %02d/%02d/%d at"
                      " %02d:%02d:%02d, the %dth day of the year\n",
    help[]          =
      "   Usage:  ZCLOCK  zone  [port [phone_number]]\n\n"
      "Options:  zone  is the time zone, valid zones are\n"
      "                AST  ADT  Atlantic    EST  EDT  Eastern\n"
      "                CST  CDT  Central     MST  MDT  Mountain\n"
      "                PST  PDT  Pacific     KST  KDT  Alaskan\n"
      "                HST  HDT  Hawaii      SST  SDT  Samoan\n"
      "                UTC  GMT  Greenwich   YST  YDT  Yukon\n\n"
      "          port  is the communication port, valid ports are "
      "COM1 thru COM4\n\n"
      "    phone_number is an alternate dialing pattern. The"
      " default is 1-202-653-0351.\n"
      "                This argument can be any modem commands "
      "which are valid after\n"
      "                an ATD. An example of dialing the "
      "observatory via a PBX\n"
      "                is T9,1-202-653-0351.\n";


/* ******************************************************************* *
 *      main()                                                        *
 * ******************************************************************* */

void    main(int ac,                        /* DOS cmd line token count */
             char *av[])                     /* ..token strings          */
{


printf(copyright);                          /* give copyright message   */

initialization(ac, av);                     /* init and parse cmd line  */
set_up_comm();                              /* set up communications    */
place_call();                              /* call the observatory     */
process_message();                         /* set CMOS clock           */
                                           /* ..and return to DOS      */
}



/* ******************************************************************* *
 *      initialization() -- init interrupts and parse command line    *
 * ******************************************************************* */
```

```
void    initialization(int  ac,              /* DOS cmd line token count */
                       char *av[])            /* ..token strings          */
{

ctrlbrk(control_break);                       /* set up ctrl break handler*/

if ((pos_found = parse_parms(ac, av,          /* find positionals/switches*/
        &pos_parms)) > 3)                     /* q. too may positionals?  */
    quit_with(too_many);                      /* a. yes .. give error/quit*/

if (pos_found == 0)                           /* q. missing parameters?   */
    quit_with(help);                          /* a. yes .. give help/quit */

validate_timezone();                          /* check time zone          */
validate_port();                              /* ..and comm port          */

}


/* ****************************************************************** *
 *       validate_timezone() -- validate timezone parameter         *
 * ****************************************************************** */
void    validate_timezone(void)
{
int     i;                                    /* index                    */
char    *p,                                   /* work pointer             */
        *q;                                   /* time zone operand        */

touppers(q = pos_parms[0]);                   /* uppercase time zone      */

if (NOT strcmp(q, yukon[0]) ||                /* q. Yukon standard time?  */
        NOT strcmp(q, yukon[1]))              /* ..or Yukon daylite sav'g?*/
    q[0] = 'K';                               /* a. yes .. make into new  */
                                              /* ..Alaskan Time (KST/KDT) */

if ((strlen(q) != 3) ||                       /* q. operand right length? */
        NOT (p = strstr(time_zones, q)) &&    /* ..and good time zone?    */
        NOT strstr(GMT_zones, q))             /* ..or GMT/UTC zone?       */
    quit_with(bad_tz, q);                     /* a. no .. give error/quit */

if (p)                                        /* q. regular time zone?    */
    {
    i = (p - time_zones) / 4;                 /* a. yes .. get entry nbr  */
    zone_offset = (-4 - (i / 2)) + (i & 1);   /* GMT offset in hours      */
    }
}


/* ****************************************************************** *
 *       validate_port() -- validate communications port parameter  *
 * ****************************************************************** */
void    validate_port(void)
{
char    *p;                                   /* comm port string pointer */
int     far *port_table = MK_FP(0x40, 0);     /* BIOS serial port table   */

if (pos_found > 1)                            /* q. port name given?      */
```

```
    {
    touppers(p = pos_parms[1]);               /* a. yes .. make uppercase */

    if ((strlen(p) > 5) ||                    /* q. wrong length for name?*/
            strncmp("COM", p, 3) ||           /* ..or bad format?         */
            p[3] < '1' || p[3] > '4' ||       /* ..or invalid port number?*/
            (p[4] != '\0' && p[4] != ':'))    /* ..or bad string term?    */
        quit_with(bad_port, p);               /* a. yes .. give error/quit*/

    port = p[3] - '1';                        /* get int 14h port number  */
    }
if (NOT (hw_port = port_table[port]))         /* q. port available?       */
    quit_with(no_port, port + 1);             /* a. no .. give error/quit */

mcr_port = hw_port + 4;                        /* set up mcr i/o address   */

}


/* ********************************************************************* *
 *      set_up_comm() -- initialize communications port and modem        *
 * ********************************************************************* */
void    set_up_comm(void)
{

outp(mcr_port, inp(mcr_port) & ~DTR);         /* turn DTR and RTS off     */
wait(9);                                      /* ..wait 1/2 second        */

_bios_serialcom(_COM_INIT, port,              /* set up comm port for ..  */
        _COM_1200 | _COM_NOPARITY |           /* ..1200 baud, no parity   */
        _COM_CHR8 | _COM_STOP1);              /* ..8 data bits, 1 stop bit*/

outp(mcr_port,  mcr_val = (inp(mcr_port)      /* capture current mcr      */
        | DTR));                              /* turn on DTR and RTS      */
wait(9);                                      /* ..and wait 1/2 second    */

}


/* ********************************************************************* *
 *      place_call() -- call Naval Observatory and get a line            *
 * ********************************************************************* */
void    place_call(void)
{
char    dial_buf[40];                         /* dial buffer              */

strcpy(dial_buf, "ATD");                      /* copy in dial command     */
strcat(dial_buf, (pos_found >= 3) ?           /* ..then phone number      */
        pos_parms[2] : "12026530351");
strcat(dial_buf, "\r");                       /* ..finally a <cr>         */

printf(modem_init);                           /* give user status message */

if (send_string("ATE0V1X1\r"))                /* q. modem accept init?    */
    quit_with(not_ready);                     /* a. no .. give error/quit */

wait(18);                                     /* wait a second            */
```

```
    printf(modem_dial);                         /* give user status message */

    if (send_string(dial_buf))                  /* q. send dial command ok? */
        quit_with(time_out);                    /* a. no .. give error/quit */

    get_line();                                 /* get modem response       */
    wait(18);                                   /* ..and wait a second      */

    if (strncmp(i_buf, "CONNECT", 7) &&         /* q. get connect response? */
            NOT (_bios_serialcom(_COM_STATUS,   /* ..or carrier detected on */
                port, 0) & CARRIER_DET))        /* ..communications port?   */
        quit_with(no_connect);                  /* a. no .. give error/quit */
     else
        printf(connected);                      /* else .. give ok status   */

    }


/* ******************************************************************** *
 *      · process_message() -- parse time message and set CMOS clock    *
 * ******************************************************************** */
void    process_message(void)
{
int     i,                                      /* loop counter             */
        dy1, dy2;                               /* day in year              */
long    julian;                                 /* julian date              */
struct  dosdate_t d;                            /* date structure           */
struct  dostime_t t;                            /* ..and time structure     */

t.hsecond = 0;                                  /* hundredths always zero   */
for (i = 0; i < MSG_ATTEMPTS; i++)              /* try to get a good msg in */
    {
    get_line();                                 /* wait for a comm message  */
/*
 *  The Observatory's message should be in following format:
 *
 *      jjjjj ddd hhmmss UTC <cr> <lf>
 *
 *      where jjjjj  when prepended with 24 becomes the Julian day number
 *                   (1721118 is March 1, 1 BC)
 *            ddd    is the day of the year
 *            hhmmss is the time
 *            UTC    stands for Universal coordinated time
 *
 */

    if (strlen(i_buf) != 20 ||                  /* q. proper length?        */
            i_buf[5] != ' ' ||                  /* ..and spaces in          */
            i_buf[9] != ' ' ||                  /* .. all the right         */
            i_buf[16] != ' ' ||                 /* .. places?               */
            strcmp(&i_buf[17], "UTC"))          /* ..and proper format?     */
        continue;                               /* a. no .. try again       */

    sscanf(i_buf, "%D %d %2d%2d%2d",            /* parse ..                 */
            &julian,                            /* ..julian day             */
            &dy1,                               /* ..day of year            */
            &t.hour, &t.minute, &t.second);     /* ..and time fields        */

    julian += 2400000L;                         /* prepend assumed digits   */
```

```
dy2 = jul2greg(julian,                  /* convert julian date to    */
        &d.month, &d.day, &d.year,      /* ..gregorian date (m/d/y)  */
        &d.dayofweek);                  /* ..and day of week         */

if (dy1 != dy2)                         /* q. day of year match?     */
    continue;                           /* a. no .. try again        */

if (t.hour < abs(zone_offset))          /* q. need to back up a day?*/
        {
    dy2 = jul2greg(--julian,            /* a. yes .. back up by one  */
        &d.month, &d.day, &d.year,      /* ..and convert to new      */
        &d.dayofweek);                  /* ..date and day of week    */

    t.hour += zone_offset + 24;         /* fix up hour for prev day  */
        }

 else
    t.hour += zone_offset;              /* else .. just apply offset*/

get_line();                             /* wait for "mark" message   */

if (i_buf[0] != '*')                    /* q. "mark"?                */
    continue;                           /* a. no .. try again        */

if (_dos_setdate(&d))                   /* q. set date ok?           */
    quit_with(bad_date,                 /* a. no .. give error msg   */
        &d.month, &d.day, &d.year);     /* ..with new date           */

if (_dos_settime(&t))                   /* q. set time ok?           */
    quit_with(bad_time,                 /* a. no .. give error msg   */
        &t.hour, &t.minute, &t.second); /* ..with new time           */

if ((_osmajor < 3) ||                   /* q. DOS 1.x or 2.x?        */
        (_osmajor == 3 && _osminor <= 2))/* ..or 3.0 thru 3.2?       */
        {                               /* a. yes .. set CMOS clock  */
    r.h.ah = 2;                         /* get real time clock time  */
    int86(0x1a, &r, &r);                /* call BIOS to get ..       */
                                        /* ..daylight savings flag   */

    if (r.x.cflag)                      /* q. error getting clock?   */
        {                               /* a. yes .. give error      */
        printf(rtc_error);             /* ..and stop trying         */
        break;
        }

    r.h.ah = 3;                         /* set real time clock time  */
    r.h.ch = BCD(t.hour);               /* ..with current hour       */
    r.h.cl = BCD(t.minute);             /* ..minutes                 */
    r.h.dh = BCD(t.second);             /* ..seconds                 */
    int86(0x1a, &r, &r);                /* call BIOS to set time     */

    if (r.x.cflag)                      /* q. error setting clock?   */
        {                               /* a. yes .. give error/quit*/
        printf(rtc_error);             /* ..and stop trying         */
        break;
        }

    r.h.ah = 5;                         /* set real time clock date  */
    r.h.ch = BCD(d.year / 100);         /* ..with current century    */
    r.h.cl = BCD(d.year % 100);         /* ..year                    */
    r.h.dh = BCD(d.month);              /* ..month                   */
    r.h.dl = BCD(d.day);                /* ..day                     */
    int86(0x1a, &r, &r);                /* call BIOS to set time     */
```

```c
            if (r.x.cflag)                      /* q. error setting date?   */
                printf(rtc_error);              /* a. yes .. give error/quit*/
            }

        break;                                  /* ..then quit loop         */
        }

    outp(mcr_port, inp(mcr_port) & ~DTR);       /* tell modem to hang up     */

    if (i == MSG_ATTEMPTS)                       /* q. get any good messages?*/
        quit_with(no_good);                      /* a. no .. give error/quit */

    rc = 0;                                       /* show everything ok..     */
    quit_with(setting, days[d.dayofweek],         /* ..give final message..   */
            d.month, d.day, d.year,               /* ..showing date           */
            t.hour, t.minute, t.second,           /* ..and time               */
            dy2);                                 /* ..and day within year    */
    }


/* ********************************************************************* *
 *         send_string() -- send a string out the comm port            *
 * ********************************************************************* */

int     send_string(char *s)                    /* string to send out       */
{
int     rc = 0;                                 /* return code              */

while (*s)                                       /* run thru whole string    */
    {
    while (NOT (_bios_serialcom(_COM_STATUS,/* while waiting for UART to*/
            port, 0) & SEND_READY))             /* ..finish w/last character*/
        kbhit();                                /* check keyboard           */

    if (((rc = _bios_serialcom(_COM_SEND,       /* q. send character ok     */
            port, *s++)) & COMM_ERROR) != 0)/* ..without a timeout?     */
        break;                                  /* a. no .. stop loop here   */
    }

return(rc & COMM_ERROR);                         /* return w/last status     */

}


/* ********************************************************************* *
 *         get_line() -- read a line from the comm port                *
 * ********************************************************************* */

void    get_line(void)
{
int     len,                                     /* unprocessed buffer length*/
        elapsed = 819,                           /* 45sec timeout            */
        far *timer = MK_FP(0x40, 0x6c);          /* BIOS timer tick counter  */
char    c;                                       /* last char read           */
long    start, work;                             /* start tick count         */

start = *timer;                                  /* get current time         */
i_ptr = i_buf;                                   /* reset input pointer      */

for (len = sizeof(i_buf); len > 0 &&            /* for each received char.. */
        elapsed > 0;)                            /* ..while not timed out     */
```

```
        {
        if (_bios_serialcom(_COM_STATUS,        /* q. something ready       */
              port, 0) & DATA_READY)            /* ..to be read in?         */
            {
            *i_ptr++ = c = _bios_serialcom(      /* a. yes .. receive it      */
                _COM_RECEIVE, port, 0);          /* ..from the comm port      */
            outp(mcr_port, mcr_val);             /* ..and make RTS on again   */

            if (c == '\r' || c == '\n')          /* q. get a <cr> or <lf>?    */
                {                                /* a. yes .. check if 1st    */
                if ((i_ptr - i_buf) > 1)         /* q. 1st char in buffer?    */
                    {
                    i_ptr--;                     /* a. no .. back up pointer */
                    break;                       /* ..and stop loop here      */
                    }
                  else
                    {
                    i_ptr = i_buf;               /* else .. restart buffer    */
                    len = sizeof(i_buf);         /* ..and reset length        */
                    }
                }
              else
                len--;                           /* decrement available       */
            }

        if ((work = *timer) != start)            /* q. time pass?             */
            {                                    /* a. yes .. see how much    */
            if (work < start)                    /* q. clock go past midnite?*/
                elapsed--;                       /* a. yes .. count as 1 tick*/
              else
                elapsed -= (int)(work - start);  /* else .. count everything */

            start = work;                        /* start again w/curr time   */
            }

        kbhit();                                 /* check keyboard            */
        }

    *i_ptr = '\0';                               /* null terminate string     */

    if (elapsed <= 0)                            /* q. time out waiting?      */
        quit_with(timed_out);                    /* a. yes .. give error/quit*/

    }


/* ****************************************************************** *
 *      jul2greg() -- convert from base date to month/day/year      *
 * ****************************************************************** */

int     jul2greg(long  n,                        /* base date                */
                 UCHAR *m,                        /* month..                  */
                 UCHAR *d,                        /* ..day                    */
                 UINT  *y,                        /* ..year with century      */
                 UCHAR *dow)                      /* day of week, 0=Sunday    */
{
long    dd;                                       /* work variable            */
int     doy,                                      /* day of year              */
        f;                                        /* leapyear flag            */

n -= 1721118L;                                    /* base calcs on 3/1/1 BC   */
*dow = (n - 5) % 7;                               /* compute day of week      */
```

```
*y = (UINT)((4 * n - 1) / 146097L);          /* get century number        */
n = 4 * n - 1 - (146097L * *y);              /* ..remove that many days   */
dd = n / 4;                                  /* get to the year           */
n = (4 * dd + 3) / 1461;                     /* ..within the century      */
*y = (UINT)(100 * *y + n);                   /* ..then year with century  */
dd = 4 * dd + 3 - 1461 * n;                  /* get to days within 4 yrs  */
f = ((dd % 4) == 3) ? 1 : 0;                 /* set leapyear flag         */
dd = (dd + 4) / 4;                           /* get days within base yr   */
*m = (5 * dd - 3) / 153;                     /* get month                 */
doy = (int)(dd + 59 + f);                    /* get day in calendar year  */
dd = 5 * dd - 3 - (153 * *m);                /* get to the day ..         */
*d = (dd + 5) / 5;                           /* ..within the month        */

if( *m < 10)                                 /* q. need to adjust month?  */
    *m += 3;                                 /* a. yes .. normalize nbr   */

 else
    {
    *m -= 9;                                 /* adjust for March base     */
    (*y)++;                                  /* ..date and fix year too   */
    doy %= (365 + f);                        /* ..and day in year         */
    }

return(doy);                                 /* and return w/day of year  */

}



/* *********************************************************************** *
 *        wait() -- wait n timer ticks                                     *
 * *********************************************************************** */

void    wait(UINT n)                         /* time to wait in ticks     */
{
int     far *timer = MK_FP(0x40, 0x6c);      /* BIOS timer tick counter   */
long    start, work;                         /* start tick count          */

start = *timer;                              /* get current time          */

while (n > 0)                                /* loop till n ticks past    */
    {
    if ((work = *timer) != start)            /* q. time pass?             */
        {                                    /* a. yes .. see how much    */
        if (work < start)                    /* q. clock go past midnite? */
            n--;                             /* a. yes .. count as 1 tick */
        else
            n -= (UINT)(work - start);       /* else .. count everything  */

        start = work;                        /* start again w/curr time   */
        }

    else
        kbhit();                             /* else .. check keyboard    */

    }
}
```

```
/* ********************************************************************* *
 *        touppers() -- uppercase a string                             *
 * ********************************************************************* */

void    touppers(char *s)                   /* string to uppercase      */
{

    while (*s)                              /* for the whole string..   */
        *s++ = toupper(*s);                 /* ..uppercase each char     */

}



/* ********************************************************************* *
 *        quit_with() -- give an error message, then return to DOS     *
 * ********************************************************************* */

void    quit_with(char *msg, ...)           /* string to print          */
{                                                                        
va_list list;                               /* variable list            */

    if (mcr_port)                           /* q. valid port available? */
        outp(mcr_port, inp(mcr_port) & ~DTR);  /* a. yes .. hang up modem */

    va_start(list, msg);                    /* set up variable list     */
    vprintf(msg, list);                     /* give error message ..    */
    exit(rc);                               /* ..and then quit          */

}



/* ********************************************************************* *
 *        parse_parms() -- parse command line parms                    *
 * ********************************************************************* */

int     parse_parms(int  ac,                /* argument count           */
                char *av[],                 /* command line arguments   */
                char ***parms_array)        /* positional parms array   */

{
int     i,                                  /* loop counter             */
        parms_fnd = 0,                      /* positional parms found   */
        slash_fnd = 0;                      /* slash found in token     */
char    *p, *q,                             /* character pointer        */
        c;                                  /* work character           */

    *parms_array = (char **) malloc(        /* set up for max nbr tokens*/
            sizeof(char *) * ac);

    if (parms_array == NULL)                /* q. memory available?     */
        quit_with(no_mem);                  /* a. no .. quit with msg    */

    for (i = 1; i < ac; i++)                /* for each cmd line token  */
        {
        p = av[i];                          /* set up pointer to token  */

        while (*p)                          /* process token            */
            {
            if (*p == '/' || slash_fnd)     /* q. option?               */
                {                           /* a. yes .. process request*/
```

```
            if (NOT slash_fnd)              /* q. embedded slash?       */
                p++;                        /* a. no .. bump past slash */

            c = toupper(*p);                /* get char and upcase it   */
            slash_fnd = 0;                  /* reset switch             */

            if (c == '?')                   /* q. help request?         */
                quit_with(help);            /* a. yes .. give help      */

            if ((q = strchr(p, '/')) != 0)  /* q. any more switches?    */
                *q = 0;                     /* a. yes .. isolate bad one*/

            quit_with(bad_op, --p);         /* ..and exit w/error msg   */
            }
        else
            {
            (*parms_array)[parms_fnd++] = p;/* save positional string   */

            if (*(p += strcspn(p, "/")))    /* q. any switches left?    */
                {
                *p++ = 0;                   /* a. yes .. make a string  */
                slash_fnd = 1;              /* ..show nxt char a switch */
                }
            }
        }
    }

*parms_array = (char **) realloc(           /* readjust array size      */
            *parms_array,                   /* ..for what was found     */
            sizeof(char *) * parms_fnd);

return(parms_fnd);                          /* rtn w/nbr of positionals */

}



/* ********************************************************************* *
 *        control_break() -- control break intercept routine           *
 * ********************************************************************* */

int     control_break(void)
{


if (mcr_port)                               /* q. valid port available? */
    outp(mcr_port, inp(mcr_port) & ~DTR);   /* a. yes .. hang up modem   */

printf(stop_here);                          /* give error message ..    */
return(0);                                  /* ..and return to DOS      */

}
```

2

COLLECTING PROGRAM STATISTICS WITH INFORMER

INFORMER monitors the execution of another program, and collects and reports statistics that describe that program's operation.

In the early days of personal computing, when complex operating systems had, say, 15 functions, it was fairly easy to determine exactly how a program performed a given task. But today the picture is quite different. Various combinations of undocumented functions, windows of varying size, Extended Memory Support (XMS), Expanded Memory Support (EMS), and TSRs can make analyzing programs a nightmare. So every piece of information you can manage to acquire about a program helps you to see how to get a job done.

INFORMER is designed to make information collection a simpler task. By intercepting the interrupts used to request services from DOS, the BIOS, and other support programs, INFORMER is able to report the exact services a program uses, as well as how often it calls them. Whether you want to know some performance

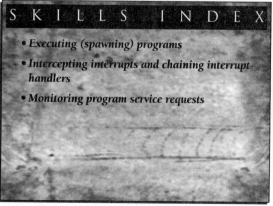

SKILLS INDEX

- *Executing (spawning) programs*
- *Intercepting interrupts and chaining interrupt handlers*
- *Monitoring program service requests*

characteristics, or how a program performs a function, or simply satisfy your curiosity, INFORMER will monitor a program you specify, and tell you what services that program used.

■ USING INFORMER

INFORMER is very easy to use. At the command prompt, simply type **INFORMER** followed by the normal command line for the program you wish to monitor. For example, to monitor the operation of the CHKDSK program, enter

```
INFORMER CHKDSK
```

If you invoke INFORMER without specifying a program to execute, you are presented with a short help message.

First, INFORMER displays its copyright notice. Immediately following that, INFORMER runs the CHKDSK program, and CHKDSK displays its normal report. INFORMER's report then follows, showing the statistics gathered during CHKDSK's execution. Figure 2.1 is an example of the report produced by INFORMER after monitoring CHKDSK's execution.

INFORMER's full syntax is as follows:

```
INFORMER [/output] program [options]
```

The *output* argument specifies the file name where INFORMER is to write its report. If you do not specify the *output* argument, INFORMER writes its report to the standard output. If specified, however, the *output* argument must be the first argument on the command line, and must be preceded by a forward slash. For example, this command tells INFORMER to monitor CHKDSK, and send INFORMER's report to the printer:

```
INFORMER /PRN CHKDSK
```

■ **Note.** *Using DOS redirection will capture both INFORMER's output and the program's output, as explained later in this section.*

The *program* argument tells INFORMER which program to execute and monitor. The *program* argument must specify the file name of a .COM or .EXE file. (You do not need to specify the extension.) The file must exist and must be located in the current directory or in a directory referenced by the PATH environment variable. Although INFORMER can monitor the execution of DOS external commands (such as CHKDSK.EXE), internal commands such as DIR and ERASE are a part of COMMAND.COM

FIGURE 2.1

Sample

INFORMER

report

```
INFORMER 1.00 • Copyright (c) 1992, Michael Holmes and Bob Flanders
PC Magazine C Lab Notes • Inform on a program's execution

Volume DDRIVE      created 12-16-1991 6:58p
Volume Serial Number is 264C-1A01

   71059456 bytes total disk space
      75776 bytes in 3 hidden files
      75776 bytes in 33 directories
   20453376 bytes in 731 user files
   50454528 bytes available on disk

       2048 bytes in each allocation unit
      34697 total allocation units on disk
      24636 available allocation units on disk

     655360 total bytes memory
     387760 bytes free

--------------- Informer Statistics ---------------
      Command Line: chkdsk
        Started at: 19:46:41 on 05/18/1992
      Completed at: 19:46:43
      Elapsed Time:  0:00:01.59
  Termination Code: 0

Interrupt Usage
     1027 Int 21 - DOS interrupt
        2 Int 25 - Disk read interrupt

Int 21 (DOS) Breakdown by Function
        2 Fnc 0D - Disk reset
        3 Fnc 0E - Select disk
       35 Fnc 11 - Search first using FCB
      834 Fnc 12 - Search next using FCB
        2 Fnc 19 - Get default disk number
        2 Fnc 1A - Set disk transfer area
        2 Fnc 25 - Set interrupt vector
        1 Fnc 30 - Get DOS version
        1 Fnc 32 - Get drive parameter block
        2 Fnc 35 - Get interrupt vector
        1 Fnc 36 - Get disk space
        2 Fnc 38 - Get/set country information
       68 Fnc 3B - Change current directory
       52 Fnc 40 - Write to file with handle
        9 Fnc 44 - IOCTL
        1 Fnc 47 - Get current directory
        2 Fnc 48 - Allocate memory
        1 Fnc 4A - Adjust memory block size
        1 Fnc 4C - Quit with exit code
        1 Fnc 52 - Get list of lists
        2 Fnc 60 - Resolve path string
        1 Fnc 62 - Get PSP address
        1 Fnc 63 - 2-byte character support
        1 Fnc 68 - Commit file

Usage by Classification
     1006 - Disk Calls
        3 - Memory Management Calls
       20 - Operating System Calls

Input/Output Byte Counts
   read  written
      0      453 - File
```

and cannot be monitored by INFORMER. If you attempt to monitor an internal command with INFORMER, you'll get an error message telling you that the requested program was not found.

Command line arguments for the program being monitored must appear after the *program* argument on the command line. For example, to monitor CHKDSK and specify CHKDSK's /F option, you can use this command:

```
INFORMER CHKDSK /F
```

When you do not specify the */output* argument, you can capture both the monitored program's output and INFORMER's report by redirecting standard output. For example, to monitor CHKDSK, and redirect both CHKDSK's and INFORMER's output to the printer, use this command:

```
INFORMER CHKDSK >PRN
```

■ INFORMER's Report

As shown in Figure 2.1, INFORMER displays its report after the monitored program finishes running. The report produced by INFORMER consists of five sections: summary information, Interrupt Usage, Breakdown by Function, Usage (of functions) by Classification, and Input/Output Byte Counts.

The summary section shows some general statistics about the monitored program. This section includes the command line used to execute the program, the time and date when the program started and completed, the length of time the program ran, and the monitored program's termination code. (If a program starts and stops on the same day, no date is displayed on the "Completed at" line.)

The Interrupt Usage section comes next and shows the number of times that the monitored program invoked specific interrupts. INFORMER monitors the following nine interrupts:

- Timer hardware (interrupt 0x08)

- Video BIOS (0x10)

- BIOS serial support (0x14)

- BIOS keyboard support (0x16)

- BIOS printer support (0x17)

- DOS functions (0x21)

- Absolute sector reads (0x25)

- Absolute sector writes (0x26)

- EMS support (0x67)

Of these nine, all but the timer interrupt may appear in the Interrupt Usage section of the report. The number of timer interrupts is shown indirectly, via the elapsed time information in the summary section.

The Interrupt Usage section helps you determine the interrupts most heavily used by a program and, conversely, those not used at all. Sometimes you may be surprised by what you find. For example, you may notice that there are no video interrupts recorded in Figure 2.1 and wonder how CHKDSK gets its report to the screen. In this case, the output was redirected to a file with the command

```
INFORMER CHKDSK >INFORMER.RPT
```

Since all screen output was sent to a file, no video interrupts were issued. INFORMER only reports on interrupts that have a nonzero count.

The Int 21 (DOS) Breakdown by Function section shows the number of calls to individual DOS functions. For example, in Figure 2.1, DOS function 0x4C (quit with exit code) is invoked once. You may find the DOS function breakdown section of particular interest when you are trying to determine how a program performs some function.

Figure 2.2 shows another output example. Here the DOS ASSIGN command was used to redirect requests for drive A to drive C (assign a=c). Following the ASSIGN command, INFORMER is used to monitor the execution of the command CHKDSK A:. In this example, CHKDSK responds with an error message indicating that it cannot check an ASSIGNed drive.

Although DOS provides no documented function for determining if a drive is ASSIGNed or not, the DOS function breakdown section of INFORMER's report provides us with a clue about how CHKDSK determines this information. As shown, CHKDSK issued several DOS calls, most of which are well documented but do not provide the information needed to determine if a drive is ASSIGNed. CHKDSK also issues three DOS calls that are not documented: get list of lists (0x52), resolve path string (0x60), and two-byte character support (0x63). Further investigation shows that resolve path string (0x60) can be used to determine the true name of an ASSIGNed drive. As you can see, although INFORMER doesn't provide all of the answers about how a program works, it can provide a few hints about how a task is accomplished.

FIGURE 2.2

INFORMER's
report of a
CHKDSK
against a drive
created with
ASSIGN

```
C>assign a=c

C>informer chkdsk a:

INFORMER 1.00 • Copyright (c) 1992, Michael Holmes and Bob Flanders
PC Magazine C Lab Notes • Inform on a program's execution

Cannot CHKDSK a SUBSTed or ASSIGNed drive

--------------- Informer Statistics ---------------
    Command Line: chkdsk a:
      Started at: 19:48:45 on 05/18/1992
    Completed at: 19:48:47
    Elapsed Time:  0:00:01.59
Termination Code: 0

Interrupt Usage
      164 Int 10 - Video interrupt
       21 Int 21 - DOS interrupt
        1 Int 25 - Disk read interrupt

Int 21 (DOS) Breakdown by Function
        1 Fnc 0D - Disk reset
        1 Fnc 19 - Get default disk number
        1 Fnc 30 - Get DOS version
        1 Fnc 36 - Get disk space
        1 Fnc 40 - Write to file with handle
        8 Fnc 44 - IOCTL
        1 Fnc 4A - Adjust memory block size
        1 Fnc 4C - Quit with exit code
        1 Fnc 52 - Get list of lists
        2 Fnc 60 - Resolve path string
        1 Fnc 62 - Get PSP address
        2 Fnc 63 - 2-byte character support

Usage by Classification
       11 - Disk Calls
      164 - Video Calls
        1 - Memory Management Calls
       10 - Operating System Calls

Input/Output Byte Counts
    read  written
       0       82 - Video
       0       41 - File

C>
```

The Usage by Classification section summarizes the types of services requested and the resources used by the monitored program. As INFORMER gathers statistics, it places the requests in one of seven classifications: console calls, disk calls, printer calls, video calls, memory management calls, serial communications, and operating system calls.

As implemented, INFORMER classifies all file I/O, both FCB-based and handle-based, as disk calls—even if the FCB or handle references a device (such as the serial port, video, and so on). When the underlying device driver issues the BIOS calls, however, INFORMER classifies the resulting statistics properly. For example, if a program writes 50 bytes to the standard output device, and standard output is not redirected, the Usage by Classification section will record 1 disk call and 50 video calls, even though no disk I/O occurred.

The Input/Output Byte Counts section recaps the number of characters read or written to various files or devices. This section notes five categories: keyboard, video, serial, printer, and file. For each category, INFORMER maintains a count of bytes read and written (except for keyboard, where INFORMER only maintains the count of bytes read). Only nonzero counts are reported.

Once again, the numbers shown in this section may surprise you. For example, if you monitored a program that wrote a 25-byte message to standard output, the input/output byte counts would reflect 25 bytes written both to a file and to video. This is clearly demonstrated in Figure 2.2. In this case, CHKDSK only performed file I/O when it wrote the message "Cannot CHKDSK a SUBSTed or ASSIGNed drive" to standard output. The Input/Output Byte Counts section reflects the 41 bytes contained in the message as both file I/O and video I/O.

■ Watch Out for TSRs

INFORMER monitors a program by intercepting certain interrupts, counting the number of times the monitored program issues those interrupts, and restoring the interrupt vector to its original value. Most TSRs also intercept one or more interrupts before terminating—but they don't restore them. If you were to monitor a program that terminated after changing an interrupt used by INFORMER, the TSR might malfunction after INFORMER restored the original value of that interrupt vector, resulting in unpredictable side effects.

■ **Caution!** *Although INFORMER can monitor most any application program, you must be careful not to monitor programs that change interrupt vectors without restoring them. Most of these programs fall into the terminate-and-stay-resident (TSR) category.*

■ INSIDE INFORMER

Unlike most utilities, INFORMER spends most of its time doing nothing! Although it sets up the environment and produces the report, INFORMER delegates the actual task of gathering the statistics to the program being monitored, *without that program's knowledge.*

Initialization

When loaded, INFORMER prints its copyright message and then verifies the command line arguments by calling check_arguments(). First, check_arguments() determines if you have explicitly requested help with the /? option. If so, check_arguments() calls quit_with() to display the help message and return to DOS. Next, check_arguments() determines if you have requested that INFORMER's report be sent to a file and, if so, points log_name to the specified file name. INFORMER checks the file name for validity just before producing its report.

Finally, check_arguments() builds the argument list that will be passed to the monitored program. The argument list is an array of string pointers, each pointing to a single argument for the command line. As check_arguments() builds the argument list, it also creates the cmd_line variable used to display the command line in the summary section of INFORMER's report.

INFORMER's Structures

INFORMER gathers statistics into four global structure arrays. The int_list[] array contains an entry for each interrupt that is intercepted, and contains six members: interrupt number, interrupt type, a pointer to the name of the interrupt, a pointer to the new interrupt handler, a pointer to the old interrupt handler, and a count variable. INFORMER uses this array to install and remove the interrupt handler and to gather the interrupt usage statistics.

The int_type[] array contains an entry for each class listed under the Usage by Classification section of INFORMER's report. There are only two members in this structure: the count variable and the description.

The io_cnt[] array contains an entry for each type of I/O statistic gathered by INFORMER. The three members of this structure are a pointer to a description, the input byte count, and the output byte count.

Finally, int21_cnt[] contains an entry for each of the 256 possible function codes passed in the AH register when DOS is called. Associated with int21_cnt[] is the int21_list[] array, which has an entry for every currently known DOS call. This array only describes the possible DOS functions. The structure has two entries: the type of function and the associated text. Each int21_list[] entry corresponds with one of the entries in the int21_cnt[] array.

Intercepting the Interrupts

As mentioned earlier, INFORMER gathers statistics by intercepting specific interrupts and counting the number of times the monitored program invokes those interrupts.

See the Endnote, "Interrupts and Interrupt Vectors," for more information about how interrupts work.

INFORMER calls install_handlers() to modify the required interrupt vectors. For each entry in the int_list[] array, install_handlers() saves the value found in the interrupt vector referenced by the entry, and installs a pointer to the INFORMER's corresponding routine. After all of the interrupts have been intercepted, install_handlers() retrieves the current date and time.

▪ Let the Execution Begin

Having installed its interrupt handlers, INFORMER is ready to run the monitored program. To do so, INFORMER calls the spawnvp() routine to execute the program. The spawnvp() function requires the name of the program to execute, as well as a pointer to a list of pointers to the command line argument.

The spawnvp() function searches the current directory and then the directories named in the PATH environment variable, to find the program to execute. Then spawnvp() loads the program into memory and passes control to it. When the program completes, control is returned to INFORMER.

There are two other functions—the exec...() family of functions and the system() function—that may seem appropriate for executing another program, but each has a drawback not shared by the spawn...() family. The system() function executes another program, but does so by first executing another copy of COMMAND.COM. Using the system() function would thus return statistics not only on the target program, but also on COMMAND.COM. The exec...() family of functions initially appears to be an appropriate alternative, but further investigation shows that these functions do not return to the calling program (in this case, INFORMER) when the child program completes.

As mentioned earlier, INFORMER spends most of its time doing nothing. During the execution of the monitored program, INFORMER is taking up memory, and its routines are being executed, but it is the monitored program that has control of the system. In effect, the monitored program is informing on itself!

Each time the monitored program invokes one of the interrupts monitored by INFORMER, the associated interrupt service routine, such as int10_new(), increments one or more counters before passing control to the original interrupt handler. For example, each time video interrupt 0x10 is issued, int10_new() gets control and counts the number of times the interrupt has been invoked. Also, int10_new() checks the function code passed in the AH register. If the code requests a read from or write to the video buffer, the associated video I/O count is incremented. These values are subsequently reported in the Input/Output Byte Counts section.

The most complicated interrupt handler is int21_new(). When either program (INFORMER or the monitored program) issues interrupt 0x21, int21_new() is invoked. When it gets control, int21_new() checks to see if the collection of statistics is enabled. If so, int21_new() increments the count of interrupt 0x21 calls in int_list[], and the count by interrupt 0x21 function in int21_cnt[]. The int21_new() handler also adds the number of bytes read or written if the function invoked is a file read or a file write.

If gathering of statistics is not enabled, int21_new() waits for a function 0x4b (load/execute a program) before enabling the collection of statistics. This is the last DOS interrupt called by the spawnvp() routine used by INFORMER. Because of this, INFORMER can call interrupt 0x21 freely without skewing the statistics. After the statistics have been collected, int21_new() passes control to the old interrupt handler via the _chain_intr() function.

■ Disadvantages of Interrupt Handlers in C

There are some ends you can't reach when writing interrupt handlers entirely in C. One disadvantage is the interrupt handlers' incompatibility with some applications that use EMS. According to the EMS standard, a program can determine if EMS memory is installed in one of two ways: by opening the guaranteed device name EMMXXXX0; or by retrieving the far address found in interrupt vector 0x67, and checking for the string EMMXXXX0 starting ten bytes after the retrieved address. The first of these methods works fine with a C interrupt handler. Unfortunately, the second method is best implemented as an assembly routine, where you can control the information located at the entry point of the EMS interrupt handler. If a program uses the second method, it will not detect the presence of EMS when monitored by INFORMER.

Another difficulty encountered when writing an interrupt handler in C occurs when you want to intercept an interrupt and perform processing before and after invoking the old handler. Although C provides a facility for invoking an old handler based solely on the address of the old handler, you must be careful to observe certain restrictions when doing so.

First, upon entry to an interrupt routine, the C interface code pushes the values contained in the CPU registers onto the stack so they can be accessed by your code. This is clearly shown in several of INFORMER's interrupt handlers. However, since any intervening code generated by the C compiler modifies CPU registers, the interrupt handler must be sure to set or restore CPU registers before calling the lower level interrupt.

Often, an interrupt handler will return a value needed by the calling routine. If your interrupt handler invokes a lower level interrupt, and you must return a value to the calling routine, you must place the value in the appropriate variable on the stack before returning to the caller.

Finally, it is impossible to invoke an interrupt handler from C that changes the BP register. If BP changes, C loses addressability to its stack frame, and will likely cause your program to crash. To invoke such a handler would require an assembly language routine.

INFORMER bypasses these restrictions by using _chain_intr() to call lower level interrupt handlers. When an interrupt handler calls _chain_intr(), _chain_intr() restores the contents of the registers from the stack and passes control to the old handler. When it finishes running, the old handler returns directly to the code that invoked the C interrupt handler.

Restoring the Old Vectors

Immediately after the monitored program finishes executing, INFORMER calls remove_handlers() to restore the original values to the interrupt vectors. The remove_handlers() routine clears the enabled variable, shutting off the gathering of further statistics, and retrieves the date and time for INFORMER's report. Next, it backs out the get return code call that spawnvp() issues at the completion of the monitored program. Finally, remove_handlers() restores the interrupt vectors saved in the int_list[] array.

Reporting the Statistics

INFORMER's last action is to call user_report(), which displays the results of the statistics gathered. The user_report() routine first checks to assure spawnvp() found the program requested. If not, an error message is displayed and INFORMER returns to DOS. Otherwise, user_report() attempts to open the report file if one was specified. If the attempt fails, the output file defaults to standard output.

Most of the code contained in user_report() simply prints the information contained in INFORMER's structures, but there are a few items of interest. The user_report() routine computes the elapsed time based on the number of times the timer interrupt (0x08) was called. Unlike the other interrupts monitored by INFORMER, the timer interrupt is a hardware interrupt and is invoked approximately 18.2 times per second. The user_report() routine uses this information to convert the number of timer interrupt ticks to hundredths of seconds, and subsequently converts that number to an elapsed time.

As mentioned earlier, certain DOS functions are also credited to various entries in the Usage by Classification section. However, the collection of this statistic is not done at the invocation of int21_new(). To avoid additional overhead during the monitored program's execution, user_report() classifies DOS functions as it prints the Breakdown by Function section of the report. As user_report() checks each entry in the int21_cnt[] array, it adds that entry to the appropriate int_type[] entry. Later, when user_report() prints the Usage by Classification section, the counts will reflect what is accumulated by the various DOS functions.

As user_report() proceeds, it only prints nonzero statistics for each section of the report. When complete, user_report() calls quit_with() to return to DOS.

■ SUMMARY

INFORMER demonstrates the ability to intercept and process interrupts, chain to existing interrupt handlers, and execute and monitor other programs. INFORMER also shows some deficits in a C program's ability to implement certain types of interrupt handlers. Here are two enhancements you may wish to add:

- Rewrite the int67_new() routine in assembler so that all applications can use EMS, if it is available.

- Capture and display more statistics about subfunctions invoked with DOS interrupt 0x21, such as memory utilization, type of IOCTL functions used, and so forth.

INTERRUPTS AND INTERRUPT VECTORS

Almost all programs request services from other software. A program may request DOS services, BIOS services, or services from other software such as memory managers. In the majority of cases, these services are requested by invoking an interrupt.

At location 0:0 in memory, there is a table of 256 32-bit entries, known as the *interrupt vector table*. Each vector location may contain a far address pointer to a routine that gets control when the associated interrupt is issued. Several of these interrupts have predefined meanings in the DOS environment.

Figure 2.3 depicts the interrupt vector table as it exists normally, and when INFORMER is executing. In the first illustration, the interrupt vectors point directly to the associated routines in the BIOS and DOS; however, when INFORMER runs, it changes those interrupt vectors, causing them to reference code within INFORMER. When the monitored program invokes an interrupt, it unknowingly passes control to INFORMER's interrupt handler. After INFORMER's interrupt handler has completed processing, it passes control to the original interrupt handler so the function requested by the monitored program is completed. ■

FIGURE 2.3

*Illustration of
system
interrupt
vectors with
and without
INFORMER*

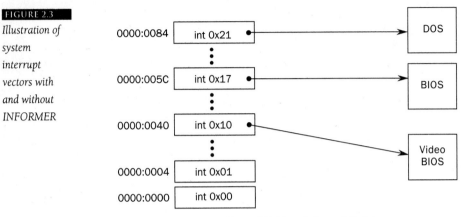

Normal System Interrupt Pointers

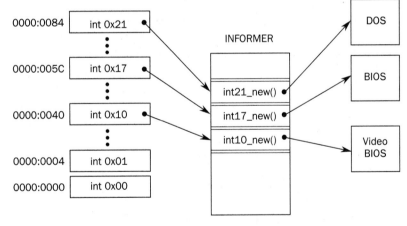

System Interrupt Vectors during INFORMER

LISTING

INFORMER 1.00

```
/* ******************************************************************* *

   INFORMER 1.00, Copyright (c) 1992, Michael Holmes and Bob Flanders
   PC Magazine C Lab Notes, Inform on a program's execution

 * ******************************************************************* *

   This code for Borland C++ version 3.0. (MSC version on diskette)

        Compile with:  BCC -O2 -ms informer.c

   To compile for Microsoft C, you need to change the following:
          - interrupt routine function prototypes
          - change #pragma as necessary

 * ******************************************************************* */


#pragma   pack(1)                          /* pack to byte alignment   */
#include <stdio.h>                         /* standard i/o library     */
#include <stdlib.h>                        /* ANSI compatibility       */
#include <dos.h>                           /* DOS rtn definitions      */
#include <string.h>                        /* string functions         */
#include <stdarg.h>                        /* argument functions       */
#include <process.h>                       /* exec functions           */

#define NOT !                              /* logical not              */
#define DATE(x) x.month, x.day, x.year                /* date fields   */
#define TIME(x) x.hour, x.minute, x.second, x.hsecond /* time fields   */
#define UINT  unsigned int                 /* unsigned integer type    */
#define INT_PARMS UINT bp, UINT di,         /* interrupt calling conv  */\
          UINT si, UINT ds, UINT es, UINT dx, UINT cx,              \
          UINT bx, UINT ax, UINT cs, UINT ip, UINT flags

/* ******************************************************************* *
 *        routine definitions                                         *
 * ******************************************************************* */

void    quit_with(char *, ...),            /* quit with error message  */
        interrupt int08_new(INT_PARMS),    /* timer interrupt          */
        interrupt int10_new(INT_PARMS),    /* video interrupt          */
        interrupt int14_new(INT_PARMS),    /* serial interrupt         */
        interrupt int16_new(INT_PARMS),    /* keyboard                 */
        interrupt int17_new(INT_PARMS),    /* printer interrupt        */
        interrupt int21_new(INT_PARMS),    /* DOS interrupt            */
        interrupt int25_new(INT_PARMS),    /* Absolute disk read       */
        interrupt int26_new(INT_PARMS),    /* Absolute disk write      */
        interrupt int67_new(INT_PARMS),    /* EMS interrupt            */
        check_arguments(int, char **),     /* check cmd line arguments */
        install_handlers(void),            /* install interrupt rtns   */
        remove_handlers(void),             /* de-install interrupt rtns*/
        user_report(void);                 /* final report             */
int     control_break(void);               /* control break handler    */
```

```
/* **************************************************************** *
 *       globals                                                    *
 * **************************************************************** */

int     rc = 1,                             /* errorlevel return code  */
        pgm_token = 1,                      /* program name token      */
        enabled = 0;                        /* flag for new int handlers*/

char    *log_name,                          /* log file name           */
        cmd_line[128];                      /* command line buffer     */

long    int21_cnt[256];                     /* DOS subfunction counts  */

struct                                      /* usage by classification */
    {
    long int_tcnt;                          /* count for this int type */
    char *int_tdes;                         /* description             */
    } int_type[] =
        { { 0, "Console Calls" },
          { 0, "Disk Calls" },
          { 0, "Printer Calls" },
          { 0, "Video Calls" },
          { 0, "Memory Management Calls" },
          { 0, "Serial Communications" },
          { 0, "Operating System Calls" }
        };

#define INT_NONE -1
#define INT_CON    0
#define INT_DISK   1
#define INT_PRT    2
#define INT_VID    3
#define INT_MEM    4
#define INT_COMM   5
#define INT_DOS    6
#define INT_TYPE sizeof(int_type) / sizeof(int_type[0])


struct                                      /* i/o byte counts         */
    {
    char *io_desc;                          /* description             */
    long io_read,                           /* bytes read              */
         io_write;                          /* bytes written           */
    } io_cnt[] =
        { { "Keyboard" },
          { "Video" },
          { "Serial" },
          { "Printer" },
          { "File" }
        };

#define IO_KB      0
#define IO_VID     1
#define IO_COMM    2
#define IO_PRT     3
#define IO_FILE    4
#define IO_CNT     sizeof(io_cnt) / sizeof(io_cnt[0])

struct                                      /* interrupt list          */
    {
    int  int_nbr;                           /* interrupt number        */
    char int_itype,                         /* interrupt type          */
         *int_text;                         /* description             */
```

```
        void (interrupt far *int_new)(),        /* new routine address    */
             (interrupt far *int_old)(void);    /* old int address        */
        long int_cnt;                           /* int usage count        */
        } int_list[] =
             { { 0x08, INT_NONE, "Timer",        int08_new },
               { 0x10, INT_VID,  "Video",        int10_new },
               { 0x14, INT_COMM, "Serial I/O",   int14_new },
               { 0x16, INT_CON,  "Keyboard",     int16_new },
               { 0x17, INT_PRT,  "Printer",      int17_new },
               { 0x67, INT_MEM,  "EMS",          int67_new },
               { 0x21, INT_NONE, "DOS",          int21_new },
               { 0x25, INT_DISK, "Disk read",    int25_new },
               { 0x26, INT_DISK, "Disk write",   int26_new }
             };

#define INT_08     0                            /* int_list entries        */
#define INT_10     1
#define INT_14     2
#define INT_16     3
#define INT_17     4
#define INT_67     5
#define INT_21     6
#define INT_25     7
#define INT_26     8
#define INT_LIST   sizeof(int_list) / sizeof(int_list[0])


        struct                                  /* int 21 subfunctions     */
           {
           char int21_type;                     /* type of function        */
           char *int21_text;                    /* description of function */
           } int21_list[] =
               { { INT_DOS,  "Program termination" },
                 { INT_CON,  "Keyboard input" },
                 { INT_VID,  "Display output" },
                 { INT_CON,  "AUX input" },
                 { INT_CON,  "AUX output" },
                 { INT_PRT,  "Printer output" },
                 { INT_CON,  "Direct console I/O" },
                 { INT_CON,  "Direct STDIN input, no echo" },
                 { INT_CON,  "Keyboard input, no echo" },
                 { INT_VID,  "Print string" },
                 { INT_CON,  "Buffered keyboard input" },
                 { INT_CON,  "Check standard input status" },
                 { INT_CON,  "Clear keyboard buffer" },
                 { INT_DISK, "Disk reset" },
                 { INT_DISK, "Select disk" },
                 { INT_DISK, "Open disk file" },
                 { INT_DISK, "Close disk file" },
                 { INT_DISK, "Search first using FCB" },
                 { INT_DISK, "Search next using FCB" },
                 { INT_DISK, "Delete file via FCB" },
                 { INT_DISK, "Sequential disk file read" },
                 { INT_DISK, "Sequential disk record write" },
                 { INT_DISK, "Create a disk file" },
                 { INT_DISK, "Rename file via FCB" },
                 { INT_DOS,  "Internal Use" },
                 { INT_DOS,  "Get default disk number" },
                 { INT_DOS,  "Set disk transfer area" },
                 { INT_DISK, "Get allocation for default drive" },
                 { INT_DISK, "Get allocation for specific drive" },
                 { INT_DOS,  "Internal Use" },
                 { INT_DOS,  "Internal Use" },
                 { INT_DOS,  "Get default drive parm block" },
```

```
{ INT_DOS,  "Internal Use" },
{ INT_DISK, "Random disk record read" },
{ INT_DISK, "Random disk record write" },
{ INT_DISK, "Get file size" },
{ INT_DISK, "Set random record field" },
{ INT_DOS,  "Set interrupt vector" },
{ INT_MEM,  "Create PSP" },
{ INT_DISK, "Random block read" },
{ INT_DISK, "Random block write" },
{ INT_DOS,  "Parse filename" },
{ INT_DOS,  "Get date" },
{ INT_DOS,  "Set date" },
{ INT_DOS,  "Get time" },
{ INT_DOS,  "Set time" },
{ INT_DOS,  "Set verify flag" },
{ INT_DOS,  "Get disk transfer area" },
{ INT_DOS,  "Get DOS version" },
{ INT_DOS,  "Terminate and stay resident" },
{ INT_DOS,  "Get drive parameter block" },
{ INT_DOS,  "Extended ^Break/Get boot drive" },
{ INT_DOS,  "Get CritSectFlag pointer" },
{ INT_DOS,  "Get interrupt vector" },
{ INT_DOS,  "Get disk space" },
{ INT_DOS,  "Get/set SWITCHAR" },
{ INT_DOS,  "Get/set country information" },
{ INT_DISK, "Create a subdirectory" },
{ INT_DISK, "Remove a directory entry" },
{ INT_DISK, "Change current directory" },
{ INT_DISK, "Create a file with handle" },
{ INT_DISK, "Open disk file with handle" },
{ INT_DISK, "Close a file with handle" },
{ INT_DISK, "Read from file with handle" },
{ INT_DISK, "Write to file with handle" },
{ INT_DISK, "Delete a file" },
{ INT_DISK, "Move file pointer" },
{ INT_DISK, "Get/put file attributes" },
{ INT_DISK, "IOCTL" },
{ INT_DISK, "Create duplicate handle" },
{ INT_DISK, "Force duplicate handle" },
{ INT_DOS,  "Get current directory" },
{ INT_MEM,  "Allocate memory" },
{ INT_MEM,  "Free memory" },
{ INT_MEM,  "Adjust memory block size" },
{ INT_DISK, "Load or execute" },
{ INT_DOS,  "Quit with exit code" },
{ INT_DOS,  "Get exit code of subprogram" },
{ INT_DISK, "Find first ASCIIZ" },
{ INT_DISK, "Find next ASCIIZ" },
{ INT_DOS,  "Set PSP segment" },
{ INT_DOS,  "Get PSP segment" },
{ INT_DOS,  "Get list of lists" },
{ INT_DOS,  "Translate BIOS parameter block" },
{ INT_DOS,  "Get verify flag" },
{ INT_MEM,  "Create PSP" },
{ INT_DISK, "Rename a file" },
{ INT_DISK, "Get/set file's date/time" },
{ INT_MEM,  "Get/set memory allocation strategy" },
{ INT_DOS,  "Get extended error code" },
{ INT_DISK, "Create unique file" },
{ INT_DISK, "Create new file" },
{ INT_DISK, "Lock/unlock file access" },
{ INT_NONE, "Internal Use" },
{ INT_DOS,  "DOS 3.1 + Microsoft Networks" },
{ INT_DOS,  "Network" },
```

```
            { INT_DOS,   "Resolve path string" },
            { INT_NONE,  "Unused" },
            { INT_DOS,   "Get PSP address" },
            { INT_DOS,   "2-byte character support" },
            { INT_NONE,  "Unused" },
            { INT_DOS,   "Country-dependent support" },
            { INT_DOS,   "Get/set global code page table" },
            { INT_DOS,   "Set handle count" },
            { INT_DISK,  "Commit file" },
            { INT_DISK,  "Get/set disk serial number" },
            { INT_NONE,  "Unused" },
            { INT_NONE,  "Unused" },
            { INT_DISK,  "Extended open/create" }
        };

#define INT21_LIST sizeof(int21_list) / sizeof(int21_list[0])


struct   dosdate_t start_d, end_d;          /* date fields        */
struct   dostime_t start_t, end_t;          /* ..and time fields  */


/* *********************************************************************** *
 *          messages and strings                                           *
 * *********************************************************************** */

char     copyright[]      = "INFORMER 1.00 \xfe Copyright (c) 1992, "
                            "Michael Holmes and Bob Flanders\n"
                            "PC Magazine C Lab Notes \xfe "
                            "Inform on a program's execution\n\n",
         stop_here[]      = "\nStopping at user's request\n",
         not_found[]      = "Requested program not found\n",
         bad_log[]        = "Could not open output log file %s\n",
         header[]         = "\n--------------- Informer Statistics "
                            "---------------\n",
         cmd_msg[]        = "    Command Line: %s",
         time_msg[]       = "\n    %s: %2d:%02d:%02d",
         date_msg[]       = " on %02d/%02d/%d",
         starting[]       = "   Started at",
         ending[]         = "Completed at",
         run_time[]       = "\n     Elapsed Time: %2d:%02d:%02d.%02d",
         term_msg[]       = "\nTermination Code: %d\n",
         int_hdr[]        = "\nInterrupt Usage\n",
         int_msg[]        = "%8ld Int %02X - %s interrupt\n",
         int21_hdr[]      = "\nInt 21 (DOS) Breakdown by Function\n",
         int21_msg[]      = "%8ld Fnc %02X - %s\n",
         type_hdr[]       = "\nUsage by Classification\n",
         type_msg[]       = "%8ld - %s\n",
         io_hdr[]         = "\nInput/Output Byte Counts\n"
                            "     read  written\n",
        *io_msg[2]      = { "%8ld %8s - %s\n",
                            "%8ld %8ld - %s\n" },
         null_line[]      = "",
         help[]           =
            " Usage:  INFORMER  [/output]  program  [options]\n\n"
            "Options:  output  specifies the filename where INFORMER "
            "writes its report\n"
            "          program is the program INFORMER runs and "
            "monitors\n"
            "          options are the command line arguments for the "
            "monitored program\n";
```

```
/* ***************************************************************** *
 *        main()                                                     *
 * ***************************************************************** */

void     main(int   ac,                       /* DOS cmd line token count */
              char *av[])                      /* ..token strings          */
{


printf(copyright);                            /* give copyright message   */

check_arguments(ac, av);                      /* check arguments          */
install_handlers();                           /* install interrupt rtns   */
rc = spawnvp(P_WAIT, av[pgm_token],           /* run requested program    */
             &av[pgm_token]);                 /* ..with user's arguments  */
remove_handlers();                            /* de-install interrupt rtns*/
user_report();                                /* give user feedback..     */
                                              /* ..and return to DOS      */

}



/* ***************************************************************** *
 *        check_arguments() -- check command line arguments          *
 * ***************************************************************** */

void     check_arguments(int   ac,            /* DOS cmd line token count */
                         char *av[])          /* ..token strings          */
{
int      i;                                   /* loop control             */
char     *p, *q;                              /* string pointers          */


if (NOT strcmp(av[1], "/?"))                  /* q. user needs help?      */
    quit_with(help);                          /* a. yes .. give help/quit */

if (av[1][0] == '/')                          /* q. user wants a log file?*/
    {
    log_name = &av[1][1];                     /* a. yes .. save name      */
    i = 2;                                    /* ..and skip to next token */
    }
 else
    i = 1;                                    /* else .. start w/first one*/

if (ac <= i)                                  /* q. missing program name? */
    quit_with(help);                          /* a. yes .. give help/quit */

if ((p = strchr(q = av[i], '/')) != 0)        /* q. cmd & switch together?*/
    {
    av[--i] = malloc(p - q + 1);              /* a. yes .. get space for..*/
    strncpy(av[i], q, p - q);                 /* ..another copy of the cmd*/
    av[i][p - q] = '\0';                      /* ..and null terminate it  */
    av[i + 1] = p;                            /* ..make /switch be a token*/
    }

for (pgm_token = i; i < ac; i++)              /* for each argument        */
    {
    if (strchr(av[i], ' '))                   /* q. token contain blanks? */
        {
        p = malloc(strlen(av[i]) + 3);        /* a. yes .. get new string */
        sprintf(p, "\"%s\"", av[i]);          /* surround string w/quotes */
        av[i] = p;                            /* ..and store new address  */
        }
```

```
        if (pgm_token != i)                 /* q. 1st item on line?    */
            strcat(cmd_line, " ");          /* a. no .. put a space 1st */

        strcat(cmd_line, av[i]);            /* ..then add the argument  */
        }
}


/* *********************************************************************** *
 *        install_handlers() -- install interrupt handlers               *
 * *********************************************************************** */
void    install_handlers(void)
{
int     i;                                  /* loop control            */


for (i = 0; i < INT_LIST; i++)              /* for each interrupt      */
    {
    int_list[i].int_old = _dos_getvect(     /* get old interrupt ..    */
                int_list[i].int_nbr);       /* ..vector address        */

    _dos_setvect(int_list[i].int_nbr,       /* install new ..          */
                int_list[i].int_new);       /* ..interrupt handler     */
    }
_dos_getdate(&start_d);                     /* get start date..        */
_dos_gettime(&start_t);                     /* ..and start time        */

}



/* *********************************************************************** *
 *        remove_handlers() -- remove interrupt handlers                 *
 * *********************************************************************** */
void    remove_handlers(void)
{
int     i;                                  /* loop control            */


enabled = 0;                                /* stop collecting data    */

_dos_getdate(&end_d);                       /* get ending date..       */
_dos_gettime(&end_t);                       /* ..and time              */

int21_cnt[0x4d]--;                          /* back out "get rc" call  */
int_list[INT_21].int_cnt--;                 /* ..from int 21 counts    */

for (i = 0; i < INT_LIST; i++)              /* for each interrupt      */
    _dos_setvect(int_list[i].int_nbr,       /* restore old ..          */
                int_list[i].int_old);       /* ..interrupt handler     */

}



/* *********************************************************************** *
 *        user_report() -- give user the final report                    *
 * *********************************************************************** */
void    user_report(void)
{
```

```
int     i,                              /* loop control            */
        hdr = 0,                        /* int 21 header flag       */
        hh, mm, ss;                     /* hours, minutes, seconds  */
long    hs;                             /* ..and hundredths seconds */
FILE    *log;                           /* output log file handle   */

if (rc == -1)                           /* q. find requested pgm?   */
    quit_with(not_found);               /* a. no .. quit w/error msg*/

if (log_name)                           /* q. log file specified?   */
    {                                   /* a. yes .. try opening it */
    if (NOT (log = fopen(log_name, "w")))  /* q. log open sucessfully? */
        quit_with(bad_log, log_name);   /* a. no .. quit w/error msg*/
    }
 else
    log = stdout;                       /* use console as log file  */

fprintf(log, header);                   /* give summary header      */
fprintf(log, cmd_msg, cmd_line);        /* ..command line           */
fprintf(log, time_msg, starting,        /* ..start time             */
            TIME(start_t));
fprintf(log, date_msg, DATE(start_d));  /* ..and start date         */
fprintf(log, time_msg, ending, TIME(end_t));/* ..end'g time         */

if (strncmp((void *) &start_d,          /* q. date change while     */
            (void *) &end_d,            /* ..we were running the    */
            sizeof(struct dostime_t)))  /* ..user's program?        */
    fprintf(log, date_msg, DATE(end_d));   /* a. yes .. give end'g date*/

hs = int_list[INT_08].int_cnt * 1000 / 182; /* ticks to hundredth secs  */
hh = (int) (hs / 360000L);              /* get hours                */
hs %= 360000L;                          /* ..then remove from total */
mm = (int) (hs / 6000);                 /* get minutes              */
hs %= 6000;                             /* ..then remove from total */
ss = (int) (hs / 100);                  /* get seconds              */
hs %= 100;                              /* ..leaving hundredths secs*/

fprintf(log, run_time, hh, mm, ss, hs); /* give run-time message    */
fprintf(log, term_msg, rc);             /* ..termination code       */

fprintf(log, int_hdr);                  /* give int header message  */

for (i = 1; i < INT_LIST; i++)          /* for each interrupt       */
    if (int_list[i].int_cnt)            /* q. any of that interrupt?*/
        {
        fprintf(log, int_msg,           /* a. yes .. display message*/
                int_list[i].int_cnt,    /* ..and count              */
                int_list[i].int_nbr,    /* ..and interrupt number   */
                int_list[i].int_text);  /* ..and interrupt name     */

        if (int_list[i].int_itype != INT_NONE)     /* q. classifiable?*/
            int_type[int_list[i].int_itype].int_tcnt /* a. yes .. build */
                += int_list[i].int_cnt;            /* ..counts by type*/
        }

for (i = 0; i < INT21_LIST; i++)        /* for each known function  */
    if (int21_cnt[i] > 0)               /* q. function used?        */
        {                               /* a. yes .. report on count*/
        if (NOT hdr)                    /* q. header given yet?      */
            {
            fprintf(log, int21_hdr);    /* a. no .. display header   */
            hdr++;                      /* ..and show header given   */
            }
```

```
            fprintf(log, int21_msg,              /* a. yes .. report count    */
                    int21_cnt[i], i,
                    int21_list[i].int21_text);

            if (int21_list[i].int21_type != INT_NONE)      /* q. collect?  */
                int_type[int21_list[i].int21_type].int_tcnt /* yes .. add   */
                    += int21_cnt[i];                       /* ..to totals   */
            }

    fprintf(log, type_hdr);                      /* give usage hdr message    */
    for (i = 0; i < INT_TYPE; i++)               /* print each type of call   */
        if (int_type[i].int_tcnt)                /* q. counter non-zero?      */
            fprintf(log, type_msg,               /* a. yes.. give usage stats*/
                    int_type[i].int_tcnt,
                    int_type[i].int_tdes);

    fprintf(log, io_hdr);                        /* give i/o cnts hdr msg     */
    for (i = 0; i < IO_CNT; i++)                 /* print each byte cnt type */
        if (io_cnt[i].io_read ||                 /* q. anything to report..   */
                io_cnt[i].io_write)              /* ..inbound or outbound?    */
            {                                    /* a. yes .. print a line    */
            if (i == IO_KB)                      /* q. byte cnt for keyboard?*/
                fprintf(log, io_msg[0],          /* a. yes .. give read cnts  */
                    io_cnt[i].io_read, "",
                    io_cnt[i].io_desc);
            else
                fprintf(log, io_msg[1],          /* else .. print read..      */
                    io_cnt[i].io_read,           /* ..and write counts        */
                    io_cnt[i].io_write,
                    io_cnt[i].io_desc);
            }

    if (log_name)                                /* q. log file being used?   */
        fclose(log);                             /* a. yes .. close log file  */

    rc = 0;                                      /* reset return code         */
    quit_with(null_line);                        /* ..and return to DOS       */

    }


/* *********************************************************************** *
 *       quit_with() -- give an error message, then return to DOS          *
 * *********************************************************************** */

void    quit_with(char *msg, ...)                /* string to print          */
{
va_list list;                                    /* variable list            */


va_start(list, msg);                             /* set up variable list     */
vprintf(msg, list);                              /* give error message ..    */
exit(rc);                                        /* ..and then quit          */

}


/* *********************************************************************** *
 *       int08_new() -- timer interrupt appendage                          *
 * *********************************************************************** */

#pragma option -Od                               /* no optimization          */
#pragma argsused                                 /* hold unused argument messages */
```

```
void    interrupt int08_new(INT_PARMS)
{

if (enabled)                            /* q. collecting data?      */
    int_list[INT_08].int_cnt++;         /* a. yes .. tally ticks    */

_chain_intr(*int_list[INT_08].int_old); /* jump to old int handler  */

}


/* ********************************************************************* *
 *       int10_new() -- video interrupt                                  *
 * ********************************************************************* */

#pragma argsused                        /* hold unused argument messages  */

void    interrupt int10_new(INT_PARMS)
{

switch (ax >> 8)                        /* based on function code   */
    {
                                        /* read functions           */
    case 0x08:                          /* character & attributes    */
    case 0x0d:                          /* pixel                    */
        io_cnt[IO_VID].io_read++;       /* bump read byte count      */
        break;                          /* ..and continue           */

                                        /* write functions           */
    case 0x09:                          /* character & attribute     */
    case 0x0a:                          /* character only            */
    case 0x0c:                          /* pixel                    */
    case 0x0e:                          /* tty mode                 */
        io_cnt[IO_VID].io_write++;      /* bump write byte count     */
        break;                          /* ..and continue           */

    case 0x13:                          /* write string             */
        io_cnt[IO_VID].io_write += cx;  /* add characters written    */
    }

int_list[INT_10].int_cnt++;             /* tally video int requests */
_chain_intr(*int_list[INT_10].int_old); /* jump to old int handler  */

}


/* ********************************************************************* *
 *       int14_new() -- serial i/o                                       *
 * ********************************************************************* */

#pragma argsused                        /* hold unused argument messages  */

void    interrupt int14_new(INT_PARMS)
{

switch (ax >> 8)                        /* based on function code   */
    {
    case 0x01:                          /* write character          */
        io_cnt[IO_COMM].io_write++;     /* bump write byte count     */
```

```
            break;                                  /* ..and continue        */

        case 0x02:                                  /* read character        */
            io_cnt[IO_COMM].io_read++;              /* bump read byte count  */
            break;                                  /* ..and continue        */
        }
    int_list[INT_14].int_cnt++;                     /* tally by serial i/o ints */
    _chain_intr(*int_list[INT_14].int_old);         /* jump to old int handler  */

    }


/* ********************************************************************* *
 *        int16_new() -- keyboard interrupt                            *
 * ********************************************************************* */

#pragma argsused                      /* hold unused argument messages      */

void    interrupt int16_new(INT_PARMS)
{

if (NOT (ax & 0xef00))                              /* q. getting a character? */
    io_cnt[IO_KB].io_read++;                        /* a. yes .. cnt keystrokes */

int_list[INT_16].int_cnt++;                         /* tally by keyboard calls  */
_chain_intr(*int_list[INT_16].int_old);             /* jump to old int handler  */

}


/* ********************************************************************* *
 *        int17_new() -- printer interrupts                            *
 * ********************************************************************* */

#pragma argsused                      /* hold unused argument messages      */

void    interrupt int17_new(INT_PARMS)
{

if (NOT (ax & 0xff00))                              /* q. printing a character? */
    io_cnt[IO_PRT].io_write++;                      /* a. yes .. cnt each one   */

int_list[INT_17].int_cnt++;                         /* tally printer interrupts */
_chain_intr(*int_list[INT_17].int_old);             /* jump to old int handler  */

}


/* ********************************************************************* *
 *        int21_handler() -- interrupt 21 handler                      *
 * ********************************************************************* */

#pragma argsused                      /* hold unused argument messages      */

void    interrupt int21_new(INT_PARMS)
{
```

```c
    if (enabled)                            /* q. collecting data?     */
        {
        int_list[INT_21].int_cnt++;         /* a. yes ..count all ints */
        int21_cnt[ax >> 8]++;               /* ..and tally by subfunc  */

        switch (ax >> 8)                     /* based on function code  */
            {
            case 0x3f:                       /* read from file/device   */
                io_cnt[IO_FILE].io_read += cx;  /* count bytes read     */
                break;                       /* ..and continue          */

            case 0x40:                       /* write to file/device    */
                io_cnt[IO_FILE].io_write += cx; /* count bytes written  */
                break;                       /* ..and continue          */
            }
        }

     else if (ax == 0x4b00)                  /* q. load/execute call?   */
        enabled++;                           /* a. yes ..start collecting*/

    _chain_intr(*int_list[INT_21].int_old);  /* then jump to old int21  */


    }



/* ********************************************************************* *
 *        int25_handler() -- absolute disk reads                       *
 * ********************************************************************* */

#pragma argsused                   /* hold unused argument messages    */

void     interrupt int25_new(INT_PARMS)
{


int_list[INT_25].int_cnt++;                 /* count disk reads        */
_chain_intr(*int_list[INT_25].int_old);     /* then jump to old int25  */


}



/* ********************************************************************* *
 *        int26_handler() -- absolute disk writes                      *
 * ********************************************************************* */

#pragma argsused                   /* hold unused argument messages    */

void     interrupt int26_new(INT_PARMS)
{


int_list[INT_26].int_cnt++;                 /* count disk writes       */
_chain_intr(*int_list[INT_26].int_old);     /* then jump to old int26  */


}
```

```
/* ********************************************************************** *
 *        int67_handler() -- EMS interrupt handler                        *
 * ********************************************************************** */

#pragma argsused                         /* hold unused argument messages    */

void    interrupt int67_new(INT_PARMS)
{


int_list[INT_67].int_cnt++;                  /* count EMS calls         */
_chain_intr(*int_list[INT_67].int_old);      /* then jump to old int67  */


}
```

3

RUNNING PROGRAMS ON OTHER NODES WITH NETRUN

NETRUN accepts a command line on one network node, and then receives and executes that command line on a second network node attached to a Novell NetWare local area network (LAN).

We can still recall one of the earliest arguments used to persuade a customer to buy a local area network (LAN) instead of a minicomputer: Adding a node to the network would increase the network's total computing power, but adding a new user to a mini would divide the available computing power among an ever-increasing community of users. And in all that persuasive talk, you never heard, "Oh, by the way, to run a program on the new LAN node, you'll have to walk down the hall and type a command."

Even today, most networks do not provide a utility for requesting execution of a program on another computer, letting you continue to work while the command executes. For example, compiling large programs often monopolizes your computer for several minutes. So if you need your computer to continue working, you will find yourself monopolized as well.

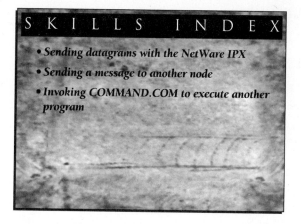

SKILLS INDEX

- *Sending datagrams with the NetWare IPX*
- *Sending a message to another node*
- *Invoking COMMAND.COM to execute another program*

NETRUN can help alleviate this problem. With NETRUN, you can submit commands on one network node for execution on another node. By offloading the execution of time-consuming programs onto another node, your computer remains available for your own use as these programs execute elsewhere. NETRUN also demonstrates one of the fundamentals of network programming: passing messages between network nodes.

■ USING NETRUN

NETRUN uses a simple command syntax, but there are some prerequisites for using the program. You must be running Novell NetWare 286 or 386, and, of course, you need to have a minimum of two nodes running DOS. The two nodes must be connected to the same NetWare server—NETRUN will not send a command across an internetwork bridge. (If you're not familiar with LAN technology, see the Endnote "Network Jargon" for definitions of many common terms.)

To exchange messages, NETRUN must be running on two nodes. One node is called the NETRUN *server*. This is the server that waits for the arrival of a command, sends back a positive acknowledgment message, executes the requested command, informs the requestor that the command has completed, and awaits the arrival of the next command. The syntax for starting NETRUN in server mode is

```
NETRUN /S
```

Once you've started the NETRUN server, you can execute NETRUN on the second node. This node is called the NETRUN *requestor*. Every five seconds, the requestor broadcasts the command you've requested until it receives a positive acknowledgment message that the command has been successfully received by a NETRUN server. Once it receives acknowledgment, the requestor terminates and returns to DOS. To send a command to the NETRUN server, use the following command:

```
NETRUN cmd-line
```

where *cmd-line* represents the command line you want executed on the NETRUN server. For example, to execute the DIR *.C command on the NETRUN server, enter this command:

```
NETRUN DIR *.C
```

Whether started as a server or requestor, NETRUN always starts by displaying its copyright notice. If run as a server, NETRUN then displays a message that it is in server mode, and settles in to wait for the arrival of a command request.

When run as a requestor, NETRUN displays the command line, and begins to transmit over the network. To let you know it is operating, NETRUN displays a period character each time it transmits the command line. When the requestor receives a positive acknowledgment message from the NETRUN server, it displays a message showing the *job number* assigned by the server, and returns to DOS. The job number is simply the number of requests received by the NETRUN server since the server was started. Figure 3.1 shows the relationship between the NETRUN requestor and NETRUN server as commands are executed.

To stop either the NETRUN server or NETRUN requestor, press the Ctrl-Break keycombination. When you do this, the NETRUN server displays the number of commands it has processed since NETRUN was started in server mode. Similarly, if you enter Ctrl-Break at the NETRUN requestor before the positive acknowledgment message arrives, the requestor displays a message that it has stopped executing by request of the user.

■ The NETRUN Environment

Although the command syntax of NETRUN is simple, there are some factors to be considered before you use NETRUN.

Running NETRUN in server mode on several network nodes means *all* of the NETRUN servers will execute *all* commands sent by *all* NETRUN requestors. And though the NETRUN requestor may be run simultaneously on many nodes, only one command at a time can be run by a NETRUN server. So if two users issue commands using the NETRUN requestor, the commands are executed one at a time by the NETRUN server. If user A issues a command before user B, and user A's command takes a significant amount of time to complete, user B's node will continue to retransmit its command until the NETRUN server becomes available to process the request. Of course, if user B becomes impatient, the command can be canceled with Ctrl-Break.

NETRUN provides no function for capturing output or redirecting input. For example, if you issue the command NETRUN DIR, DIR sends its output to the server screen, and you receive the completion message from the NETRUN server, but you have no way of seeing the directory listing at the requestor. You can't redirect DIR's output using the command

```
NETRUN DIR >DIR.TXT
```

because this redirects the NETRUN requestor's output, not the NETRUN server's.

FIGURE 3.1

*Relationship of
NETRUN
requestor to
NETRUN
server*

NETRUN Requestor

NETRUN Server

```
16:50 C:\NETRUN> netrun /s
NETRUN 1.00 • Copyright (c) 1992,
Bob Flanders and Michael Holmes
PC Magazine C Lab Notes • Run a
program at another network station

NETRUN is in server mode.  Ctrl-Break
to stop.
    User:  BOB[2]
 Command:  dir *.c
    Job:  1
```

Request #1

```
16:54 C:\UTIL> netrun dir *.c
NETRUN 1.00 • Copyright (c) 1992,
Bob Flanders and Michael Holmes
PC Magazine C Lab Notes • Run a
program at another network station

Sending to NETRUN server: dir *.c  .
Job 1 started by NETRUN server
```

```
Volume in drive C is MOH SYS
Directory of C:\NETRUN

NETRUN  C     27886  5-27-92  3:03p
        1 File(s)   4087808 bytes free

Completed Job:  1
 Last command:  dir *.c
    From User:  BOB[2]
-----------------------------------
NETRUN is in server mode.  Ctrl-Break
to stop.
    User:  BOB[2]
 Command:  set
    Job:  2
```

Request #2

```
16:55 C:\UTIL> netrun set
NETRUN 1.00 • Copyright (c) 1992,
Bob Flanders and Michael Holmes
PC Magazine C Lab Notes • Run a
program at another network station

Sending to NETRUN server: set  .
Job 2 started by NETRUN server
```

```
COMSPEC=C:\COMMAND.COM
PROMPT=$T$H$H$H ($P)
PATH=C:\;C:\DOS;C:\UTIL;Z:.;Y:.;X:.;
USERNAME=Michael

Completed Job:  2
 Last command:  set
    From User:  BOB[2]
-----------------------------------
NETRUN is in server mode.  Ctrl-Break
to stop.
*C
NETRUN terminating, 2 commands
processed.

16:56 C:\NETRUN>
```

To capture the output from a command run on a NETRUN server, use a batch program that redirects the appropriate command's output to a file. Place the .BAT file on a drive accessible by both the NETRUN requestor and server, and send a command to execute the batch program.

- **Note.** *Avoid using NETRUN to execute programs that require keyboard input. If you do, the program will stop the NETRUN server until the requested input has been entered.*

NETRUN provides no security and no built-in method of logging in to or out of a NetWare server. It's best to set up NETRUN with access to one or more common directories so that authorized users can send files to and receive files from NETRUN. These directories should be protected from unauthorized access. For example, you might place a new directory such as SYS:\NETRUN on the server, and create a NETRUN group having read, write, create, erase, modify, and file scan privileges for that new directory. You might also add a new user, NETRUNSERVER, with a login script that maps SYS:\NETRUN to a drive, makes the mapped drive the current drive, and executes NETRUN /S. If you place the NETRUN.EXE program in the NETRUN directory, only users who are members of the NETRUN group will have access to the program. Those users will also have the right to place files in the NETRUN directory (such as .BAT files, data files, and other files needed by a program executed under NETRUN).

■ INSIDE NETRUN

NETRUN is a combination of two straightforward programs: the server and the requestor. As noted earlier, the server waits for and processes requests sent by the requestor. The requestor simply broadcasts command lines until it receives a positive acknowledgment from a NETRUN server.

When you execute NETRUN, it displays its copyright notice and verifies the command line syntax by calling check_arguments(). The check_arguments() routine notes if you specified /? as the first argument, and if so, displays a help message and returns to DOS. Next, check_arguments() tests if you specified /S, requesting server mode. Since NETRUN does not accept any other command line arguments when you specify /S, check_arguments() tests for other arguments when it finds /S on the command line. If check_arguments() finds any other command line arguments, quit_with() is invoked to display a help message and return to DOS. Otherwise, check_arguments() sets the server variable to nonzero (indicating server mode), and returns to main().

If /S is not found on the command line, NETRUN assumes requestor mode, and check_arguments() tests if you specified a command line to send to the NETRUN server. If not, check_arguments() calls the quit_with() function to display the help message and return to DOS. Otherwise, check_arguments() concatenates the arguments from the command line into a single string suitable for passing to the system() routine, and returns to main().

■ NetWare's Addressing Scheme

NETRUN then opens two *sockets*, one for sending and one for receiving. NetWare uses sockets to address different processes within the same node. Sockets are one part of the addressing scheme in the Internetwork Packet Exchange (IPX) protocol used by the NETRUN server and requestor to communicate. (See the Endnote "NetWare's Protocols" for more information about protocols available under NetWare.)

NETRUN uses the IPX protocol because it provides an easy way to broadcast messages. When an application sends a message using IPX, it must include three pieces of information: the destination network, the destination node, and the destination socket.

The destination network is simply the network containing the destination node, and is addressed using a number assigned during network configuration. NETRUN sets this field to zero, telling NetWare to send the packet to nodes on the same physical network. Internetwork bridges ignore NETRUN's packets because of the zero in the destination node field. (To send messages across internetwork bridges you must know the network numbers of the destination nodes.)

The destination network field contains the physical address of the node that is to receive the message. If all of the bytes within the field contain the value 0xff, the message is broadcast to all nodes on the destination network. NETRUN does not target its messages to individual nodes; rather, it broadcasts all of its messages to all nodes on the net. Only nodes that are listening, however, will receive the broadcast packets.

The destination socket determines which process within a node will receive a message. Certain socket numbers are reserved by NetWare. For example, NetWare uses socket number 451 for file service packets. If you were to send a packet using socket 451, NetWare would likely reject the packet unless you formatted it as a valid file service request.

NETRUN uses socket number 0xb0bf to listen for packets on the NETRUN server, and socket number 0xb0c0 to listen for packets on the NETRUN requestor. Although both the NETRUN server and requestor could use a single socket for all sends and receives, in that case both the server and requestor would receive their own packets, because the packets are broadcast to all nodes on the net. Using a single socket would require additional code to recognize and ignore packets generated by the sending node.

NETRUN reserves its socket numbers by calling open_socket(). The open_socket() function first retrieves the connection number and user name of the current station by calling get_username().

■ Getting the Node's Login Name

The get_username() routine performs three functions: getting the current node's connection number, ensuring that NetWare is active on the current node, and getting the user name for the current node. The connection number is retrieved from NetWare by invoking DOS interrupt 0x21 with the get connection number function (0xdc00) in the AX register. The connection number, which may range from 1 to 100, is returned in the AL register. If AL contains zero after this function, get_username() calls quit_with() to display a message that the node is not connected to the network, and returns to DOS.

If the node is connected to the network, get_username() uses NetWare's get connection information function (0x16) to retrieve the name of the user on the current node. The get connection information function requires two operands: a request buffer and a reply buffer.

The request buffer must be in the format of a conn_packet structure, and contains three fields: the buffer length, a function code, and a connection number. Many functions supported by NetWare accept the address of a buffer where the first field is a 16-bit value containing the number of bytes *that follow the length field*. For example, if a buffer contains a 2-byte (16-bit) length field and a 4-byte (32-bit) count field, the total length of the buffer is 6, but the length field would be set to 4 since only 4 bytes follow the length field. For NetWare's get connection information function, the buffer length must be set to 2; the function code must be set to 0x16, telling NetWare that this is a get connection information request; and the connection number is set to the value returned by the get connection number function discussed earlier.

The reply buffer must be in the format of a name_packet structure, and contains five fields: the buffer length, the object ID, the object type, the object name, and the login time. Although several pieces of information are returned by get connection information, NETRUN is interested only in the object name. When the get connection information function is invoked, only the buffer length must be set to 63, which is the number of bytes following the length field in the name_packet structure.

Once get_username() has set up the buffers, it calls DOS interrupt 0x21 with the connection service function (0xe3). The connection service function accepts the addresses of the conn_packet and the name_packet structures. The conn_packet structure's function code field contains 0x16, which requests connection information. In response to this request, NetWare fills in the name_packet structure with information about the connection number specified in the conn_packet structure. NETRUN uses the n_name[] member of the name_packet structure that contains the login name for the current node. After retrieving the login name, get_username() returns to open_socket().

■ **Opening the Sockets**

Next, open_socket() enters a for loop, and issues the NetWare function to open (and therefore reserve) sockets number 0xb0bf and 0xb0c0. If either of these sockets is in use on *this node*, the open request fails, and NETRUN displays an error message and returns to DOS. Since a socket number can only be opened once on each node, NETRUN cannot be used to invoke itself. If NETRUN does invoke itself, the second copy fails, with the "Network socket in use" message. After the sockets have been successfully opened, open_sockets() starts a *listen* on the appropriate socket by calling listen_buffer().

■ **Listening for Messages**

When you write a program using the IPX protocol, that program does not call a function to actually receive a message. Rather, the application calls a function that sets up a *listen* for a message. Once the listen is established, NetWare returns control to the application, and the application can periodically check if a message has arrived. The listen_buffer() routine initiates a listen for NETRUN. (See the Endnote "Anatomy of IPX Send and Listen" for a more detailed explanation of send and listen packets with the IPX protocol.)

The listen_buffer() routine sets up the LISTEN message buffer ECB (event control block) structure to receive a packet on the appropriate socket (0xb0bf for the server, 0xb0c0 on the requestor). Once the function to start a listen has been executed, the associated control structure (ECB, IPX header, and message block) must not be tampered with until a message has arrived to fulfill the listen request, or the program cancels the listen by invoking a separate NetWare function. Altering the structure before the listen is fulfilled or canceled usually results in a crashed node, requiring a reboot to recover.

Once NETRUN starts the listen, a field in the ECB structure can be tested to determine if a packet satisfying the request has arrived. When the listen has been fulfilled, NetWare clears the LISTEN.ecb.e_use field to zero. After starting the listen, listen_buffer() returns to open_sockets(), and open_sockets() returns to main().

- ## The NETRUN Server

  After opening the sockets, NETRUN tests the server variable and, if it is nonzero, calls process_commands(), which starts the NETRUN server code. If the server variable is zero, NETRUN calls send_commands() to send the requested command to a NETRUN server.

  The process_commands() routine starts by displaying a message showing that the node is in NETRUN server mode. Then process_commands() enters an infinite loop that discards any characters entered at the keyboard and checks to see if a command request has arrived. (NETRUN discards keyboard input while awaiting a command, to prevent invalid and potentially harmful keyboard data from reaching the next command executed.) The only way to exit the NETRUN server is to press Ctrl-Break. Once a command has arrived, process_commands() calls run_command().

  The run_command() routine displays a message showing which user sent the command, the command that was sent, and the job number for the command. Next, run_command() sends the received command back to the sender as a positive acknowledgment, and passes the m_msg field of the message block to system().

  The system() routine loads a new copy of COMMAND.COM, which, in turn, executes the requested command. Since COMMAND.COM actually executes the requested command, the command that is passed to NETRUN can refer to an .EXE, .COM, or .BAT program, or a DOS internal command.

- **Note.** *There are several other methods of executing programs under C, such as the exec() and spawn() routines, but NETRUN uses the system() call so that batch programs and DOS internal commands may be executed. Although the system() routine is easier to use than exec() and spawn(), it has the disadvantage of using slightly more memory, leaving less for the executed program.*

  When the command finishes executing, run_command() sends a completion message to the node that requested the command, by calling broadcast_msg(). The function used by broadcast_msg() is the same function used by the NetWare SEND utility, which lets you send a message to a user at another node. NetWare displays the completion message unless the user has disabled the receipt of broadcast messages with the CASTOFF command.

  After sending the completion message, run_command() redisplays the job number, the command line, and the name of the user who sent the command. This lets you determine the last command executed by the NETRUN server, even if the executed command cleared the server's screen. Finally, run_command() initiates a listen for a new command by calling listen_buffer(), and returns to process_commands().

- ### The NETRUN Requestor

  If the server variable contains zero, NETRUN executes in requestor mode, and transmits the command line to the NETRUN server by calling send_command(). The Endnote "Anatomy of IPX Send and Listen" explains the setup performed by send_command() in preparation for sending a message. After the setup is complete, send_command() displays the command line being sent to the NETRUN server, and enters a while loop, repeatedly sending the command until it is acknowledged by the NETRUN server.

  To indicate each attempt, send_command() displays a single period character, and then broadcasts the request using an IPX send. Then send_command() checks to see that the send request completed, by calling wait_til(), which returns zero if the request completes within five seconds.

  If five seconds pass without the send completing, send_command() calls IPX requesting cancellation of the send function. (Note that the code to cancel the send is purely precautionary. Only under the most unusual circumstances will a send fail, such as extremely heavy network traffic or a hardware failure. If the send does fail, NETRUN cancels the send request so the control block structure can be reused in the next send attempt.)

  When the send function completes, send_command() calls wait_til() to test if the listen completes. A NETRUN requestor's listen only completes when the NETRUN server returns its positive acknowledgment. When the NETRUN requestor receives the positive acknowledgment, it breaks out of the while loop, displays the number of the job started on the NETRUN server, and returns to main(). Then main() releases the reservations on the open sockets by calling close_sockets(), and returns to DOS.

- ### What about Ctrl-Break?

  The NETRUN requestor normally terminates when it receives a positive acknowledgment from a NETRUN server. The Ctrl-Break key-combination may also be used to forcibly exit the NETRUN requestor. (Ctrl-Break is the *only* method for exiting the NETRUN server.) The control_break() routine receives control only when you press Ctrl-Break. When it receives control, control_break() calls close_sockets(), displays a message (if running as a NETRUN requestor), and returns a zero, which causes a return to DOS.

  It was noted earlier that an active listen must be completed or canceled, or the results are unpredictable, but control_break() does neither. Fortunately, closing a socket that has an active request automatically cancels any requests against that socket, so close_socket() implicitly cancels any listen request, leaving the system in a stable condition.

■ SUMMARY

NETRUN demonstrates the procedures needed to allow programs to communicate across a NetWare LAN. Here are a few enhancements you may wish to add to NETRUN:

- Add a name argument to the NETRUN server command, and allow the requestor to specify a NETRUN server.

- Allow the NETRUN requestor to specify a login name and password, and the NETRUN server to log in under the new name. This will preserve network security.

NETWARE'S PROTOCOLS

NETWARE supplies two network communications protocols: Internetwork Packet Exchange (IPX) and Sequenced Packet Exchange (SPX).

IPX is the lowest level of protocol included with NetWare, and provides great flexibility in packet routing. IPX does not require a connection to be established between communicating nodes. Therefore, packets may easily be broadcast for all nodes to hear. IPX's main disadvantage is that it does not guarantee delivery of the messages; nor does it guarantee that the messages will be delivered in the order sent.

SPX performs most of the functions of IPX, and also guarantees message delivery and message order. However, although SPX's use of IPX functions provides added functionality, SPX is slower than IPX. SPX can guarantee delivery because it requires that a connection be established with a remote node before messages can be sent. Unfortunately, this makes broadcasting a message with SPX exceptionally difficult. In order to do so, an application needs to establish a session with every node that is to receive the message, and send the message to each node separately.   ∎

ANATOMY OF IPX SEND AND LISTEN

The most complicated function performed by NETRUN is the sending of messages over the network. Transmission of messages with the Internetwork Packet Exchange (IPX) protocol is by no means an easy matter. Before examining the mechanics of IPX message transmission, you'll want to understand the underlying philosophy.

IPX provides a mechanism for *peer-to-peer* communications in a NetWare network. This means a program running on a network node can communicate with another program running on a different node, without accessing the file server. Under IPX, the peer-to-peer relationship can be *one-to-one* (message to a particular node/socket) or *one-to-many* (broadcast to a particular node/socket). NETRUN uses the one-to-many (broadcast) technique for sending messages across the network, allowing the NETRUN server to run on any node and still receive requests for command execution.

There are three parts of an IPX address: a network number, a node address, and a socket number. All three are necessary, but the socket number is of particular interest. Before any sends or listens can occur with IPX, a socket must be opened. Then the program can send a packet or listen for a packet on that socket number. Even when the network number and node address are correct, the message can't be delivered without a socket number.

When a program requests a send or a listen, the program passes a structure known as an event control block (ECB) to NetWare. NetWare uses an ECB as the point of interface with an application after certain functions have been invoked. For example, when an application requests a listen, NetWare informs the application that the listen has completed by placing data in the ECB. NetWare processes the request and immediately returns to the program, often before the processing completes. The application program must examine periodically the contents of the ECB to determine if the request completed or not. Although NETRUN does this, it only has one outstanding request at any given moment. A more complex application program might have several active requests outstanding, servicing the requests as they are fulfilled.

Once all processing for a particular socket is complete, the socket can be closed. Even if there are outstanding requests against that socket, they are automatically canceled when the applications closes the associated socket.

■ Sending and Listening, Up Close

To best understand the process of a send and listen, we will examine the steps necessary to transmit a single message. Figure 3.2 illustrates the layout of the structure for the control blocks IPX requires and the messages that NETRUN sends.

■ LISTENING

For the transmission of a message to be successful, some node on the network must be listening. To start a listen, the following steps are required:

1 *Open a socket.* Opening a socket is a simple operation, and is clearly shown in the open_sockets() routine. Both the sending and listening stations must use the same socket number, or the messages will never be received.

2 *Build the control block structure.* There are two control blocks that the program must provide to IPX: the event control block (ECB) and the IPX packet header. In the ECB, the socket field (e_socket), fragment count (e_fragcnt), fragment size (e_fragsize), and fragment address (e_fragaddr) must be set to

the socket number, number of fragments, size of the fragment, and IPX header address, respectively. A *fragment* is a discrete section of a message to be sent or received. Although not shown in Figure 3.2, you may have several copies of the last two fields of the ECB (e_fragaddr and e_fragsize) following the ECB. The e_fragcnt field contains the number of e_fragaddr and e_fragsize fields that follow the ECB. For our purposes, we will consider a message that has a single fragment.

The e_fragaddr field contains the address of an IPX packet header. Although you need not fill in any of the information in the IPX header during a listen, you must provide ample space to contain the header and any information that may follow the header. The information that follows the IPX header may be in any format—it's your message. Figure 3.2 shows the format of the messages passed by NETRUN.

3 *Ladies and gentlemen, start your listens.* After the control block structure is built, a listen must be initiated. This is done by setting register BX to 4, setting registers ES:SI to the address of the ECB, and invoking interrupt 0x7a. In response, NetWare starts a listen and returns to the calling program. (At this point, the program may continue with other functions, or simply wait in a loop for the listen to complete when a message is received.)

■   **SENDING A PACKET**

On the sending node, the process is slightly different. The control structure is the same, but the sending node must fill in more information before it sends the message. The steps are as follows:

1 *Open the socket.* The sending program, too, must open a socket. The socket number must be the same as the socket used on the destination node.

2 *Build the control block structure.* Similar to the listening program, the sending program must build the control block structure that supports the message being sent; however, the sending program must include some additional information. The sending program fills in the following fields in the ECB: e_socket, e_fragcnt, e_fragaddr, and e_fragsize. (These fields have the same meaning as for a listen function.) In addition, the sender must fill in the e_iaddr (immediate address) field. To do this, the sending program calls NetWare's get local target function, as shown in NETRUN's send_command() routine. The e_iaddr field tells NetWare how to route the message so that it arrives at the destination.

FIGURE 3.2

*IPX send/listen
control block
structure*

```
struct ecb_block                              /*event control block         */
  long e_link;                                   /* network link field      */
  char far *e_esr;                               /* ESR address             */
  char e_use,                                    /* in use flag             */
       e_code;                                   /* completion code         */
  int  e_socket;           = socket;            /* socket number           */
  long e_iwrk;                                   /* IPX work space          */
  char e_dwrk[12],                               /* driver work space       */
       e_iaddr[6];                               /* immediate address       */
  int  e_fragcnt;          = 1                   /* fragment count          */
  char far *e_fragaddr;                          /* fragment address        */
  int  e_fragsize;         = FRAGSIZE           /* fragment size           */


struct ipx_header                             /*IPX Header                  */
  int  i_chks,             = 0xffff            /* checksum                */
       i_len;              = SWAP (FRAGSIZE)   /* length                  */
  char i_tc,                                     /* transport control       */
       i_packet;           = 4                   /* packet type             */
  long i_dnet;                                   /* destination network     */
  char i_dnode[6];         = 0xffffffffffff     /* ..node                  */
  int  i_dsocket;          = socket             /* ..socket nbr            */
  long i_snet;                                   /* source network          */
  char i_snode[6];                               /* ..node                  */
  int  i_ssocket;          = socket             /* ..socket nbr            */
```

The user message area immediately
follows the IPX header.

```
struct message                                /*user message buffer        */
  int  m_len;              = LENGTHOF (msg)    /* message length          */
  char m_station,          = station          /* station number          */
       m_name[48],         <- user_name       /* login name              */
       m_msg[128];         <- command line    /* area for command        */
  int  m_sequence;                               /* job sequence number     */
```

In the IPX header, the sending program must fill in the following fields:

i_len   Packet length (the length of the IPX header plus any message data)

i_packet   Packet type (per NetWare, this field should be set to zero for an unknown type, or 4 for a "Packet Exchange Packet")

i_dnet   Network number containing the destination node (NETRUN uses zero, meaning the same physical network)

i_dnode   Destination node (NETRUN sets all the bytes in this field to 0xff, telling NetWare to broadcast the message)

i_dsocket   Destination socket number (sockets 1 through 0x4000 are reserved, and should not be used)

Of course, if any information is to follow the IPX header, the sending program is responsible for filling it in.

3 *Call the send function.* Having filled in the required fields, the sending program can then call the send function. When it does, the BX register must contain a 3, and the ES:SI registers must contain the address of the ECB describing the send. Once again, NetWare may return before the send completes, but will post the completion of the event in the ECB's e_use field.

- **Another Way to Process**
As you might expect, there is an alternative to periodically checking the ECB for the completion of an operation. In the ECB, there is a field call e_esr (event service routine). When the operation associated with the ECB completes, NetWare checks the value in the e_esr field. If the value is nonzero, NetWare calls the routine whose address is found in e_esr. This routine can perform any processing necessary to clean up after the operation completes, such as returning the ECB to a list of free ECBs, posting some other control structure, and so on.

- **Note**. *Be careful not to place garbage in the e_esr field, either before invoking the function or while the program is waiting for an operation to complete, because NetWare will transfer control to the address in this field, whether the value is valid or not.*

- **It's All Over but the Closing**

  When the send completes on the sending node, or the receive completes on the listening node, the programs should close the sockets. If either program terminates without closing the sockets, the sockets will remain open, and you will have to reboot the node (or run a program to close the sockets) before the sockets can be reopened.

  Of course, there is an exception to this rule. The open socket function supports an option that marks a socket to automatically close when the program terminates. If so marked, the socket closes when the program returns to DOS. Generally, the only programs that need to mark a socket as permanent are terminate-and-stay-resident (TSR) programs that use IPX. TSR software needs to use the permanent option to keep the socket open when the program returns to DOS using DOS's TSR function.

- **When It Absolutely, Positively Has to Get There**

  Just because a send completes successfully does not mean that the message has arrived at the listening node. IPX only guarantees that the message makes it out of the sending node. If a node is not listening, the message is lost. If the transmission media garbles the message, the message is lost.

  If your application requires assurance of packet delivery, there are two alternatives: You can require a reply from the listening node, or use the SPX protocol. When a message arrives at a listening machine, the IPX header is set up to be returned to the sender. This is evident in NETRUN's run_command() routine, which does practically no setup before returning the received message to the sender. The other alternative, the SPX protocol, provides guaranteed, sequenced delivery of packets. This protocol is documented in manuals available from Novell.   ■

ENDNOTE

NETWORK JARGON

When writing and using network programs, you are likely to encounter any of the following terms:

ACKNOWLEDGMENT: An acknowledgment is an indication that a transmission has been received successfully (positive acknowledgment) or unsuccessfully (negative acknowledgment). NETRUN sends a positive acknowledgment from the NETRUN server to the NETRUN requestor when a command has been received.

BRIDGE: A bridge is a combination of hardware and software that allows networks to communicate with each other.

BROADCAST: A message is broadcast when it is sent to all nodes on a network. The NETRUN requestor, for example, broadcasts its execution requests.

EVENT CONTROL BLOCK (ECB): An event control block is a data structure used by NetWare to communicate with an application program after the application requests a send or receive function.

INTERNETWORK: An internetwork is two or more networks connected via an internetwork bridge. Under NetWare, each of the networks will have a different network number. NETRUN will only communicate between nodes that are attached to the same network.

IPX: Internetwork Packet Exchange (IPX) is the lowest-level protocol provided with NetWare. IPX provides transmission of messages across the network, but does not guarantee the delivery of the messages or the order in which the messages are recieved. *See SPX*.

LISTEN: The NetWare listen function sets up a control block structure to receive a message using IPX. A listen remains active until a message is received or the application explicitly cancels the listen request.

NetWare: NetWare is a local area network (LAN) operating system produced by Novell, Inc. Included with NetWare are the operating system and utilities needed to operate and administer a local area network.

NetWare FILE SERVER: The NetWare file server is a machine that runs the NetWare operating system, and has one or more hard drives containing data files to be shared among network users.

NETWORK: A network is a set of computers connected by hardware that allows the computers to communicate with each other.

NODE: A node is a single computer connected to a network.

SOCKET NUMBER: A socket number is a value chosen by a network application and used to identify which process on a node will receive a message. NETRUN uses socket numbers 0xb0bf and 0xb0c0.

SPX: Sequenced Packet Exchange (SPX) is a NetWare protocol that guarantees delivery of messages, and ensures that the messages are received in the order sent. SPX uses IPX to transmit the messages between network nodes. *See IPX.*   ■

NETRUN 1.00

```
/* ********************************************************************* *

    NETRUN 1.00, Copyright (c) 1992, Bob Flanders and Michael Holmes
    PC Magazine C Lab Notes, Run a program at another network station

 * ********************************************************************* *

    This code for Borland C++ version 3.0. (MSC version on diskette)

        Compile with:  BCC -O2 -mt netrun.c

    To compile for Microsoft C, you need to change the following:
         - handle MK_FP() and FP_SEG() macro differences
         - change control break handling for ctrlbrk() and control_break()

 * ********************************************************************* */


#pragma  pack(1)                              /* pack to byte alignment    */
#include <stdio.h>                            /* standard i/o library      */
#include <stdlib.h>                           /* commonly used routines    */
#include <dos.h>                              /* DOS rtn definitions       */
#include <string.h>                           /* string functions          */
#include <conio.h>                            /* console i/o functions     */

#define NOT !                                 /* logical not               */
#define UINT unsigned                         /* unsigned integer          */
#define SWAP(x) ((x >> 8) | (x << 8))         /* byte swapping             */
#define SET(x,y) memset(x, y, sizeof(x))      /* memset an area            */
#define LENGTHOF(x) sizeof(x) - sizeof(int)   /* control block length      */

#define WAIT        91                        /* 91 ticks (5 sec) wait     */
#define SOCKET      0xB0BF                     /* NETRUN socket number      */
#define IPXINT      0x7a                       /* IPX interrupt number      */

                                              /* IPX functions             */
#define IPX_OPEN          0                   /*   open a socket           */
#define IPX_CLOSE         1                   /*   close a socket          */
#define IPX_GET_TARGET    2                   /*   get local target fnc    */
#define IPX_SEND          3                   /*   send function           */
#define IPX_LISTEN        4                   /*   listen for message      */
#define IPX_CANCEL        6                   /*   cancel event            */

#define CONN_SERVICE    0xe3                   /* connection service        */
#define CONN_GET_NAME   0x16                   /* get connection info fnc   */
#define CONN_GET_NBR    0xdc00                 /* get connection number     */

#define MSG_BROADCAST   0xe1                   /* broadcast a message       */
```

```
/* ********************************************************************* *
 *         routine definitions                                          *
 * ********************************************************************* */

void      quit_with(char *),                  /* quit with error message  */
          check_arguments(int, char **),      /* check cmd line arguments */
          get_username(void),                 /* get network username     */
          process_commands(void),             /* handle incoming requests */
          open_sockets(void),                 /* open network socket      */
          close_sockets(void),                /* close network socket     */
          listen_buffer(void),                /* set up buffer to listen  */
          send_command(void),                 /* send command packet      */
          broadcast_msg(void),                /* broadcast reply message  */
          run_command(void);                  /* run user's command       */
int       control_break(void),                /* control break handler    */
          wait_til(UINT, char *);             /* event completion test    */


/* ********************************************************************* *
 *         globals                                                      *
 * ********************************************************************* */

int       rc = 1,                             /* errorlevel return code   */
          station,                            /* network connection nbr   */
          socket;                             /* open socket number       */

UINT      cmds_received;                       /* server mode cmds rec'd   */

char      server,                             /* server mode switch       */
          cmd_line[128];                      /* target command line      */

extern
UINT      _heaplen = 1024;                     /* specify very small heap  */


/* ********************************************************************* *
 *         structures                                                   *
 * ********************************************************************* */

struct   SREGS    s;                          /* segment registers        */
union    REGS     r;                          /* other registers          */

struct conn_packet                            /* connection request packet*/
    {
    int  c_len;                               /* packet length            */
    char c_fnc;                               /* function code            */
    char c_station;                           /* station number           */
    } conn_pkt;

struct name_packet                            /* logon name reply packet  */
    {
    int  n_len;                               /* packet length            */
    long n_uid;                               /* unique id                */
    int  n_type;                              /* type                     */
    char n_name[48],                          /* login name               */
         n_log[8];                            /* log time                 */
    } name_pkt;

struct bc_packet                              /* broadcast msg packet      */
    {
    int  b_len;                               /* packet length            */
    char b_fnc,                               /* function code            */
         b_cnt,                               /* station count            */
         b_station,                           /* station number           */
```

```
              b_mlen,                      /* message length         */
              b_msg[128];                  /* message text           */
         } bc_pkt;

    struct bcr_packet                      /* broadcast reply packet */
         {
         int  r_len;                       /* packet length          */
         char r_cnt,                       /* station count          */
              r_status;                    /* completion status      */
         } bcr_pkt;

    struct ecb_block                       /* event control block    */
         {
         long e_link;                      /* network link field     */
         char far *e_esr;                  /* ESR address            */
         char e_use,                       /* in use flag            */
              e_code;                      /* completion code        */
         int  e_socket;                    /* socket number          */
         long e_iwrk;                      /* IPX work space         */
         char e_dwrk[12],                  /* driver work space      */
              e_iaddr[6];                  /* immediate address      */
         int  e_fragcnt;                   /* fragment count         */
         char far *e_fragaddr;             /* fragment address       */
         int  e_fragsize;                  /* fragment size          */
         };

    struct ipx_header                      /* IPX Header             */
         {
         int  i_chks,                      /* checksum               */
              i_len;                       /* length                 */
         char i_tc,                        /* transport control      */
              i_packet;                    /* packet type            */
         long i_dnet;                      /* destination network    */
         char i_dnode[6];                  /* ..node                 */
         int  i_dsocket;                   /* ..socket nbr           */
         long i_snet;                      /* source network         */
         char i_snode[6];                  /* ..node                 */
         int  i_ssocket;                   /* ..socket nbr           */
         };

    struct message                        /* user message buffers   */
         {
         int  m_len;                       /* message length         */
         char m_station,                   /* station number         */
              m_name[48],                  /* login name             */
              m_msg[128];                  /* area for command       */
         int  m_sequence;                  /* job sequence number    */
         };

    struct                                /* IPX message blocks     */
         {
         struct ecb_block   ecb;           /* event control block    */
         struct ipx_header  ipx;           /* IPX header             */
         struct message     msg;           /* user data              */
         } msg_buffer[2];                  /* message buffers/packets */

    #define FRAGSIZE (sizeof(SEND.ipx) + sizeof(SEND.msg))  /* fragment size*/
    #define LISTEN msg_buffer[0]           /* receiving buffer       */
    #define SEND   msg_buffer[1]           /* sending buffer         */
```

```
/* ******************************************************************* *
 *       messages and strings                                          *
 * ******************************************************************* */

char    copyright[]      = "NETRUN 1.00 \xfe Copyright (c) 1992, "
                           "Bob Flanders and Michael Holmes\n"
                           "PC Magazine C Lab Notes \xfe "
                           "Run a program at another network station\n\n",
        stop_here[]      = "\nStopping at user's request\n",
        no_network[]     = "Network not loaded\n",
        in_use[]         = "Network socket in use\n",
        running[]        = "\n   User: %s[%u]\n"
                           "Command: %s\n"
                           "    Job: %u\n\n",
        sending[]        = "Sending to NETRUN server: %s  ",
        started_job[]    = "\nJob %u started by NETRUN server\n",
        one_dot[]        = ".",
        job_done[]       = "NETRUN completed job %u: %s",
        end_of_job[]     = "\nCompleted Job: %u\n"
                           " Last command: %s\n"
                           "    From User: %s[%u]\n"
                           "--------------------------------------------\n",
        waiting[]        = "NETRUN is in server mode. Ctrl-Break to stop.\n",
        totals[]         = "NETRUN terminating, %d commands processed.\n",
        help[]           =
                  " Usage: NETRUN   /S\n"
                  "        NETRUN   cmd_line\n\n"
                  "Options: /S        specifies NETRUN server mode\n"
                  "         cmd_line is the command to execute on the NETRUN "
                  "server\n";

/* ******************************************************************* *
 *       main()                                                        *
 * ******************************************************************* */

void    main(int  ac,                      /* DOS cmd line token count */
             char *av[])                    /* ..token strings         */
{

printf(copyright);                         /* give copyright message  */

check_arguments(ac, av);                   /* check arguments         */
ctrlbrk(control_break);                    /* set up ctrl break handler*/
open_sockets();                            /* open network sockets    */

if (server)                                /* q. server mode?         */
   process_commands();                     /* a. yes .. wait for cmds */
else
   send_command();                         /* else, just send command */

close_sockets();                           /* close network sockets   */

}


/* ******************************************************************* *
 *       check_arguments() -- check command line arguments             *
 * ******************************************************************* */

void    check_arguments(int  ac,           /* DOS cmd line token count */
                        char *av[])         /* ..token strings          */
```

```
{
int     i;                               /* loop control            */
char    *p;                              /* string pointer          */


if (NOT strcmp(av[1], "/?"))             /* q. user needs help?     */
    quit_with(help);                     /* a. yes .. give help/quit */

if (NOT stricmp(av[1], "/S"))            /* q. run in server mode?  */
    {
    server++;                            /* a. yes .. set flag      */

    if (ac != 2)                         /* q. any other arguments? */
        quit_with(help);                 /* a. yes .. give help/quit */

    return;                              /* ..and return to caller  */
    }

if (ac < 2)                              /* q. missing program name? */
    quit_with(help);                     /* a. yes .. give help/quit */

for (i = 1; i < ac; i++)                 /* for each argument       */
    {
    if (strchr(av[i], ' '))              /* q. token contain blanks? */
        {
        p = malloc(strlen(av[i]) + 3);   /* a. yes .. get new string */
        sprintf(p, "\"%s\"", av[i]);     /* surround string w/quotes */
        av[i] = p;                       /* ..and store new address */
        }

    if (i != 1)                          /* q. 1st item on line?    */
        strcat(cmd_line, " ");           /* a. no .. put a space 1st */

    strcat(cmd_line, av[i]);             /* ..then add the argument */
    }
}


/* **********************************************************************  *
 *      process_commands() -- handle server mode processing             *
 * **********************************************************************  */

void    process_commands(void)
{

printf(waiting);                         /* tell user we are waiting */

while (1)                                /* loop 'til ctrl-break    */
    {
    if (kbhit())                         /* q. user hit a key?      */
        getch();                         /* a. yes .. get/discard key */

    if (NOT LISTEN.ecb.e_use)            /* q. something available? */
        run_command();                   /* a. yes .. run user cmd  */
    }

}
```

```
/* ********************************************************************* *
 *        run_command() -- run user command                            *
 * ********************************************************************* */

void    run_command(void)
{

printf(running, LISTEN.msg.m_name,            /* give server info like   */
            LISTEN.msg.m_station,             /* ..sequence, user name   */
            LISTEN.msg.m_msg,                 /* ..station number        */
            ++cmds_received);                 /* ..and command to run    */

                                              /* set up reply to command */
LISTEN.ipx.i_dsocket =                        /* ..destination and source */
    LISTEN.ipx.i_ssocket = socket + 1;        /* ..socket number         */
LISTEN.msg.m_sequence = cmds_received;        /* ..job number            */

r.x.bx = IPX_SEND;                            /* bx = send function code */
r.x.si = (unsigned) &LISTEN;                  /* si -> ECB               */
s.es = FP_SEG(&LISTEN);                       /* es:si -> ECB            */
int86x(IPXINT, &r, &r, &s);                   /* send reply to command   */

system(LISTEN.msg.m_msg);                     /* execute received command */
broadcast_msg();                              /* ..tell user we're done  */

printf(end_of_job, cmds_received,             /* show job number..       */
            LISTEN.msg.m_msg,                 /* ..last command          */
            LISTEN.msg.m_name,                /* ..and last user         */
            LISTEN.msg.m_station);            /* ..and user's station    */
printf(waiting);                              /* ..and waiting message   */

listen_buffer();                              /* prepare to rcv another  */

}


/* ********************************************************************* *
 *        send_command() -- send command line to NETRUN server         *
 * ********************************************************************* */

void    send_command(void)
{

                                              /* set up event control blk */
SEND.ecb.e_socket = socket;                   /* ..socket number         */
SEND.ecb.e_fragcnt = 1;                       /* ..fragment count        */
SEND.ecb.e_fragaddr = (char far *)&SEND.ipx;  /* ..user data area        */
SEND.ecb.e_fragsize = FRAGSIZE;               /* ..and fragment size     */

                                              /* set up IPX header       */
SEND.ipx.i_chks = 0xffff;                     /* ..checksum (disabled)   */
SEND.ipx.i_len = SWAP(FRAGSIZE);              /* ..packet length         */
SEND.ipx.i_packet = 4;                        /* ..packet type           */
SET(SEND.ipx.i_dnode, 0xff);                  /* ..destination net & node */
SEND.ipx.i_dsocket =                          /* ..destination and source */
    SEND.ipx.i_ssocket = socket;              /* ..socket number         */

                                              /* set up user message area */
SEND.msg.m_len = LENGTHOF(SEND.msg);          /* ..message length        */
SEND.msg.m_station = station;                 /* ..station number        */
strcpy(SEND.msg.m_name, name_pkt.n_name);     /* ..user name             */
strcpy(SEND.msg.m_msg, cmd_line);             /* ..and the command       */
```

```
r.x.bx = IPX_GET_TARGET;                  /* bx = get local target     */
r.x.si = (unsigned) &SEND.ipx.i_dnet;     /* si -> destination addr    */
r.x.di = (unsigned) SEND.ecb.e_iaddr;     /* di -> intermediate addr   */
s.es = FP_SEG(&SEND);                     /* es:si -> ECB              */
int86x(IPXINT, &r, &r, &s);               /* get local target address  */

printf(sending, cmd_line);                /* give status to user       */

while (1)                                 /* loop 'til message rcv'd   */
    {
    printf(one_dot);                      /* put out one dot per msg   */

    r.x.bx = IPX_SEND;                    /* bx = send function code   */
    r.x.si = (unsigned) &SEND;            /* si -> ECB                 */
    s.es = FP_SEG(&SEND);                 /* es:si -> ECB              */
    int86x(IPXINT, &r, &r, &s);           /* send ECB to listen        */

    if (wait_til(WAIT, &SEND.ecb.e_use))  /* q. send complete ok?      */
        {                                 /* a. no..cancel event       */
        r.x.bx = IPX_CANCEL;              /* bx = cancel event fnc     */
        r.x.si = (unsigned) &SEND;        /* si -> sending ECB         */
        s.es = FP_SEG(&SEND);             /* es:si -> ECB              */
        int86x(IPXINT, &r, &r, &s);       /* cancel send function      */

        continue;                         /* do send again             */
        }

    if (NOT wait_til(WAIT,                /* q. receive response..     */
                &LISTEN.ecb.e_use))       /* ..from NETRUN server?     */
        break;                            /* a. yes .. exit loop..     */
    }                                     /* ..server running request  */

printf(started_job, LISTEN.msg.m_sequence); /* give start of job info  */

}


/* ********************************************************************* *
 *       open_sockets() -- establish network sockets                   *
 * ********************************************************************* */

void    open_sockets(void)
{
int     i;                                /* loop control              */

get_username();                           /* get connection & username */
socket = SOCKET;                          /* save the base socket nbr  */

for (i = 0; i < 2; i++)                   /* loop opening sockets      */
    {
    r.x.bx = IPX_OPEN;                    /* bx = open socket fnc      */
    r.h.al = 0;                           /* al = open till end of job */
    r.x.dx = socket + i;                  /* dx = socket number        */
    int86(IPXINT, &r, &r);                /* open the socket           */

    if (r.h.al)                           /* q. open socket ok?        */
        quit_with(in_use);                /* a. no .. give error/quit  */
    }

listen_buffer();                          /* prepare to receive a msg  */

}
```

```
/* **************************************************************** *
 *       get_username() -- get connection number and user name     *
 * **************************************************************** */

void    get_username()
{

r.x.ax = CONN_GET_NBR;                      /* ah = get station number */
int86(0x21, &r, &r);                        /* get station number      */

if (NOT (station = r.h.al))                 /* q. network loaded?      */
    quit_with(no_network);                  /* a. no .. give error/quit */

conn_pkt.c_len = LENGTHOF(conn_pkt);        /* request packet length   */
conn_pkt.c_fnc = CONN_GET_NAME;             /* get connection name info */
conn_pkt.c_station = station;               /* our connection number   */
name_pkt.n_len = LENGTHOF(name_pkt);        /* reply packet length     */
r.x.si = (int) &conn_pkt;                   /* request packet          */
r.x.di = (int) &name_pkt;                   /* reply packet            */
r.h.ah = CONN_SERVICE;                      /* use connection services */
int86(0x21, &r, &r);                        /* get this station's name */

}


/* **************************************************************** *
 *       listen_buffer() -- prepare a buffer to receive a message  *
 * **************************************************************** */

void    listen_buffer(void)
{

LISTEN.ecb.e_use = 1;                       /* preset to not-in-use    */
LISTEN.ecb.e_socket = socket +              /* set up socket number    */
            (server ? 0 : 1);
LISTEN.ecb.e_fragcnt = 1;                   /* ..fragment count        */
LISTEN.ecb.e_fragsize = FRAGSIZE;           /* ..fragment size         */
LISTEN.ecb.e_fragaddr = (char far *) &LISTEN.ipx;   /* ..user data area */

r.x.bx = IPX_LISTEN;                        /* bx = listen function code*/
r.x.si = (UINT) &LISTEN;                    /* si -> ECB               */
s.es = FP_SEG(&LISTEN);                     /* es:si -> ECB            */
int86x(IPXINT, &r, &r, &s);                 /* listen a buffer         */

}


/* **************************************************************** *
 *       close_socket() -- close network socket                    *
 * **************************************************************** */

void    close_sockets()
{
int     i;                                  /* loop control            */

if (socket)                                 /* q. any sockets open?    */
    {                                       /* a. yes ..               */
    for (i = 0; i < 2; i++)                 /* loop, closing sockets   */
        {
        r.x.bx = IPX_CLOSE;                 /* bx = close socket fnc   */
```

```c
        r.x.dx = socket + i;              /* dx = socket number       */
        int86(IPXINT, &r, &r);            /* close the socket         */
        }

    socket = 0;                           /* reset open socket flag   */
    }

if (server)                               /* q. server mode?          */
    printf(totals, cmds_received);        /* a. yes .. print totals   */

}


/* ********************************************************************* *
 *        broadcast_msg() -- broadcast completion message to user      *
 * ********************************************************************* */

void    broadcast_msg(void)
{

bc_pkt.b_len = LENGTHOF(bc_pkt);          /* request packet length    */
bc_pkt.b_fnc = 0;                         /* send a broadcast message */
bc_pkt.b_cnt = 1;                         /* station count            */
bc_pkt.b_station = LISTEN.msg.m_station;  /* station number           */
sprintf(bc_pkt.b_msg, job_done,           /* format message data      */
        LISTEN.msg.m_sequence,            /* ..with sequence number   */
        LISTEN.msg.m_msg);                /* ..and command executed   */
bc_pkt.b_mlen = strlen(bc_pkt.b_msg);     /* message length           */

bcr_pkt.r_len = LENGTHOF(bcr_pkt);        /* reply packet length      */
r.x.si = (int) &bc_pkt;                   /* request packet           */
r.x.di = (int) &bcr_pkt;                  /* reply packet             */
r.h.ah = MSG_BROADCAST;                   /* send a broadcast message */
int86(0x21, &r, &r);                      /* get station name         */

}


/* ********************************************************************* *
 *        wait_til() -- wait for timeout or event completion           *
 * ********************************************************************* */

int     wait_til(UINT count,              /* countdown tick counter   */
                 char *flag)              /* event complete flag      */
{
long    far *timer = MK_FP(0x40, 0x6c),   /* BIOS timer tick counter  */
        work;                             /* current tick value       */

work = *timer;                            /* get current time         */

while (count && *flag)                    /* loop 'til out of time    */
    {                                     /* ..or operation completes */
    if (work != *timer)                   /* q. a tick pass?          */
        {
        work = *timer;                    /* a. yes .. save new value */
        count--;                          /* ..and decrement t/o cnt  */
        }

    if (kbhit())                          /* q. user hit a key?       */
        getch();                          /* a. yes .. get/discard key*/
    }
```

```
    return(*flag);                          /* rtn w/status flag      */

    }


/* *********************************************************************** *
 *      quit_with() -- give an error message, then return to DOS         *
 * *********************************************************************** */

void    quit_with(char *msg)
{

printf(msg);                                /* give error message     */
exit(rc);                                   /* ..and then quit        */

}


/* *********************************************************************** *
 *      control_break() -- control break intercept routine               *
 * *********************************************************************** */

int     control_break(void)
{

close_sockets();                            /* close any open sockets */

if (NOT server)                             /* q. non-server mode?    */
    printf(stop_here);                      /* a. yes .. give error msg */

return(0);                                  /* ..and return to DOS    */

}
```

4

LISTING FILES WITH LASERPRT

LASERPRT prints files on Hewlett-Packard LaserJet-compatible printers in landscape mode, two pages per sheet, and side by side. It saves not only time and paper, but also money by reducing the cost of operating the printer.

There is probably no single tool used as universally by programmers as the code listing. Unfortunately, since the earliest days of computing, programmers have had to wait for their program listings. Even on today's speedy laser printers, pages are produced at what seems to be an increasingly slower pace. Once they're printed, you usually need to look at the listing for a few minutes, fix a problem or two, and reprint the whole program. When a deadline is looming, you can't afford to lose more time waiting for yet another printout.

Although it doesn't solve all your woes, LASERPRT can help. LASERPRT reduces print time by cutting in half the number of pages used to print your programs—or, for that matter, just about any other text files you print.

SKILLS INDEX

- **Using Hewlett-Packard's printer control language (PCL)**
- **Understanding page layout**

■ USING LASERPRT

LASERPRT employs a very simple command syntax. If all you want to do is print a file, you only need to specify the name of that file on the command line. For example, to print the file named READ.ME, enter the command

```
LASERPRT READ.ME
```

With this syntax, LASERPRT reads the file READ.ME and sends the listing to LPT1. Here is the complete syntax for LASERPRT:

```
LASERPRT input [output] [/Tn] [/H]
Where input is the name of the file to print (wildcards are OK)
      output is the optional output file or device (LPT1 is the default)
      Tn specifies the tab width (/T8 is the default)
      /H suppresses the printing of page headers
```

The *input* argument specifies the files LASERPRT is to print. Using DOS wildcards, you can specify more than one file at a time, and each file will be printed as if it were specified separately. For example, to print all of the C source files contained in the current directory, you can use this command:

```
LASERPRT *.c
```

The *output* argument sends LASERPRT's output to the file (or DOS device) of your choice. Using this option, you can redirect LASERPRT's output to a different printer (such as LPT2), a disk file, or any DOS device. This is useful when your machine is not connected to a laser printer and you wish to take a file to a machine that is. For example, to format all the .TXT files in the current directory, and send the printer-ready output to the file A:PRNTOUT.DAT, use this command:

```
LASERPRT *.TXT A:PRNTOUT.DAT
```

If you do not specify the *output* argument, LASERPRT assumes the DOS device is LPT1.

■ **Caution.** *You must be careful when using the* output *argument. LASERPRT does not check for the existence of the* output *argument before performing the open. If you specify the name of an existing file, the file will be overwritten with LASERPRT's output.*

To customize how LASERPRT interprets tab characters, use the /Tn option, specifying n as a number from 1 to 16. Generally, DOS text files assume a tab stop after every 8 characters (that is, at positions 9, 17, 25, and so on). Word processors usually default to 5. Some program editors use 4 as the default tab width, but LASERPRT uses 8. If you specify /T4, LASERPRT will place the tab stops at positions 5, 9, 13, and so on. This can be very useful for compressing listings, but beware: It can cause misalignment in the printout if the value chosen for *n* does not agree with the tab settings used by your program editor.

The /H option causes LASERPRT to suppress the printing of header information at the top of every page. Normally, the headers printed by LASERPRT contain the date and time of the file, the name of the file, and the page number. This option is useful when printing text files that contain embedded page numbering.

As each file is printed, LASERPRT displays the name of the file and how many pages were contained in the file. Figure 4.1 shows LASERPRT's screen output after printing several C source files. Figure 4.2 is a sample of LASERPRT's output when used to print the source code of the LASERPRT program.

Screen output
produced by
LASERPRT

```
C:\SOURCE>e:laserprt *.c

LASERPRT 1.00 ■ Copyright (c) 1992, Michael Holmes and Bob Flanders
PC Magazine C Lab Notes ■ Print two-up listings

Processing: ZCLOCK.C      34855  05/20/1992  15:24    751 lines in  12 pages
Processing: INFORMER.C    33587  05/23/1992  03:14    774 lines in  12 pages
Processing: NETRUN.C      27884  05/27/1992  20:02    600 lines in  10 pages
Processing: LASERPRT.C    18754  06/15/1992  17:53    523 lines in   8 pages
Processing: PHONE.C       31726  06/11/1992  09:06    721 lines in  11 pages
Processing: SYNC.C        58430  06/11/1992  15:40   1303 lines in  20 pages
Processing: UP2DATE.C     56381  05/14/1992  14:46   1299 lines in  20 pages
Processing: CHKSTRUC.C    69705  05/16/1992  12:08   1528 lines in  24 pages
Processing: CAL.C         41320  06/15/1992  01:06    929 lines in  15 pages

   Totals: 9 files processed, 8428 lines on 132 pages printed

C:\SOURCE>
```

■ What Can Be Printed with LASERPRT

LASERPRT can print only files that contain ASCII text. It treats a few special characters as commands, including carriage return (0x0d), line feed (0x0a), tab (0x09), backspace (0x08), form feed (0x0c), and Ctrl-Z (0x1a). If the file contains any other special characters, LASERPRT sends those characters to the printer without translation, and the final printout may not be what you expect. For example, if you were to redirect a word processor's printed output to a disk file and subsequently

FIGURE 4.2

Sample printout from LASERPRT

```
06/29/1992  14:39     Filename: LASERPRT.C          Page  1

/* ********************************************************** *

    LASERPRT 1.00, Copyright (c) 1992, Michael Holmes and Bob Flanders
    PC Magazine C Lab Notes, Print a two-up listing

 *
    This code for both Borland C++ version 3.0. and MSC version 6/7.

       For Borland compile with:  BCC -O2 -ms laserprt.c
       For MSC compile with:      CL  /AS laserprt.c

 * ********************************************************** */

#pragma pack(1)                       /* pack to byte alignment   */
#include <stdio.h>                    /* standard I/O library     */
#include <stdlib.h>                   /* commonly used routines   */
#include <dos.h>                      /* DOS rtn definitions      */
#include <string.h>                   /* string functions         */
#include <stdarg.h>                   /* argument functions       */
#include <ctype.h>                    /* character classifications*/

#define NOT          !                /* logical not              */
#define UINT         unsigned         /* unsigned integer         */
#define MAX_PATH     70               /* max filename string      */
#define ESC          "\x1b"           /* escape character         */

/* ********************************************************** *
 *   routine definitions                                      *
 * ********************************************************** */
void  quit_with(char *, ...);         /* quit with error message  */
      initialization(int, char **);   /* init and parse cmd line  */
      print_file(struct find_t *);    /* print a file             */
int   parse_parms(int, char *w, int,  /* parse command line       */
           struct cmd_parm *, char ***),
      main(int, char **);             /* main line routine        */
FILE  *open_file(struct find_t *fb);  /* file to open             */

/* ********************************************************** *
 *   globals                                                  *
 * ********************************************************** */
long  grand_total_lines;              /* total lines printed      */
      grand_total_pages,              /* total pages printed      */
int   col,                            /* current column           */
      tabs = 8,                       /* default tab setting      */
      processed;                      /* files processed          */

char  **pos_parms,                    /* positional parms array   */
      *path,                          /* base path for wildcards  */
      *prt_name,                      /* printer output filename  */
      i_buf[128],                     /* input buffer             */
      *i_ptr;                         /* input pointer            */
      file_dt[18];                    /* date and time string     */

FILE  *prt_file;                      /* printer file handle      */
struct find_t find_blk;               /* find control block       */

/* ********************************************************** *
 *   command line switches                                    *
```

```
06/29/1992  14:39     Filename: LASERPRT.C          Page  2

char  *sw_tab,                        /* switch parameters        */
      sw_headers;

struct cmd_parm                       /* command line parm        */
{
      char cp_ltr,                    /* switch letter            */
           *cp_entry,                 /* pointer to data          */
           cp_flag;                   /* value flag               */
};

struct cmd_parm parm_table[] =        /* LASERPRT cmd line parms  */
{
   { 'H', &sw_headers },              /* H - page headers         */
   { 'T', (char *) &sw_tab, 1 }       /* T - tab columns          */
};
#define PARM_TABLE_CNT  sizeof(parm_table) / sizeof(struct cmd_parm)
                                      /* number of table entries  */
/* ********************************************************** *
 *   messages and strings                                     *
 * ********************************************************** */
char  copyright[]    = "LASERPRT 1.00 \xfe Copyright (c) 1992, "
                       "Michael Holmes and Bob Flanders\n"
                       "PC Magazine C Lab Notes \xfe "
                       "print two-up listings\n\n",
      too_many[]     = "Too many parameters\n",
      bad_value[]    = "Bad value for /%c parameter\n",
      bad_opt[]      = "Invalid parameter /%s\n",
      create_error[] = "Could not open print file %s\n",
      open_err[]     = "Error opening file %s -- file skipped\n",
      no_matches[]   = "No files found %s\n",
      process[]      = "Processing: %-12s\b\b %s",
      finished[]     = "%2ld lines invalid pass\n",
      date_fmt[]     = "%02d/%02d/%d %02d:%02d\n",
      report[]       = "\n  Totals: %d files processed, "
                       "%d lines on %d pages printed\n",
      no_mem[]       = "Not enough memory for processing\n",
      help[]         = "  Usage: LASERPRT input [output] [/Tn] [/H]\n\n"
                       "  where: input is the file to be printed "
                       "(wildcards are ok)\n"
                       "         output is the optional output file "
                       "(LPT1 is the default)\n\n"
                       "  Options: /Tn specifies the tab width "
                       "(/T8 is the default)\n"
                       "           /H suppresses the printing of page headers\n";

/* ********************************************************** *
 *   printer control strings                                  *
 * ********************************************************** */
char  *pcs[]   = {  ESC "E",          /* initialization string    */
                    ESC "&l0O",       /* reset printer            */
                    ESC "&l16.66H",   /* landscape orientation    */
                    ESC "&l5.14C",    /* 16.66 char/inch font      */
                    ESC "&l6E",       /* vertical motion index    */
                    ESC "&l71f",      /* top margin lines         */
                    ESC "(s-3B",      /* lines per page           */
                                      /* stroke weight            */
```

print that file with LASERPRT, the output would likely be unreadable (or at least very badly formatted).

■ INSIDE LASERPRT

When designing software such as LASERPRT, there are two obvious methods for implementing the program. The first (and more difficult) method involves formatting an entire printed page in memory and sending it to the printer. The second, simpler method works cooperatively with the printer's capabilities, allowing the printer to format the pages. With this method, the program does little more than keep track of the current position on the page and insert printer commands into the data stream at the appropriate places. LASERPRT uses the second technique.

Before we look at LASERPRT's logic, it's important to understand the printer's capabilities and how they're invoked using the Hewlett-Packard (HP) printer control language, or PCL.

■ Printer Control Language (PCL)

One of the most significant advantages of using a laser printer is the printer's ability to receive an entire page of information before actually printing the page. As a result, the program doesn't have to build the whole print image before sending it to the printer. For example, it is possible to send the information for a portion of a page, reposition the *cursor* (the name used by HP in defining the next print position), and then send the balance of the information for that page. LASERPRT uses this capability to print the left half of a page, reposition the cursor, and print the right half. LASERPRT performs this task using PCL. PCL is the native language of HP LaserJet (and compatible) printers, and is sent to the printer as part of the data stream. PCL instructs the printer to perform functions such as setting margins, selecting a font, and selecting the next print position. (Figure 4.3 is a detailed illustration of LASERPRT's page layout and PCL usage.)

The printer can differentiate PCL from other print data because PCL commands always start with an escape character (0x1b). There are literally hundreds of PCL commands, and LASERPRT uses only a small subset. (You can see these commands later in Table 4.1.)

ote:

or a detailed
olanation of
'L command
mat, see the
dnote, "HP
serJet Printer
ntrol
nguage
rmat."

FIGURE 4.3

LASERPRT's page layout and PCL usage

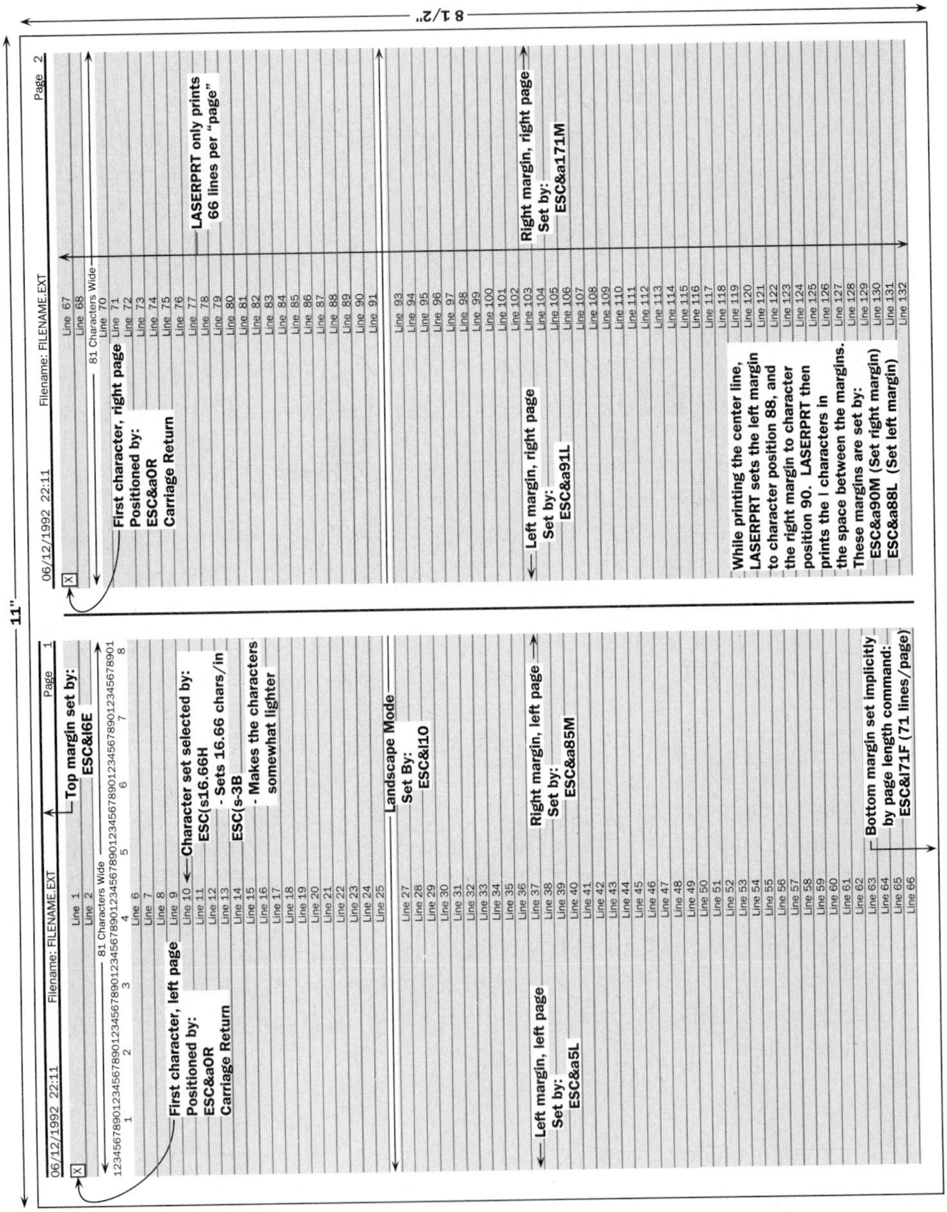

Page 1

06/12/1992 22:11   Filename: FILENAME.EXT

81 Characters Wide
1234567890123456789012345678901234567890123456789012345678901234567890123456789 01
1   2   3   4   5   6   7   8

Top margin set by:
ESC&l6E

Character set selected by:
ESC(s16.66H – Sets 16.66 chars/in
ESC(s-3B – Makes the characters somewhat lighter

Landscape Mode
Set By:
ESC&l1O

First character, left page
Positioned by:
ESC&aOR
Carriage Return

Left margin, left page
Set by:
ESC&a5L

Right margin, left page
Set by:
ESC&a85M

Bottom margin set implicitly
by page length command:
ESC&l71F (71 lines/page)

Line 1 – Line 66

Page 2

06/12/1992 22:11   Filename: FILENAME.EXT

81 Characters Wide

First character, right page
Positioned by:
ESC&aOR
Carriage Return

LASERPRT only prints
66 lines per "page"

Left margin, right page
Set by:
ESC&a91L

Right margin, right page
Set by:
ESC&a171M

While printing the center line,
LASERPRT sets the left margin
to character position 88, and
the right margin to character
position 90. LASERPRT then
prints the | characters in
the space between the margins.
These margins are set by:
ESC&a90M (Set right margin)
ESC&a88L (Set left margin)

Line 67 – Line 132

8 1/2"

11"

	Command	Action
TABLE 4.1 *PCL Commands Used by LASERPRT*		
	EscE	**Reset. Returns the printer to its default settings.**
	Esc&l1O	**Set landscape mode. Printing proceeds across the 11-inch length of the page rather than the 8½-inch width of the page.**
	Esc(s16.66H	**Select font pitch. LASERPRT uses a 16.66-characters-per-inch font.**
	Esc&l5.14C	**Set vertical motion index. Defines the number of 1/48-inch increments between the top of one line and top of the next line. This value evaluates to .1071 inches, or slightly less than 10 lines per inch.**
	Esc&l6E	**Set top margin. Six lines are reserved as the top margin.**
	Esc&l71F	**Set page length to 71 lines. Implicitly sets the bottom margin. The resulting size of the print space is based on the vertical motion index (VMI).**
	Esc(s-3B	**Select stroke weight. Causes the printer to select a font with characters that appear somewhat lighter, if such a font is available.**
	Esc&a0R	**Set cursor row position. Positions the cursor to the first printable row (or line).**
	Esc&a5L **Esc&a88L** **Esc&a91L**	**Set the left margin. Sets the left margin for the left side of the page (5), the center line (88), or the right side of the page (91).**
	Esc&a85M **Esc&a90M** **Esc&a171M**	**Set the right margin. Sets the right margin for the left side of the page (85), the center line (90), or the right side of the page (171).**
	Esc&d3D	**Set underline mode. Used when the header line is printed.**
	Esc&d@	**Reset underline mode. Turns off underline after the header line is printed.**

LASERPRT uses PCL in six operations:

- Printer initialization
- Setup for left side of the page
- Header printing
- Center line Setup
- Setup for right side of the page
- Print completion

All of the PCL commands (as well as other strings) used by LASERPRT are contained in the array pcs[].

■ Initializing the Printer

During printer initialization, LASERPRT sends seven PCL commands. The first command, reset, returns the printer to its default environment. The environment settings will vary based upon the options entered by the user using the control panel on the printer. Additionally, the reset command also forces any partial page to be printed and ejected from the printer.

■ **Note.** *The commands described here are listed with their escape codes in Table 4.1.*

LASERPRT then sends the PCL command to set landscape mode. As shown in Figure 4.3, landscape mode causes data to be printed across the 11-inch length of the paper. (When the data is printed across the 8½-inch width of the paper, the printer is in portrait mode.)

LaserJet-compatible printers are shipped with several resident fonts. LASERPRT uses the select font pitch command to select a font with a pitch of 16.66 characters per inch. At this pitch, LASERPRT can fit two 81-character lines across the page, with a reasonable margin to the left, right, and in the center between the two lines.

One of the more unusual commands used by LASERPRT is set vertical motion index (VMI). The VMI is the distance between the top of one line and the top of the next, and is specified in increments of 1/48 of an inch. LASERPRT uses the VMI value 5.14, which equals .1071 inch or just under 10 lines per inch. LASERPRT's use of this VMI guarantees that 66 lines will fit within the designated print area. Look again at Figure 4.3. With a few exceptions, each of the lines is numbered. Notice that the first 66 lines (1 through 66) are down the left-hand side of the page, and the second

66 (67 through 132) are down the right-hand side. The line spacing is selected by the set VMI command.

LASERPRT sets the top margin to 6 lines using the set top margin command. This margin provides enough space so that a three-hole punch can be used on the pages, for insertion into a three-ring binder.

In PCL, there is no set bottom margin command, but this element can be implicitly set with the set lines per page command. LASERPRT sets the number of lines per page to 71. Although only 68 lines are used by LASERPRT (including the heading line), the 71 setting ensures that the page does not eject prematurely. If the number of lines printed exceeds the lines per page setting, the printer automatically ejects the page and continues printing on the next sheet.

Finally, the stroke weight command instructs the printer to select a font with a lighter appearance. When selecting a font, the printer uses information from both the select font pitch and select stroke weight commands.

■ Preparing for the Left Page

LASERPRT sends four PCL commands to set up the left side of the page: set the left margin, set the right margin, set the cursor row, and set the cursor column. When printing the left page, LASERPRT sets the left margin to column 5 and the right margin to column 85. This allows exactly 81 characters to print between the margins. If an attempt is made to print beyond column 81, the printer truncates the characters and they are lost. Knowing this, LASERPRT keeps track of the current column position and inserts a carriage return/line feed combination into the print stream, causing excess characters to print on subsequent lines.

After setting the margins, LASERPRT sends the set cursor row position command. This places the cursor on the top line of the page, just below the top margin. Next, LASERPRT sends a carriage return. Regardless of the original position of the cursor, the cursor is moved to the left margin. (Although there is a PCL command to place the cursor at an absolute column on a line, that column number is relative to the leftmost printable position, not to the left margin.)

Preceding the commands for setup of the left page is a form feed character. LASERPRT skips this character on the first sheet, but sends it to eject subsequent sheets before sending the next group of left-page setup commands.

■ Printing the Heading

While printing the heading, LASERPRT uses two PCL commands: set underline mode on, and reset underline mode. The lines that appear at the top of each page are produced by setting underline mode on as the header line is being printed. (The center line works differently.)

- **Preparing for the Center Line and Right Page**
  The setup for the center line and right side of the page uses the same PCL commands as the setup for the left page. The only difference is the values used to set the margins, and the order in which the set margin commands are sent. For the center line, the left and right margins are set at 88 and 90 respectively. On the right page, the left and right margins are 91 and 171, respectively.

  Note that in the commands for setting up the center line and right page, the right margin is set before the left margin. If LASERPRT were to send the left margin command before the right margin command, the printer would ignore the command for the left margin because the left margin value must always be less than that of the right margin. The printer ignores any commands that attempt to transpose the left and right margins' positions.

- **When Printing Is Done**
  After all the data has been sent to the printer, LASERPRT sends another reset command to the printer. As mentioned earlier, this command causes the printer to print the final page and return the printer to its default environment.

- ## LASERPRT'S LOGIC
  When you run LASERPRT, it starts by printing its copyright message and invoking initialization(). The initialization() routine has three functions: parse the command line arguments, test the value of the tabs option, and open the output file (or device). The initialization() routine parses command line arguments by calling parse_parms().

  When you specify arguments on the command line, the C interface prepares an array of pointers; each pointer contains the address of one command line argument. If one of the arguments contains one or more options, as in the command

  ```
  LASERPRT *.C/T4
  ```

  the C interface will only indicate that one argument was specified on the command line (*.C/T4). LASERPRT uses parse_parms() to find options that are "attached" to an argument, note which argument was specified, and return the arguments without the options. Additionally, parse_parms() allows options to be specified anywhere on the command line, not just at the beginning or end. The parse_parms() routine examines the command line arguments, saving pointers to the *input* and *output* arguments and checking for the presence of the /Tn or /H options.

When called, parse_parms() starts by allocating an array of pointers large enough to contain a pointer to every argument specified on the command line. Then, for each argument on the command line, parse_parms() checks the first character to determine if it is a forward slash. If so, parse_parms() retrieves the character immediately following the slash, and tests if the character is a question mark (/?). If parse_parms() finds /?, it calls quit_with(), which prints a help message and returns to DOS. Otherwise, parse_parms() enters a loop scanning the parm_table[] array for a match of the options found on the command line. If no match is found, parse_parms() calls quit_with() to print an error message and return to DOS. If the command line option matches one found in parm_table[], parse_parms() checks the cp_flag member in the matching parm_table[] entry. When cp_flag is true, parse_parms() also stores the address of the character following the option, allowing an option (such as the /Tn option) to have an associated value.

If parse_parms() finds that an argument does not start with a forward slash, it places a pointer to that argument in the array allocated earlier. Then parse_parms() checks the argument for embedded forward slashes (that is, an "attached" option). If an option is attached to the argument, the option is stripped from the argument and parse_parms() continues the loop, checking the validity of the new option. When parse_parms() is finished, it returns the number of nonoption arguments found on the command line.

The initialization() routine determines if you specified the appropriate number of entries on the command line by testing the returned value with a set of case statements. If you specified no arguments, initialization() simply prints the help message, and returns to DOS. If only one argument was specified, LASERPRT sets the output file name to its default value of LPT1, and processing continues. If two arguments were specified on the command line, the output file name is set to the value specified as the second argument. If parse_parms() finds more than two arguments, initialization() prints an error message and returns to DOS.

After parsing the arguments, initialization() tests if the /Tn option was specified. If so, the routine validates that the value following /T is between 1 and 16. If the value is out of range, an error message is displayed and the program returns to DOS.

Finally, initialization() attempts to open the default or specified output file. If the file cannot be opened, initialization() displays an error message and returns to DOS. Since initialization() does not determine if the output file exists before opening it, it is possible to overlay a file by simply naming it as the *output* argument. Of course, if the file named has the read-only attribute set to on, the open will fail, and LASERPRT will display an error message and terminate.

Although the command line for LASERPRT is simple, and specific logic for parsing such a command line would be fairly trivial to implement, using the initialization() and parse_parms() routines allows new options to be added to the existing code easily.

■ PRINTING THE FILES

Once the initialization phase has completed, LASERPRT checks for the existence of at least one matching file by calling _dos_findfirst(). If no matching files exist, main() calls quit_with() to display an error and return to DOS. If a matching file is found, main() calls print_file() to send the file contents to the printer.

The algorithm used by print_file() is simple: The *input* file is read one character at a time. After reading a character, print_file() checks if the character is one that will change the current print position (such as a carriage return), or if the character must be interpreted (such as a tab). If the character requires no special treatment, it is sent on to the printer, as is, and print_file() notes the new print position as a result of printing the character. The print_file() routine also performs housekeeping tasks such as tracking left and right pages, sending the appropriate setup strings, and printing the center line.

■ A Closer Look at print_file()

The print_file() routine reads the input file and inserts PCL commands into the data stream sent to the printer. When called, print_file() opens the file by calling open_file(). If an error occurs, open_file() displays the file name in an error message and returns to print_file(), which returns to main(). If the open is successful, open_file() displays the name, date, time, and size of the file.

Note:

Tab expansion is the conversion of tabs into the appropriate number of spaces in the printout.

After opening the input file, print_file() enters a for loop that reads and processes one character from the file. The very first operation performed within the for loop is a test for tab expansion. If tab expansion is not in progress (the variable called *blanks* is zero) print_file() calls fgetc() to retrieve a character from the input file. If tab expansion is in progress, print_file() simply decrements the *blanks* variable and continues processing. During tab expansion, the remainder of the logic thinks that a blank has been read from the file, when, in fact, no read has taken place.

After getting the next character (whether from the file or tab expansion), print_file() checks if it is time to start a new page. Any of three conditions signal the start of a new page: if this is the first character of the file, if 66 lines have completed printing, or if a form feed character (0x0c) is encountered in the input file. If any of these conditions exist, and no previous data has been sent to the printer, print_file() sends the string containing the PCL commands that initialize the printer.

The print_file() routine must then determine if it is starting a left or a right side. Before printing a left side, a code string is sent to eject the previous page (if any), left and right margins are set, and the cursor is positioned on the first line. Before printing a right side, print_file() first sets the margins for and prints the center line; then it sets the margins for the right side and positions the cursor on the first character of the right side. After setting up all the margins, print_file() prints the header lines (if the /H option was not specified).

- ### Translating the Characters
  LASERPRT translates certain characters' codes, and keeps track of the current print position. For each character read, print_file() checks for certain characters before printing them. A backspace (0x08) causes LASERPRT to retreat one space; however, print_file() only allows backspacing to continue to the beginning of the current line. (Some text files use backspace to print underscores, strikeouts, and other characters. For example, a simple way to print <u>ABC</u> is to print the letters ABC, followed by three backspaces, followed by three underscores. Although PCL does support a command to underscore text, using character-backspace-underscore works on a larger variety of printers.)

- **Caution.** *Be aware that, if a backspace occurs after a tab, the backspace overwrites only one of the spaces produced by the tab.*

  When print_file() encounters a form feed (0x0c), it sets the ff_flag variable to 1 and continues processing. The form feed is processed when print_file() processes the next character. If print_file() encounters the form feed while printing the left side of the page, printing continues on the right side; however, if the form feed is found while printing the right side of the page, the sheet is ejected and the left side of a new page is started.

  When print_file() gets a line feed (0x0a) from the input file, the line variable is incremented, a line feed is printed, and processing continues. Similarly, when print_file() gets a carriage return (0x0d), the current column is set to zero, a carriage return is printed, and processing continues. Later, when the next character is retrieved, print_file() determines whether line 66 has completed printing, and if so, continues printing on the next page.

  When print_file() encounters a tab character (0x09), it calculates the number of blanks needed to fulfill the tab, sets the current character to a blank, and continues processing. The number of blanks needed is the width of a tab stop (as set by the /T option, or 8 by default), minus the modulus of the current column and the tab width. For example, if the tab width is 8, and the current column is 6, the number of blanks is calculated as follows:

blanks = 8 – (6 mod 8)

blanks = 8 – 6

blanks = 2

In this example, print_file() will insert two blanks into the print stream before reading in the next character from the input file. (*Note:* The current column is maintained as a zero-based value. As mentioned earlier, when the *blanks* variable is nonzero, print_file() does not read the input file, but rather decrements the *blanks* variable, and returns a blank character.)

Finally, print_file() does not process a Ctrl-Z character (0x1a) when it is found as the last character in the file. Many DOS text files end with a Ctrl-Z marking the end of the file, and this character is returned by fgetc(). (The use of Ctrl-Z was common when a file's length was defined by the number of sectors it contained. Under those conditions, the last sector of a text file was padded with Ctrl-Z to show unused space.) If print_file() encounters Ctrl-Z and it is not the last character in the file, the character is sent on to the printer without translation.

If a character retrieved from the file is not one of the special characters recognized by print_file(), the character is printed, and the col variable is incremented. When col indicates that 81 characters have been printed on a line, print_file() begins a new line and continues printing.

- ## Printing Additional Files
When print_file() finishes printing a file, the routine returns to main(). Next, main() prints a string that causes the last page to be ejected and resets the printer. By resetting the printer, LASERPRT starts with a known environment. Then, main() checks if any other files match the *input* file specification. If so, it passes that file to print_file(), and the printing process is repeated. When all input files have been processed, main() displays some final statistics and returns to DOS.

■ SUMMARY

LASERPRT demonstrates a method of using the PCL to aid in formatting listings on a LaserJet-compatible laser printer. Here are some enhancements you may want to consider adding to LASERPRT:

- Add an option to print four pages per sheet by printing on both sides of each sheet.

- Add an option instructing LASERPRT to truncate lines instead of wrapping them to the next line. This option could be used to print the first 81 columns of wide printouts, such as assembly listings.

HP LASERJET PRINTER CONTROL LANGUAGE FORMAT

The HP LaserJet Printer Control Language (PCL) controls the output produced by La-serJet and compatible printers. PCL comprises a set of escape sequences. Each se-quence must begin with the escape character (0x1b). PCL commands are divided into two groups: two-character escape sequences, and parameterized escape sequences.

- Two-character escape sequences instruct the printer to perform some spe-cific function. For example, this sequence:

  ESC E (escape, capital E)

  resets the printer to its power-on state. Another example:

  ESC 9 (escape, nine)

  clears the horizontal margins. This command sets the left margin to position zero, and the right margin to the rightmost print position on the page.

- Parameterized escape sequences contain user-specified parameters. For ex-ample, LASERPRT uses this sequence:

  ESC & l 1 O (escape, ampersand, lowercase el, one, uppercase O)

  to set the printer to landscape mode. The parameter in this command is the one. The alternative setting, portrait mode, is selected by this command:

  ESC & l 0 O (escape, ampersand, lowercase el, zero, uppercase O)

  Note that the above two commands are the same, with only the one parame-ter changed to a zero parameter.

A laser printer differentiates between a two-character escape sequence and a pa-rameterized escape sequence by examining the second character of the sequence. The second character of a two-character sequence will have a value in the range 48 to 126 decimal, or the equivalent ASCII characters from zero (0) to right bracket (]). The second character for a parameterized string falls in the range 33 to 47 decimal, or the equivalent ASCII characters left quote (') to forward slash (/).

The last character of a parameterized sequence is always in the range 64 to 94 decimal, or the equivalent ASCII characters at sign (@) to caret (^), with the greatest majority of commands ending in a capital letter.

As usual, there is an exception to the requirement for an escape character preceding every parameterized command. If the two characters following the escape are the same characters in two separate commands, the commands may be combined. This is done by changing the last character of the first command to a lowercase letter, and appending to it the fourth through the last characters from the second command. For example, the set left margin and set right margin commands in LASERPRT could be combined as follows:

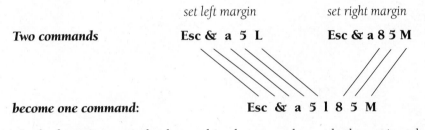

Two commands   *set left margin*   *set right margin*

                               Esc & a 5 L   **Esc & a 8 5 M**

become one command: **Esc & a 5 l 8 5 M**

In the foregoing example, the combined command to set both margins takes three characters fewer than the two commands to set each margin separately. (To maintain clarity in the code, this technique is not used in LASERPRT.) ∎

LISTING

LASERPRT 1.00

```
/* ********************************************************************* *

    LASERPRT 1.00, Copyright (c) 1992, Michael Holmes and Bob Flanders
    PC Magazine C Lab Notes, Print a two-up listing

 * ********************************************************************* *

    This code for both Borland C++ version 3.0. and MSC version 6/7.

        For Borland compile with:  BCC -O2 -ms laserprt.c
             For MSC compile with:  CL  /AS laserprt.c

 * ********************************************************************* */


#pragma   pack(1)                           /* pack to byte alignment    */
#include <stdio.h>                          /* standard i/o library      */
#include <stdlib.h>                         /* commonly used routines    */
#include <dos.h>                            /* DOS rtn definitions       */
#include <string.h>                         /* string functions          */
#include <stdarg.h>                         /* argument functions        */
#include <ctype.h>                          /* character classifications*/

#define NOT         !                       /* logical not               */
#define UINT        unsigned                /* unsigned integer          */
#define MAX_PATH    79                      /* max filename string       */
#define ESC         "\x1b"                  /* escape character          */


/* ********************************************************************* *
 *      routine definitions                                            *
 * ********************************************************************* */

void    quit_with(char *, ...),             /* quit with error message   */
        initialization(int, char **),       /* init and parse cmd line   */
        print_file(struct find_t *);        /* print a file              */
int     parse_parms(int, char **, int,      /* parse command line        */
            struct cmd_parm *, char ***),
        main(int, char **);                 /* main line routine         */
FILE    *open_file(struct find_t *fb);      /* file to open              */


/* ********************************************************************* *
 *      globals                                                        *
 * ********************************************************************* */

long    grand_total_lines;                  /* total lines printed       */

int     grand_total_pages,                  /* total pages printed       */
        col,                                /* current column            */
        tabs = 8,                           /* default tab setting       */
        processed;                          /* files processed           */

char    **pos_parms,                        /* positional parms array    */
```

```
        *path,                              /* base path for wildcards  */
        *prt_name,                          /* printer output filename  */
        i_buf[128],                         /* input buffer             */
        *i_ptr,                             /* input pointer            */
        file_dt[18];                        /* date and time string     */

FILE    *prt_file;                          /* printer file handle      */
struct  find_t find_blk;                    /* find control block       */


/* ********************************************************************** *
 *       command line switches                                           *
 * ********************************************************************** */

char    *sw_tab,                            /* switch parameters        */
        sw_headers;

struct  cmd_parm                            /* command line parm        */
    {
    char cp_ltr,                            /* switch letter            */
        *cp_entry,                          /* pointer to data          */
         cp_flag;                           /* value flag               */
    };

struct  cmd_parm parm_table[] =             /* LASERPRT cmd line parms  */
    {
    { 'H', &sw_headers },                   /* H - page headers         */
    { 'T', (char *) &sw_tab, 1 }            /* T - tab columns          */
    };

                                            /* number of table entries  */
#define PARM_TABLE_CNT  sizeof(parm_table) / sizeof(struct cmd_parm)


/* ********************************************************************** *
 *       messages and strings                                            *
 * ********************************************************************** */

char    copyright[]   = "LASERPRT 1.00 \xfe Copyright (c) 1992, "
                        "Michael Holmes and Bob Flanders\n"
                        "PC Magazine C Lab Notes \xfe "
                        "Print two-up listings\n\n",
        too_many[]    = "Too many parameters\n",
        bad_value[]   = "Missing value for /%c parameter\n",
        bad_op[]      = "Invalid parameter /%s\n",
        bad_tab[]     = "Invalid value %d for the /T parameter\n",
        create_error[] = "Could not open print file %s\n",
        open_err[]    = "Error opening file %s -- file skipped\n",
        no_matches[]  = "No files found %s\n",
        process[]     = "Processing: %-12s%8lu  %s",
        finished[]    = "%6ld lines in%4d pages\n",
        date_fmt[]    = "%02d/%02d/%d  %02d:%02d",
        report[]      = "\n    Totals: %d files processed, "
                        "%ld lines on %d pages printed\n",
        no_mem[]      = "Not enough memory for processing\n",
        help[]        =
            "  Usage:  LASERPRT input [output] [/Tn] [/H]\n\n"
            " Where:  input  is the file to be printed "
            "(wildcards are ok)\n"
            "         output  is the optional output file "
            "(LPT1 is the default)\n\n"
            "Options:  /Tn  specifies the tab width "
            "(/T8 is the default)\n"
            "          /H  suppresses the printing of page headers\n";
```

```
/* *********************************************************************** *
 *        printer control strings                                         *
 * *********************************************************************** */

char    *pcs[]          = {                     /* initialization string    */
                        ESC "E"                 /*    reset printer         */
                        ESC "&l1O"              /*    landscape orientation */
                        ESC "(s16.66H"          /*    16.66 char/inch font  */
                        ESC "&l5.14C"           /*    vertical motion index */
                        ESC "&l6E"              /*    top margin lines      */
                        ESC "&l71F"             /*    lines per page        */
                        ESC "(s-3B",            /*    stroke weight         */

                        ESC "E",                /* reset printer string     */

                                                /* middle margins           */
                        ESC "&a90M"             /*    right margin          */
                        ESC "&a88L"             /*    left margin           */
                        ESC "&a2R"              /*    row positioning        */
                            "\r",               /*    .. at left margin      */

                        "\x7c\r\n",             /* center line              */

                                                /* left page margins        */
                            "\f"                /*    form feed             */
                        ESC "&a5L"              /*    left margin           */
                        ESC "&a85M"             /*    right margin          */
                        ESC "&a0R"              /*    top row positioning    */
                            "\r",               /*    .. at left margin      */

                                                /* right page margins       */
                        ESC "&a171M"            /*    right margin          */
                        ESC "&a91L"             /*    left margin           */
                        ESC "&a0R"              /*    top row positioning    */
                            "\r",               /*    .. at left margin      */

                                                /* page headers             */
                        ESC "&d3D"              /*    underlining on         */
                        "%-24sFilename: "
                        "%-12.12s%27sPage%4u"
                        ESC "&d@\r\n\r\n",      /*    underlining off        */

                                                /* no headers               */
                        "\r\n\r\n" };

#define PCS_INIT      0                         /* initialize printer        */
#define PCS_RESET     1                         /* end of job reset          */
#define PCS_MID_PG    2                         /* middle of page margin     */
#define PCS_BAR       3                         /* center line divider       */
#define PCS_LEFT_PG   4                         /* left side of page margin  */
#define PCS_RIGHT_PG 5                          /* right side of page margin */
#define PCS_HEADING   6                         /* heading lines             */
#define PCS_NON_HEAD 7                          /* no heading lines          */


/* *********************************************************************** *
 *        main()                                                          *
 * *********************************************************************** */

int     main(int  ac,                           /* DOS cmd line token count */
             char *av[])                         /* ..token strings          */
```

```
{
UINT    find_rc;                              /* find return code         */
char    *p;                                   /* work string pointer      */

printf(copyright);                            /* give copyright message   */

initialization(ac, av);                       /* init and parse cmd line  */

path = pos_parms[0];                          /* set up base path name?   */

if ((find_rc = _dos_findfirst(path,           /* q. any files found?      */
          _A_NORMAL, &find_blk)) != 0)
    quit_with(no_matches, path);              /* a. no .. give error/quit */

if ((p = strrchr(path, '\\')) != 0)           /* q. find the last '\' ?   */
    *++p = 0;                                 /* a. yes .. kill path there*/
 else
    *path = 0;                                /* else .. no path used     */

while (NOT find_rc)                           /* find all matching files  */
    {
    print_file(&find_blk);                    /* print found file, then   */
    find_rc = _dos_findnext(&find_blk);       /* ..find next matching name*/
    }

fprintf(prt_file, pcs[PCS_RESET]);            /* do a printer reset then  */

if (processed > 1)                            /* q. do more than 1 file?  */
    printf(report, processed,                 /* a. yes .. give stats..   */
           grand_total_lines,                 /* ..files processed, lines */
           grand_total_pages);                /* ..and pages printed      */

return(0);                                    /* ..and return to DOS      */

}


/* ******************************************************************** *
 *      initialization() -- init interrupts and parse command line      *
 * ******************************************************************** */

void    initialization(int ac,                /* DOS cmd line token count */
                    char *av[])               /* ..token strings          */
{


switch (parse_parms(ac, av,                   /* parse switches and       */
          PARM_TABLE_CNT, parm_table,         /* ..positional parameters  */
          &pos_parms))                        /* ..and based on parm cnt..*/
    {
    case 0:                                   /* q. missing parameters?   */
        quit_with(help);                      /* a. yes .. give help/quit */

    case 1:                                   /* q. specified input only? */
        prt_name = "LPT1";                    /* a. yes .. use default    */
        break;                                /* ..and continue           */

    case 2:                                   /* q. user give output file?*/
        prt_name = pos_parms[1];              /* a. yes .. save name      */
        break;                                /* ..and continue           */

    default:                                  /* q. too many parameters?  */
        quit_with(too_many);                  /* a. yes .. give error/quit*/
```

```
        }

    if (*sw_tab != 0 &&                      /* q. tabs switch given?    */
                ((tabs = atoi(sw_tab)) < 1 ||    /* ..and less than 1?       */
                (tabs > 16)))                /* ..or greater than 16?    */
        quit_with(bad_tab, tabs);            /* a. yes .. give error/quit*/

    if (NOT (prt_file = fopen(prt_name, "wb")))  /* q. open output file ok?  */
        quit_with(create_error, prt_name);   /* a. no .. give error/quit */

    }


/* *********************************************************************** *
 *       print_file() -- print a file                                      *
 * *********************************************************************** */

void    print_file(struct find_t *fb)        /* file to print            */
{
int     i,                                   /* loop counter             */
        blanks = 0,                          /* tab expansion counter    */
        ff_flag = 0,                         /* form feed flag           */
        line = 0,                            /* ..and line               */
        page = 0;                            /* page counter             */
char    c;                                   /* character buffer         */
long    total_lines = 0,                     /* total lines printed      */
        file_size;                           /* file size                */
FILE    *fi;                                 /* file handle              */


    if (NOT (fi = open_file(fb)))            /* q. file open ok?         */
        return;                              /* a. no .. just return     */

    for (file_size = fb->size; file_size;)   /* while not end of file .. */
        {
        if (NOT blanks)                      /* q. expanding a tab?      */
            {                                /* a. no .. read from file  */
            c = fgetc(fi);                   /* get a character from file*/
            file_size--;                     /* ..and decrement counter  */
            }
          else
            blanks--;                        /* a. yes .. decrement count*/

        if (NOT page || line > 65 || ff_flag)  /* q. time for a page break?*/
            {                                /* a. yes .. do page routine*/
            if (NOT page)                    /* q. first cycle?          */
                fprintf(prt_file,            /* a. yes .. do prt startup */
                    pcs[PCS_INIT]);

            if (NOT (page & 1))              /* q. time for a left page? */
                fprintf(prt_file,            /* a. yes .. print one      */
                    &pcs[PCS_LEFT_PG][page ? 0 : 1]);
              else
                {
                fprintf(prt_file,            /* set up center margins    */
                    pcs[PCS_MID_PG]);        /* ..for divider line       */

                for (i = 0; i < 66; i++)     /* draw line down page ..   */
                    fprintf(prt_file,        /* ..one line at a time      */
                        pcs[PCS_BAR]);

                fprintf(prt_file,            /* finally, set up new       */
```

```
            pcs[PCS_RIGHT_PG]);           /* ..margins for right page */
        }

    fprintf(prt_file,                      /* put out ..             */
        pcs[PCS_HEADING + sw_headers],     /* ..heading lines        */
        file_dt, fb->name, "", ++page);    /* ..file date/time & name */

    total_lines += line;                   /* count lines printed     */
    col = line = ff_flag = 0;              /* clear column & line cnts */
    }

switch (c)                                 /* handle special characters*/
    {
    case '\b':                             /* backspace               */
        if (--col < 0)                     /* q. backing up too much?  */
            col = 0;                       /* a. yes .. fix to start   */
        else
            fprintf(prt_file, "\b");       /* else .. print a backspace*/

        continue;                          /* ..and continue from top  */

    case '\f':                             /* form feed               */
        ff_flag = 1;                       /* set page break needed    */
        continue;                          /* ..and continue from top  */

    case '\n':                             /* line feed               */
        line++;                            /* bump line counter        */
        fprintf(prt_file, "\n");           /* put out the line feed    */
        continue;                          /* ..and continue from top  */

    case '\r':                             /* carriage return          */
        col = 0;                           /* reset column counter     */
        fprintf(prt_file, "\r");           /* output just the return   */
        continue;                          /* ..and continue from top  */

    case '\t':                             /* tab                     */
        blanks = tabs - (col % tabs);      /* columns to skip over     */
        c = ' ';                           /* change to blank character*/
        continue;                          /* ..then continue from top */

    case 0x1a:                             /* eof character           */
        if (NOT file_size)                 /* q. last character?       */
            continue;                      /* a. yes .. skip character */
    }

if (col > 80)                              /* q. at end of line?       */
    {
    fprintf(prt_file, "\r\n");             /* a. yes .. output <cr><lf>*/
    col = 0;                               /* ..then reset counter     */
    line++;                                /* ..and increment lines    */
    }

fprintf(prt_file, "%c", c);                /* print a character        */
col++;                                     /* ..and tally columns prt'd*/
}

fclose(fi);                                /* close input file         */

total_lines += line;                       /* count last lines on page */
grand_total_lines += total_lines;          /* roll up line counters    */
grand_total_pages += page;                 /* ..and pages              */

printf(finished, total_lines, page);       /* give closing stats       */
```

```
}


/* *********************************************************** *
 *      open_file() -- open file and give file size, date and time *
 * *********************************************************** */

FILE    *open_file(struct find_t *fb)          /* file to open        */
{
char    full_name[MAX_PATH];                   /* fully qualified filename */
FILE    *fi;                                    /* file handle         */

sprintf(full_name, "%s%s", path, fb->name);    /* format full filename */

if (NOT (fi = fopen(full_name, "rb")))         /* q. file open/readable?  */
    {
    printf(open_err, full_name);               /* a. no .. give message   */
    return(0);                                  /* ..then process next file */
    }
sprintf(file_dt, date_fmt,                     /* build file date and     */
        (fb->wr_date >> 5) & 0xf,              /* ..file time string      */
        fb->wr_date & 0x1f,
        ((fb->wr_date >> 9) & 0x7f)+ 1980,
        (fb->wr_time >> 11) & 0x1f, (fb->wr_time >> 5) & 0x3f);

printf(process, fb->name, fb->size,            /* display file size along */
        file_dt);                              /* ..with date and time    */

processed++;                                    /* count files processed   */

return(fi);                                     /* return w/file handle    */

}


/* *********************************************************** *
 *      quit_with() -- give an error message, then return to DOS *
 * *********************************************************** */

void    quit_with(char *msg, ...)              /* string to print         */
{
va_list list;                                   /* variable list           */

va_start(list, msg);                           /* set up variable list    */
vprintf(msg, list);                            /* give error message ..   */
exit(1);                                        /* ..and then quit         */

}


/* *********************************************************** *
 *      parse_parms() -- parse command line parms *
 * *********************************************************** */

int     parse_parms(int  ac,                   /* argument count          */
                char *av[],                    /* command line arguments  */
                int  n,                        /* parse table entries     */
```

```
                        struct cmd_parm *t,     /* cmd line parse table    */
                        char ***parms_array)    /* positional parms array  */
{
int     i, j,                                   /* loop counter            */
        parms_fnd = 0,                          /* positional parms found  */
        slash_fnd = 0;                          /* slash found in token    */
char    *p, *q,                                 /* character pointers      */
        c;                                      /* work character          */


*parms_array = (char **) malloc(               /* set up for max nbr tokens*/
        sizeof(char *) * ac);

for (i = 1; i < ac; i++)                        /* for each cmd line token */
    {
    p = av[i];                                  /* set up pointer to token */

    while (*p)                                  /* process token           */
        {
        if (*p == '/' ‖ slash_fnd)              /* q. option?              */
            {                                   /* a. yes .. proess it     */

            if (NOT slash_fnd)                  /* q. embedded slash?      */
                p++;                            /* a. no .. bump past slash */

            c = toupper(*p);                    /* get char and upcase it  */
            slash_fnd = 0;                      /* reset switch            */

            if (c == '?')                       /* q. help request?        */
                quit_with(help);                /* a. yes .. give help ..  */

            for (j = 0; j < n; j++)             /* check each table entry  */
                if (c == t[j].cp_ltr)           /* q. find match?          */
                    break;                      /* a. yes .. exit loop     */

            if (j == n)                         /* q. no matches?          */
                {                               /* a. no .. process error  */
                if ((q = strchr(p, '/'))        /* q. any more switches?   */
                        != 0)
                    *q = 0;                     /* a. yes .. isolate bad one*/

                quit_with(bad_op, p);           /* give error message & quit*/
                }

            q = p + 1;                          /* point to next switch    */

            if (t[j].cp_flag)                   /* q. keyword with data?   */
                {                               /* a. yes .. process arg   */
                if (NOT strlen(q))              /* q. value given?         */
                    quit_with(bad_value,        /* a. no .. give an error  */
                        *p);                    /* ..message and quit      */

                if (*(p = strcspn(q, "/")       /* q. any more switches    */
                        + q))                   /* ..to worry about?       */
                    {
                    *p++ = 0;                   /* a. yes .. get to slash  */
                    slash_fnd = 1;              /* ..show nxt char a switch */
                    }

                *(char **)t[j].cp_entry = q;/* save argument string        */
                }

            else
                {
```

```
            p++;                              /* point to next switch    */
            (*t[j].cp_entry)++;               /* show slash parm used    */
            }
        }

    else
        {
        (*parms_array)[parms_fnd++] = p;/* save positional string    */

        if (*(p += strcspn(p, "/")))      /* q. any switches left?   */
            {
            *p++ = 0;                     /* a. yes .. make a string */
            slash_fnd = 1;                /* ..show nxt char a switch */
            }
        }
    }

}

return(parms_fnd);                        /* rtn w/nbr of positionals */

}
```

5

LET YOUR KEYBOARD DO THE WALKING WITH PHONE

PHONE places a call to a telephone number via a modem. Once the dialing has finished, the user

can tell the modem to disconnect, and continue the call using a telephone.

It's unusual, these days, to find a PC that isn't equipped with a modem. A relatively inexpensive piece of equipment, a modem guarantees connectivity with a wide range of systems and services. Placing a simple phone call is one of the often-neglected capabilities of today's modems. But without the proper software, placing a call with a modem is a tedious, if not impossible task. Thanks to PHONE, this is true no more. PHONE—easily and quickly—lets you use the modem to dial a number, and then turns control over to you and your telephone.

■ USING PHONE

Few utilities are as easy to use as PHONE. In its simplest form, the command PHONE typed at the DOS prompt starts the program in *interactive mode*. After displaying its copyright message for a moment, PHONE displays the entries

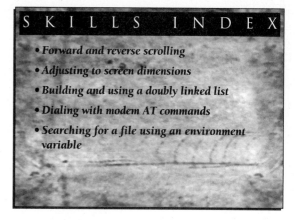

SKILLS INDEX

- *Forward and reverse scrolling*
- *Adjusting to screen dimensions*
- *Building and using a doubly linked list*
- *Dialing with modem AT commands*
- *Searching for a file using an environment variable*

in the phone book file, PHONE.DAT. (Figure 5.1 shows an example of PHONE's inter-active display.) PHONE's full syntax is as follows:

PHONE [*phone-number*]

where *phone-number* is an optional number to dial immediately (*immediate mode*).

PHONE's
interactive
display

```
                               Phone Dialer
-------------- Personal ---------------

NCI Systems, Inc                #88,1-703-941-0285
Home                            #555-1234
Carol's Extension               #0381
Roxane's Extension              #0181
Elise                           #555-0777
Matthew                         #555-7373
Jonathan                        #555-7770
Jeremy                          #555-3737
Ian                             #555-7337
Zachary                         #555-3773

------ Business Numbers ----------

>Computer Retail Wholesalers     #1-800-555-9999
Hard Disks "R" Us, Jim Doe       #1-800-555-5091,,,,5261
The Laser Gallery                #88,1-414-555-9200
Systems 'n Stuff                 #1-206-555-8086

------ Pulse dial example --------

PULSE DIAL THIS NUMBER           #P555-1212
        Move highlight bar and press ENTER to dial, ESC to exit
```

To use PHONE, you must have a modem that uses the standard AT command set. (Most modems do.) When dialing, PHONE precedes the telephone number with the command ATD, and follows with the number specified on the command line or found in the selected phone book entry.

Once you start PHONE in interactive mode, the program displays the entries found in the PHONE.DAT file, and highlights the first line of the displayed data. You have three options: You can scroll through the entries with the Up Arrow and Down Arrow keys, or dial the highlighted entry by pressing Enter, or exit to DOS by pressing the Escape key or Ctrl-Break.

Pressing Down Arrow moves the cursor toward the bottom of the screen until it reaches either the last display line or the last entry from the PHONE.DAT file. Once the highlight reaches the last display line, the PHONE.DAT entries will scroll upward on the screen until you release Down Arrow or reach the last PHONE.DAT entry. If you continue to press Down Arrow after the last entry is highlighted, PHONE sounds an error tone, letting you know you've reached the end of the phone book.

Similarly, pressing the Up Arrow key causes the highlight to move upward on the screen until it reaches the first display line or the first entry in the PHONE.DAT file. Once the top line on the screen is highlighted, the PHONE.DAT entries scroll downward until the first entry in PHONE.DAT is highlighted. If you continue to press Up Arrow, PHONE sounds an error tone, letting you know that it can scroll no further.

To dial the highlighted phone number, press the Enter key. As soon as you do, the display clears, and PHONE redisplays the copyright notice followed by the number being dialed. PHONE also displays a message asking you to wait while it dials the number. After a few moments, PHONE tells you to pick up the receiver and press any key. Doing so disconnects the modem from the telephone line. (There is no way for PHONE to know when dialing has actually completed; you'll need to listen for the completion of dialing on the modem's speaker.) Figure 5.2 shows a sample screen after PHONE has completed a call in interactive mode.

PHONE's
display after
an interactive
session

```
PHONE 1.00 ■ Copyright (c) 1992, Bob Flanders and Michael Holmes
PC Magazine C Lab Notes ■ Phone dialer

Computer Retail Wholesalers        #1-800-555-9999
Please wait while modem dials the phone number
Pick up receiver and hit any key
```

If you wish to cancel PHONE without dialing a number, you can press either the Escape key or the Ctrl-Break key-combination. In either case, PHONE clears the screen, redisplays its copyright notice, displays an appropriate message based on your action, and returns to DOS.

If you have already started a call, and you want to cancel it before PHONE completes the connection, you again have two options. As soon as PHONE completes dialing, you can press a key without picking up the telephone handset. This causes the modem to disconnect from the telephone line, but because the telephone is not off the hook (you haven't picked up the handset), the call will be disconnected. Or you can press Ctrl-Break, which causes the modem to disconnect and PHONE to return to DOS. As long as you haven't picked up the handset, the dialing will be terminated and the call disconnected.

■ SETTING UP TO USE PHONE

Before using PHONE, there are a few things that you must do. First, PHONE assumes that you've already hooked up a modem to your computer. Most modems have two outlets: one for connection to a telephone line, and another for connection to a telephone. The precise function of these outlets varies from modem to modem. For example, on some modems both outlets are always active, and you can pick up the telephone handset while the modem is connected with another system. This action usually introduces errors into the data stream, and the result can be anything from a few unsightly characters on the screen to a disconnect from the remote service. Other modems disable the telephone connector while they are active, effectively locking out use of the telephone while the modem is being used. Regardless of how your modem operates, it's best to connect the modem to the telephone, not the telephone line.

If you have a modem that does not have a second connector for a telephone, purchase a T-connector (a two-to-one connector) for your telephone wall jack. Connect the T-connector to the wall jack, and connect both the modem and the telephone to the T-connector. Be aware that with this setup, the telephone will always interfere with the modem connection should you lift the handset while the modem is in use.

■ **Note.** *The modem used by PHONE must honor the AT standard command set. Also, your modem should be configured to disconnect if the Data Terminal Ready (DTR) signal changes from on to off. (These are the conditions found in most PC modems. See your modem's manual for information on configuration.)*

■ Setting Up PHONE.DAT

After hooking up the hardware, you must create a PHONE.DAT file, using most any text editor. As shown in Figure 5.3, PHONE.DAT's first line must name the COM port to which the modem is connected. The format of the entry may be either COMn or COMn:, where n is a number from one to four. The colon is optional. A comment may follow COMn:, but it must be separated from COMn: by at least one blank space.

The lines following the COMn: entry are the phone book entries. PHONE imposes one restriction on the format of these lines: The number sign (#) must appear only once in the line—immediately preceding the telephone number to be dialed. For example, for this phone book entry:

```
John Doe          #555-4321
```

the PHONE program will dial John Doe at 555-4321 when you highlight the entry and press Enter.

```
COM2:
---------- Personal -------------

NCI Systems, Inc                   #88,1-703-941-0285
Home                               #555-1234
Carol's Extension                  #0381
Roxane's Extension                 #0181
Elise                              #555-0777
Matthew                            #555-7373
Jonathan                           #555-7770
Jeremy                             #555-3737
Ian                                #555-7337
Zachary                            #555-3773

------ Business Numbers ----------

Computer Retail Wholesalers        #1-800-555-9999
Hard Disks 'R' Us, Jim Doe         #1-800-555-5091,,,,5261
The Laser Gallery                  #88,1-414-555-9200
Systems 'n Stuff                   #1-206-555-8086

------ Pulse dial example --------

PULSE DIAL THIS NUMBER             #P555-1212
```

You may place comment lines in PHONE.DAT. Comment lines must not contain a number sign. Example of comment lines appear in Figures 5.1 and 5.3; they are "Personal," "Business Numbers," and "Pulse dial example." If you highlight one of these lines and press Enter, PHONE sounds a short beep, letting you know that there is no number to dial.

If you include lines in PHONE.DAT that are longer than 78 characters, PHONE splits the line starting at the 79th character, and treats each subsequent set of up to 78 characters as a separate phone book entry.

- ### Searching for PHONE.DAT

  When looking for the PHONE.DAT file, PHONE first searches the current directory. If PHONE.DAT is not found there, PHONE continues its search in every directory named in the PATH environment variable until PHONE.DAT is found or all directories have been searched. For example, if the PATH environment variable is set to

  ```
  PATH=C:\;C:\DOS;C:\UTILITY
  ```

  and your current path is C:\TEMP, PHONE will first search C:\TEMP, followed by C:\, then C:\DOS, and finally C:\UTILITY to find PHONE.DAT. If PHONE cannot locate PHONE.DAT in any of these directories, it displays an error message and returns to DOS.

- ### Calling an Unlisted Number

  If you wish to place a call to a specific telephone number not found in PHONE.DAT, you can do so by placing the number to call on the command line as the *phone-number* argument. Doing this puts PHONE in immediate mode, and the entries in PHONE.DAT are not displayed. For example, if you wanted to call Jane Doe (John's sister), and you know that her number (555-1234) is not in PHONE.DAT, you can issue this command:

  ```
  PHONE 555-1234
  ```

  As shown in Figure 5.4, PHONE immediately displays the number being dialed and dials that number. From this point, PHONE operates precisely as if you had pressed Enter with a PHONE.DAT entry selected.

  Although PHONE does not use the phone book file entries in immediate mode, it must still find the PHONE.DAT file, because PHONE.DAT names the COM port to which the modem is connected.

- ### Special Dialing Instructions

  Occasionally, you may need to include some special dialing instructions in the numbers sent to the modem. If either the phone book number or *phone-number* argument contains special dialing instructions, they will be executed by the modem as the number is dialed. Figure 5.3 shows a few entries with special dialing instructions, discussed in the paragraphs that follow.

  The NCI Systems entry contains a prefix code, followed by a comma. In this case, the modem will dial 88 and then wait for a short time before sending the remainder of the number. Use this dialing instruction when your telephone equipment requires a special code to dial long-distance numbers, or to acquire an outside line.

```
C:\PHONE>phone 5551234

PHONE 1.00 ■ Copyright (c) 1992, Bob Flanders and Michael Holmes
PC Magazine C Lab Notes ■ Phone dialer

Dialing: 5551234
Please wait while modem dials the phone number
Pick up receiver and hit any key


C:\PHONE>
```

The Hard Disks 'R' Us entry shows a dialing instruction that dials an 800 number, and then waits for a period of time before dialing the extension number 5261. When most modems encounter a comma in a dial command, they wait for a predetermined time, usually two seconds. (In most modems, the comma's pause-time value can be changed. See your modem documentation for more information.) Since many modern answering systems allow you to enter an extension through a touch-tone pad, this example will place a call to Hard Disks 'R' Us, wait for eight seconds, and then dial Jim Doe's extension (John and Jane's cousin).

Sometimes, older telephone equipment requires that you use pulse dialing instead of tone dialing. (Pulse dialing is a series of connects and disconnects used to transmit a telephone number to remote telephone equipment.) If you must use pulse dialing, precede the affected telephone numbers in PHONE.DAT with the letter *P*. Be aware, however, that once you use pulse dialing, many modems will continue using pulse dialing until you force a change back to tone dialing by preceding a telephone number with the letter *T*.

▪ INSIDE PHONE

Although PHONE's logic flow is quite straightforward, it employs some advanced techniques to get the job done. There are three steps in PHONE's main() routine: setting up the environment, getting the phone number, and placing the call.

When it starts, PHONE first prints its copyright notice, and calls initialization(). The initialization() routine starts by installing the control break handler. Next, initialization() checks to see if you specified any command line arguments, and if so, determines whether you requested help with the /? argument. When you specify /? on the command line, PHONE prints a short help message and returns to DOS. Any other argument specified on the command line is used by PHONE as the *phone-number* argument.

Next, initialization() opens PHONE.DAT by calling find_file() and passing the name of the file to open. In this case, initialization() passes the file name PHONE.DAT.

▪ Searching PATH's Directories

Various software products use different methods for locating files. Some require that you name the location of files when you install the product. Others require you to provide the fully qualified file name each time you wish to reference a specific file. PHONE assumes that the PHONE.DAT file will be either in the current directory or in one of the directories named by the PATH environment variable. The find_file() routine looks for a file in the current directory or, if the file is not there, searches the directories in PATH.

When called, find_file() first attempts to open the file in the current directory. If the file is not found, find_file() calls C's getenv() routine to retrieve the value associated with the PATH environment variable. If the PATH variable is not found, find_file() issues an error message and returns to DOS.

Next, find_file() calls strdup() to make a copy of the string returned by getenv(), and places the starting address of the string in both the path and m_path variables. The starting address is needed because the path variable will be altered during find_file()'s processing, and the original address of the string is thus lost. Since strdup() allocates memory when creating a copy of the string, the original address of the memory allocated by strdup() is needed for deallocation. The original address is maintained in m_path for this very purpose.

Next, find_file() enters a for loop, extracting the directories named by the PATH environment variable. Again, find_file() makes use of an interesting C library routine, strtok().

The strtok() routine extracts substrings from another string based on a set of delimiters (or "tokenizes" that string). When first called, the first argument passed to strtok() is a pointer to the string to be searched, and the second argument is a pointer to a string containing all of the possible delimiters. In subsequent calls to strtok(), the application must change the first argument to null. As strtok() encounters one of the delimiting characters, the delimiter is replaced with a null, and strtok() returns the starting address of the substring. Since find_file() used strdup() to copy the value of the PATH variable, no damage is done to the string returned by getenv().

Since strtok() knows where to continue checking after the first invocation, the routine likely uses static variables. If this is the case, strtok() can only be used to search one string at a time. When all of the substrings (or tokens) have been extracted from a string, strtok() returns a null.

As each entry from the PATH variable is returned, find_file() appends the PHONE.DAT file name to the entry from PATH. When building the fully qualified PHONE.DAT file name, find_file() checks if the last character of the PATH entry is a backslash, and if it is, does not add a backslash to that entry before building the file name. This is one instance where PHONE saves some memory by embedding the test within the call to sprintf(), as explained next.

■ Using the Ternary Operator to Save Space

Whenever you encounter a test that alters one variable in a subroutine call, C's ternary operator (?:) can save you some memory over the alternative, a discrete if statement. If the test used in sprintf() were written as an if statement, the code would appear as follows:

```
if (LAST(path) == '\\')
    sprintf(buf, "%s%s", path, s);
 else
    sprintf(buf, "%s\\%s", path, s);
```

This example requires two complete calls to sprintf(), even though only one argument has changed. A better implementation might be this:

```
if (LAST(path) == '\\')
    format = "%s%s";
 else
    format = "%s\\%s";

sprintf(buf, format, path, s);
```

In this case, memory space must be reserved for the format variable, but only one call to sprintf() is compiled, saving about 16 bytes of memory (in Borland C++ 3.0). By using the ternary operator, however, PHONE reduces the memory utilization by yet another two bytes, although the program is slightly slowed down because sprintf() must interpret the additional argument when building the string.

As find_file() retrieves each entry from the PATH variable, it builds a new file name and attempts to open that file. If any attempt succeeds, find_file() exits the for loop and returns a FILE pointer to the opened PHONE.DAT file. If PHONE.DAT is not found in any directory named by the PATH variable, find_file() prints an error message and returns to DOS.

■   **Validating the COM Port**

After finding and opening the PHONE.DAT file, initialization() retrieves the first line from the file. Using strtok(), initialization() retrieves the COMn: specification from the line and passes it to validate_port().

When a PC is first turned on or rebooted, one of the routines contained in the BIOS checks for the existence of communications ports. The standard I/O addresses for COM ports are 0x3F8 for COM1, 0x2F8 for COM2, 0x3E8 for COM3, and 0X2E8 for COM4. The BIOS builds a table at address 0x40:0 that describes the communications ports found by boot routines. This communications port table comprises four words indicating the presence of COM1 to COM4. If any of the words are zero, the corresponding communications port was not found by the BIOS.

The validate_port() routine validates the string that is passed to it, by checking that the string starts with COM, that the number following COM is in the range 1 to 4, and that the trailing character, if present, is a colon. The routine also checks to ensure that the port table entry corresponding to the named COM port is not zero. If the COM port specification fails any of these tests, validate_port() issues an appropriate error message and returns to DOS. Otherwise, the routine retrieves the entry from the communications port table and calculates the address of the modem control register (MCR). As we'll see, the MCR controls certain modem functions.

■   **Checking the Video Mode**

PHONE automatically adjusts to the screen dimensions that are active when PHONE is run. To do so, initialization() calls _gettextinfo(), which retrieves information about the current video mode. PHONE retrieves the number of lines available, and ensures that each line has at least 80 columns. If the monitor is monochrome, PHONE also resets the video attributes to those appropriate for monochrome.

Setting Up the COM Port

After initialization() finishes, main() calls set_up_comm() to initialize the communications port. First, set_up_comm() resets the Data Terminal Ready (DTR) and Request To Send (RTS) signals by modifying the modem control register (MCR). If the modem is appropriately configured, this forces the modem to disconnect should it be connected to another service when PHONE is executed.

Next, set_up_comm() sets the port's communications parameters to 1200 bits per second (bps), no parity, 8 data bits, and 1 stop bit. Although this is a relatively slow data rate, it is quite sufficient for sending an extremely small amount of data (such as a telephone number) to the modem. This also ensures that PHONE will work with the vast majority of modems. Unfortunately, because PHONE uses 1200 bps, it cannot use 300-bps modems.

After setting the data rate, set_up_comm() raises the DTR and RTS signals. This ensures that most modems will respond to the commands sent by PHONE.

DTR and RTS

te: For more
cussion of
-232
nmunications,
Chapter 1,
tting the
ck with
LOCK."

Two signals available under the RS-232 standard and controlled by the MCR are Data Terminal Ready (DTR) and Request To Send (RTS). The DTR signal tells the modem that the terminal equipment (in this case, the computer) is on and ready to communicate. The RTS signal tells the modem that the computer is ready to either send or receive some data. Although the response to RTS and DTR varies from modem to modem, PHONE raises both of these signals for compatibility with a wide range of modems.

Getting the Phone Number

When set_up_comm() returns to main(), main() checks to see if you specified a phone number on the command line. If so, main() displays a message showing the number being dialed, and proceeds to dial that number. Otherwise, main() calls display_file(), which starts the interactive mode.

Displaying PHONE.DAT

The display_file() routine starts by loading PHONE.DAT's phone book entries into memory, placing each record on a *doubly linked* list. (A doubly linked list is a set of memory blocks, each containing a forward and backward chain pointer.) To do this, display_file() calls load_file().

The load_file() routine immediately enters a while loop, reading each record from PHONE.DAT. (Remember that PHONE has already read the first record when it retrieved the COM port specification.) As it reads each record, load_file() builds a p_lines structure that contains the data from the PHONE.DAT line along with two pointers. The p_back pointer references the previous p_lines structure, and the p_fwd pointer references the next p_lines structure. Figure 5.5 shows the layout of the p_lines structures after loading the example PHONE.DAT file into memory.

FIGURE 5.5
Layout after loading PHONE.DAT in memory

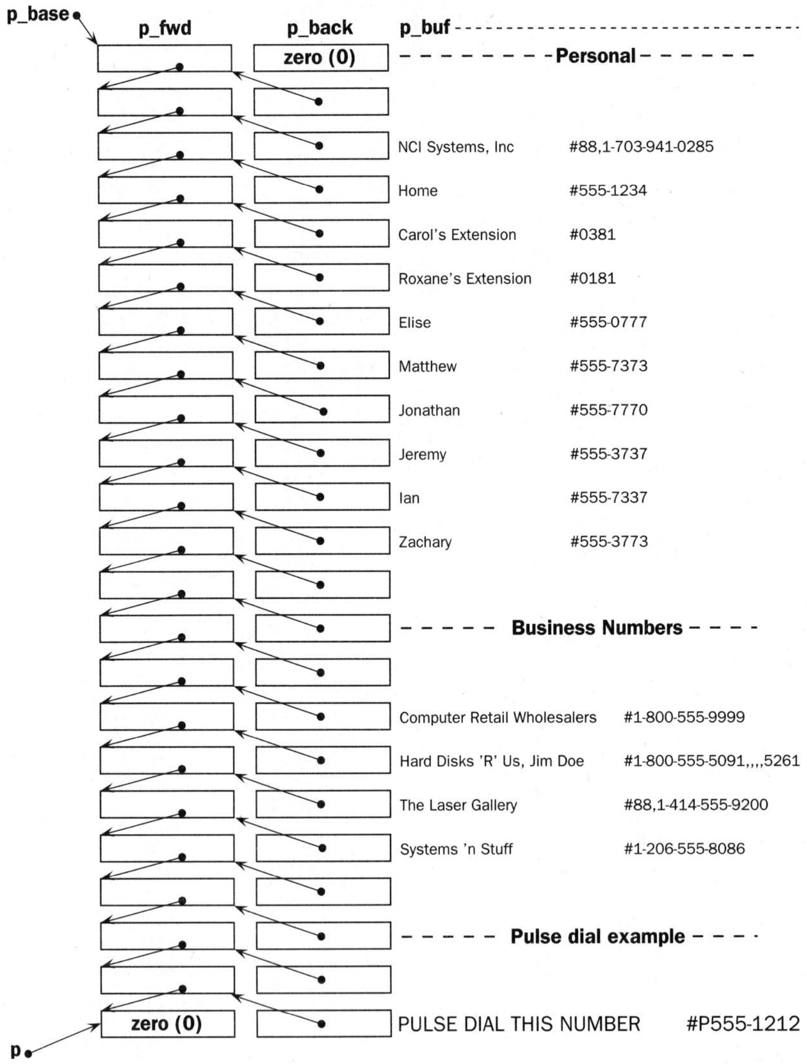

There are several algorithms that can be used when writing a scroll routine, especially when the data being viewed cannot be changed by the viewer program. If you are relatively certain that the data will fit in memory, two algorithms immediately come to mind: an array of fixed length entries, residing in a contiguous block of memory; or a linked list of variable length entries.

A list of fixed-length entries requires the program to count the number of lines needed to hold the entries, and calculate the amount of memory needed. After allocating the memory, the program simply reads each line into the corresponding array entry. The main drawback of this implementation is that the program is limited by the largest block of memory available when the program is executed. Also, since each entry has the maximum space allocated, whether used or not, fewer total entries can fit in memory.

Instead, PHONE uses a doubly linked list to manage the phone book entries, even though this is somewhat more difficult to implement. Using a doubly linked list, there is some overhead (eight bytes) for each entry, but the buffer portion of each entry contains only the space needed to hold the text portion of that entry. For a blank line, only nine bytes are allocated (eight bytes for pointers, one for the string). It is unusual for an entry line to be completely filled out, so the linked list generally requires less memory than the fixed-length entry array for the same file.

■ Building the Linked List

There are three steps to building a linked list: building the entry, checking to see if it is the first, and chaining it to the appropriate places. Building the entry requires getting a piece of storage large enough to hold the information. The load_file() routine allocates memory based on the length of the entry, and moves the line from the file into the entry's buffer.

When building a linked list, your program must handle two conditions: building the first entry and building the other entries. Linked lists usually have a *base pointer* (often referred to as an *anchor*). The base pointer for the p_lines structures is p_base. A pointer to the last entry on the chain is also helpful. This allows the addition of a new entry without searching through the list for the end of the chain. Since PHONE's linked list is built in one routine (that is, the list does not dynamically grow once PHONE.DAT has been read into memory), the variable p in load_file(), which points at the last linked entry, is an automatic variable (allocated when load_file() is called, and deallocated when load_file() returns). Before the first entry is linked, p contains zero.

After allocating an entry, load_file() checks to see if the p variable points to an existing p_lines structure. If not, this is the first entry; load_file() points the base pointer (p_base) at the newly created entry, and clears the backward pointer of that entry to zero. The first entry has now been placed on the list. The load_file() routine then sets the p variable to point at the first entry on the linked list. Figure 5.6 illustrates the steps used when building the first entry of a doubly linked list.

For all subsequent entries, load_file() allocates and builds p_lines structures to contain those entries. Since the p variable now points to an existing entry, load_file() sets the previous entry's forward pointer to the address of the new entry, and the new entry's backward pointer to the address of the previous entry. As before, load_file() sets the p variable to point at the new entry. Figure 5.7 illustrates how a new entry is added to a linked list.

The load_file() routine continues adding new entries until the whole file has been read or the system runs out of memory. If a memory allocation error occurs when load_file() is trying to build a new entry, the function displays an error and returns to DOS.

■ Starting the Display

After the file has been loaded into memory, display_file() sets up the display by calling set_up_screen(). This routine clears the screen and writes the information fixed on the top and bottom lines of the screen. Note that set_up_screen() uses the max_lines variable to determine the last line of the screen.

After setting up the base screen, set_up_screen() calls the window(). The window() routine establishes limits for subsequent calls to insline() and delline(), which scroll the window area down and up, respectively.

Once the screen is prepared, display_file() enters a loop, writing the first set of lines to the screen. The number of lines written is based on the number of lines available on the screen. The first entry of PHONE.DAT is displayed in reverse video, and subsequent lines are displayed in normal video.

■ Moving through the Entries

Having prepared the first screenful of entries, display_file() enters a loop, waiting for a key to be pressed. There are only four keys recognized by display_file(): Up Arrow, Down Arrow, Enter (or Return), and Escape.

When Up Arrow is pressed, display_file() removes the highlight from the current line. Since display_file() can only move upward if the highlight is not at the top of the screen, or if there are more entries above the currently highlighted one, display_file() checks both of these conditions. If display_file() cannot move to a previous entry, it sounds an error tone. If the highlight is not at the top of the screen, the previous line is highlighted; otherwise, display_file() scrolls the screen down one line, and highlights the previous entry.

FIGURE 5.6
Building the
first entry on a
linked list

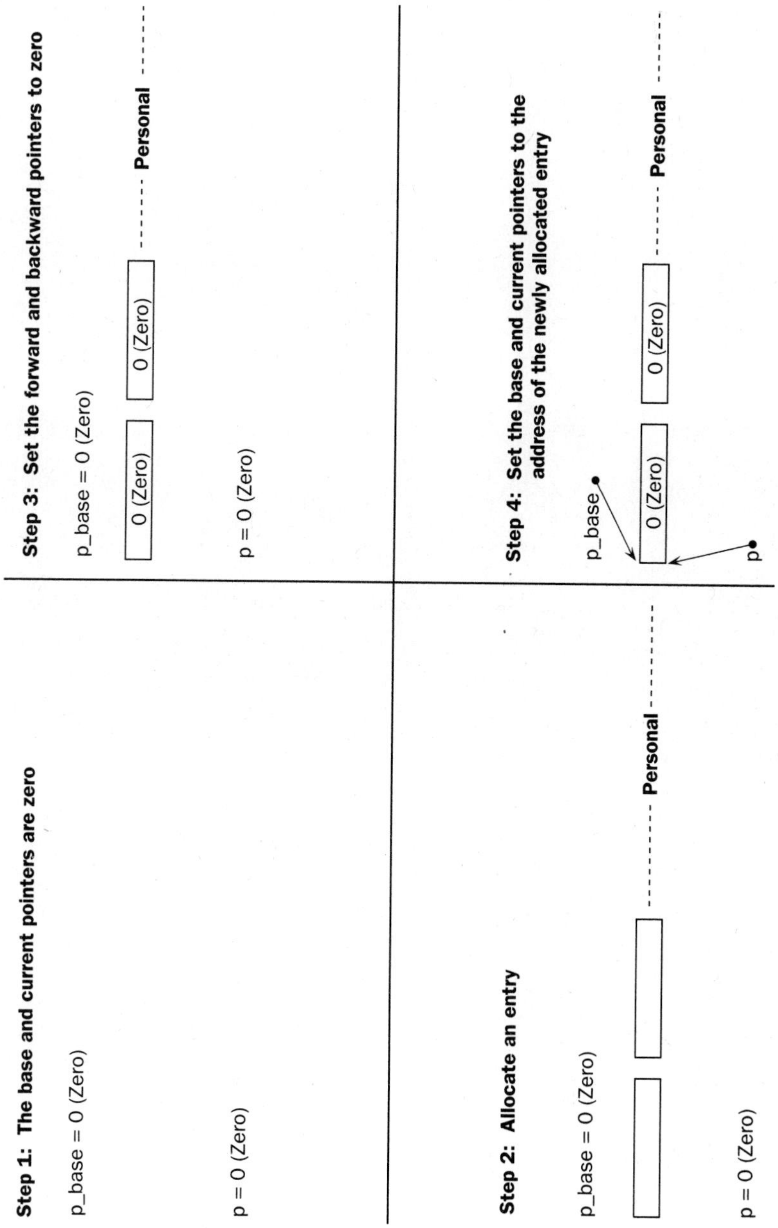

Step 1: The base and current pointers are zero

p_base = 0 (Zero)

p = 0 (Zero)

Step 2: Allocate an entry

p_base = 0 (Zero)

p = 0 (Zero)

Personal

Step 3: Set the forward and backward pointers to zero

p_base = 0 (Zero)

0 (Zero)   0 (Zero)   Personal

p = 0 (Zero)

Step 4: Set the base and current pointers to the
address of the newly allocated entry

p_base

0 (Zero)   0 (Zero)   Personal

p

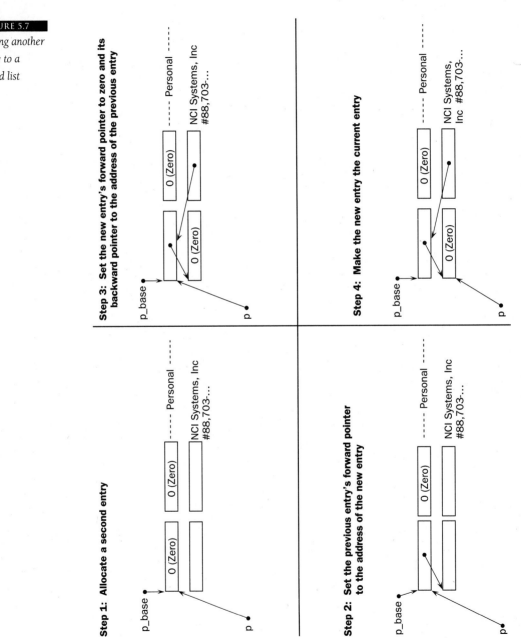

FIGURE 5.7

Adding another entry to a linked list

Down Arrow causes display_file() to work in the opposite direction; the highlight moves down the screen, and once at the bottom, the entries scroll upward until the last entry is highlighted. Again, any attempt to move down from the last entry causes an error tone, and the highlight remains where it is.

The display_file() routine does not remember which line is highlighted on the screen. Rather, it uses the wherey() function to determine the current line. The only value maintained by display_file() is the address of the highlighted p_lines structure. Since each structure contains a pointer to the next and previous entry, the address of the highlighted entry is all that display_file() needs.

■ Selecting an Entry

When you press the Enter key, display_line() checks to see that the highlighted entry has a telephone number to dial. If not, it sounds an error tone and continues. If display_line() finds a telephone number, it saves the address of the number to dial, clears the screen, redisplays the copyright notice, displays the selected entry, and returns to main().

If you press the Escape key, display_line() simply clears the screen, prints a message to show no number was requested, and exits to DOS.

■ Dialing the Number

Whether run in the immediate mode or interactive mode, the variable named phone contains the address of the requested telephone number. To place the call, main() invokes the place_call() function, passing the requested number.

First, place_call() builds the dial command by appending the request number to ATD, and appending a semicolon and carriage return to the resulting string. Next, place_call() calls send_string(), which sends the dial command to the modem. The send_string() routine enters a loop, sending each character in the dial command. Before sending each character, send_string() ensures that a character can be sent to the port by calling _bios_serialcom(), and only sends the character when the port is ready.

After sending the dial command, place_call() displays a message requesting you to wait, waits three seconds for the modem to process the command, and displays another message telling you to pick up the receiver and press any key.

■ Note.   *Before pressing a key, listen to be sure the modem has finished dialing. If the number has commas in the command, the modem may not be finished dialing even though the tones have stopped.*

When you press a key, place_call() resets DTR and RTS. If you've properly configured the modem, it will immediately disconnect from the line, leaving you to talk to whomever you called. "Hello. Do you deliver pizza?..."

■ SUMMARY

PHONE uses several important programming techniques: building and traversing linked lists, managing a full-screen display, dynamically adjusting to the size of the display, and finding files based on an environment string. Here are some enhancements you may want to add to PHONE:

- Honor the Page Up and Page Down keys, moving a full screen at a time rather than a single line at a time.

- Allow the user to add new phone book file entries, or change or delete existing entries, and rewrite PHONE.DAT when done.

- Allow the user to enter an alphabetical telephone number (such as 1-800-NCI-GUYS), and have the program translate the number to its numeric equivalent.

- Sort the phone book file entries as they are being loaded into memory.

- Allow the selection of a phone book entry from the command line.

PHONE 1.00

```
/* ********************************************************************** *

    PHONE 1.00, Copyright (c) 1992, Bob Flanders and Michael Holmes
    PC Magazine C Lab Notes, Phone dialer

 * ********************************************************************** *

    This code for Borland C++ version 3.0. (MSC version on diskette)

         Compile with:  BCC -O2 -mc phone.c

    To compile for Microsoft C, you need to change the following:
         - screen scrolling routines, insline() and delline()
         - screen color setting routines, textcolor() and textbackground()
         - logical screen definition routine, window()
         - change control break handling for ctrlbrk() and control_break()
         - change #pragma as necessary

 * ********************************************************************** */


#pragma  pack(1)                         /* pack to byte alignment   */
#pragma  warn -eff                       /* remove erroneous msgs    */
#include <stdio.h>                       /* standard i/o library     */
#include <stdlib.h>                      /* commonly used routines   */
#include <dos.h>                         /* DOS rtn definitions      */
#include <string.h>                      /* string functions         */
#include <stdarg.h>                      /* argument functions       */
#include <bios.h>                        /* BIOS manifest constants  */
#include <ctype.h>                       /* character classifications*/
#include <conio.h>                       /* console i/o routines     */

                                         /* shorthands               */
#define NOT !                            /* logical not              */
#define LAST(x)       x[strlen(x) - 1]   /* get last char in string  */
#define UINT          unsigned int       /* unsigned integer type    */

#define PHONE_DAT     "PHONE.DAT"        /* database filename        */
#define BUFSIZE       79                 /* line buffer size         */

                                         /* communications defines   */
#define SEND_READY    0x2000             /* UART ready for next char */
#define COMM_ERROR    0x9e00             /* int 14h error flags      */
#define DTR           0x03               /* DTR and RTS bits in mcr  */

                                         /* key definitions          */
#define UP            0x100 + '\x48'     /* up key                   */
#define DOWN          0x100 + '\x50'     /* down key                 */
#define RETURN        '\r'               /* return key               */
#define ESC           '\x1b'            /* escape key               */
```

```
/* ****************************************************************** *
 *         routine definitions                                        *
 * ****************************************************************** */

void    quit_with(char *, ...),              /* quit with error message  */
        initialization(int, char **),        /* init and parse cmd line  */
        validate_port(char *),               /* validate comm port parm  */
        set_up_comm(void),                   /* set up port and modem    */
        display_file(void),                  /* display phone file       */
        display_line(struct p_lines *,       /* display single phone line*/
            enum select_types),
        load_file(void),                     /* load PHONE.DAT file      */
        set_up_screen(void),                 /* display header & footer  */
        color_set(enum select_types),        /* set up screen colors     */
        close_down(void),                    /* close screen and quit    */
        place_call(char *),                  /* call for the user        */
        touppers(char *),                    /* string to uppercase      */
        wait(long);                          /* wait n timer ticks       */
int     control_break(void),                 /* control break handler    */
        send_string(char *),                 /* send string out comm port*/
        get_key(void);                       /* get any key              */
FILE    *find_file(char *, char *);          /* find and open a file     */



/* ****************************************************************** *
 *         globals                                                    *
 * ****************************************************************** */

int     rc = 1,                              /* errorlevel return code   */
        full_screen,                         /* full screen mode active  */
        text_fg = WHITE,                     /* default foreground color */
        text_bg = BLUE,                      /* ..background color       */
        hdr_fg = YELLOW,                     /* header foreground color  */
        hdr_bg = CYAN,                       /* ..background color       */
        max_lines,                           /* screen size in lines     */
        port,                                /* int 14h port number      */
        hw_port,                             /* hardware port address    */
        mcr_port,                            /* modem control reg port   */
        mcr_val;                             /* mcr value w/o DTR & RTS   */

char    *phone,                              /* string to dial           */
        buf[BUFSIZE],                        /* file buffer              */
        cmd_line[128];                       /* cmd line phone number    */

FILE    *fi;                                 /* input file               */

struct  p_lines                              /* lines in PHONE.DAT file  */
        {
        struct p_lines *p_fwd, *p_back;      /* forward and backward ptrs*/
        char   p_buf[1];                     /* line buffer              */
        } *p_base;                           /* anchor to linked list    */

enum    select_types                         /* display line types       */
        {
        selected,                            /* highlighted line         */
        unselected,                          /* normal display line      */
        unselected_special                   /* ..w/o prefix character   */
        };
```

```
/* **************************************************************** *
 *        messages and strings                                     *
 * **************************************************************** */

char      copyright[]    = "PHONE 1.00 \xfe Copyright (c) 1992, "
                           "Bob Flanders and Michael Holmes\n"
                           "PC Magazine C Lab Notes \xfe "
                           "Phone dialer\n\n",
          missing_port[] = "Port name is not the first line in "
                           "PHONE.DAT\n",
          stop_here[]    = "\nStopping at user's request\n",
          new_line[]     = "\n",
          bell[]         = "\a",
          no_memory[]    = "Not enough memory to load PHONE.DAT file\n",
          no_database[]  = "Cannot find PHONE.DAT file\n",
          no_port[]      = "System does not have a COM%d:\n",
          no_lines[]     = "Database has no lines in it\n",
          bad_port[]     = "Bad port name %s\n",
          bad_width[]    = "Screen must be at least 80 columns wide\n",
          dialing[]      = "Dialing: %s\n",
          wait_msg[]     = "Please wait while modem dials the phone "
                           "number\n",
          line_fmt[]     = "%-78.78s\r",
          time_out[]     = "Time out sending to comm port\n",
          no_request[]   = "No dialing request made\n",
          pick_up[]      = "Pick up receiver and hit any key\n",
          header[]       = "%34sPhone Dialer%34s",
          footer[]       = " Move highlight bar and press ENTER to dial, "
                           "ESC to exit ",
          help[]         =
              "  Usage:   PHONE   [phone_number]\n\n"
              "Options:   phone_number is the number to dial immediately"
              "\n\n";

/* **************************************************************** *
 *        main()                                                   *
 * **************************************************************** */

void      main(int ac,                  /* DOS cmd line token count */
               char *av[])               /* ..token strings         */
{


printf(copyright);                       /* give copyright message  */

initialization(ac, av);                  /* init and parse cmd line */
set_up_comm();                           /* set up communications   */

if (NOT phone)                           /* q. phone number given?  */
    display_file();                      /* a. no .. display file   */
 else
    printf(dialing, phone);              /* else .. display number  */

place_call(phone);                       /* place the phone call    */

rc = 0;                                  /* clear errorlevel and    */
quit_with(new_line);                     /* ..return to DOS         */

}
```

```c
/* ********************************************************************* *
 *      initialization() -- init interrupts and parse command line      *
 * ********************************************************************* */

void    initialization(int  ac,             /* DOS cmd line token count */
                       char *av[])           /* ..token strings          */
{
int     i;                                  /* loop control             */
char    *port;                              /* string ptr to port name  */
struct  text_info r;                        /* screen info structure    */


ctrlbrk(control_break);                     /* set up ctrl break handler*/

if (ac > 1)                                 /* q. arguments given?      */
    {                                       /* a. yes .. check it out   */
    if (NOT strcmp(av[1], "/?"))            /* q. help wanted?          */
        quit_with(help);                    /* a. yes .. give help/quit */

    phone = cmd_line;                       /* get addr of phone number */

    for (i = 1; i < ac; i++)                /* gather each argument..    */
        strcat(phone, av[i]);               /* ..into one string         */
    }

fi = find_file(PHONE_DAT, "r");             /* find and open database   */

if (fgets(buf, sizeof(buf), fi))            /* q. read first line ok?   */
    {                                       /* a. yes .. find port name */
    if ((port = strtok(buf, " \n")) != 0)   /* q. find a port name?     */
        validate_port(port);                /* a. yes .. validate it    */
     else
        quit_with(missing_port);            /* else .. give error & quit*/
    }

gettextinfo(&r);                            /* get current screen info  */
max_lines = r.screenheight;                 /* save maximum nbr of lines*/

if (r.screenwidth < 80)                     /* q. less than 80 columns? */
    quit_with(bad_width);                   /* a. yes .. give error/quit*/

if (r.currmode == BW80 ||                   /* q. black and white mode..*/
            r.currmode == MONO)             /* ..or monochrome mode?    */
    {
    text_bg = hdr_bg = BLACK;               /* a. yes .. set up mono..   */
    text_fg = hdr_fg = WHITE;               /* ..palette for text/hdrs  */
    }
}



/* ********************************************************************* *
 *      set_up_comm() -- initialize communications port and modem       *
 * ********************************************************************* */

void    set_up_comm(void)
{


outp(mcr_port, inp(mcr_port) & ~DTR);       /* turn DTR and RTS off     */
wait(9L);                                   /* ..wait half second       */

_bios_serialcom(_COM_INIT, port,            /* set up comm port for ..  */
        _COM_1200 | _COM_NOPARITY |         /* ..1200 baud, no parity   */
```

```
                _COM_CHR8 | _COM_STOP1);          /* ..8 data bits, 1 stop bit*/

outp(mcr_port,  mcr_val = (inp(mcr_port)    /* capture current mcr..     */
                | DTR));                     /* ..turn on DTR and RTS     */
wait(9L);                                    /* ..and wait half second    */

}



/* ********************************************************************* *
 *      display_file() -- display phone file                           *
 * ********************************************************************* */
void    display_file(void)
{
int     i;                                   /* loop counter              */
struct  p_lines *t, *b, *p;                  /* line pointers             */


load_file();                                 /* load file into structure  */
set_up_screen();                             /* ..and set up base screen  */

for (i = 0, t = b = p = p_base;              /* loop thru building..      */
            i < (max_lines - 2); i++)        /* ..initial screen          */
    {
    display_line(b, min(i, unselected));     /* ..one line at a time      */
    gotoxy(1, wherey() + 1);                 /* ..and move to next line   */

    if (b->p_fwd)                            /* q. something follows?     */
        b = b->p_fwd;                        /* a. yes .. set up next one*/
     else
        break;                               /* else .. exit loop         */
    }

if (i == (max_lines - 2))                    /* q. fill the screen?       */
    b = b->p_back;                           /* a. yes .. get last ptr    */

gotoxy(1, 1);                                /* position on first line    */

while (1)                                    /* loop 'til user quits      */
    {
    switch (get_key())                       /* handle waiting character  */
        {
        case 0:                              /* no key available          */
            continue;                        /* ..try again later         */

        case UP:                             /* up key                    */
            display_line(p, unselected);     /* unselect line             */

            if (p == t)                      /* q. cursor on top row?     */
                {                            /* a. yes .. try moving up    */
                if (p->p_back)               /* q. any previous lines?    */
                    {
                    insline();               /* a. yes .. make room       */
                    t = p = p->p_back;       /* get top line's pointer    */
                    b = b->p_back;           /* ..and bottom line's ptr   */
                    }
                 else
                    printf(bell);            /* else .. just ring bell    */
                }

            else
```

```
                    {
                    p = p->p_back;               /* get previous line pointer*/
                    gotoxy(1, wherey() - 1);     /* ..move to previous line   */
                    }

            display_line(p, selected);           /* write new current line    */
            continue;                            /* ..and get next key        */

    case DOWN:                                   /* down key                  */
            display_line(p, unselected);         /* unselect line             */

            if (p == b)                          /* q. cursor on bottom row?  */
                {                                /* a. yes .. try moving dwn  */
                if (p->p_fwd)                    /* q. any more lines?        */
                    {                            /* a. yes .. scroll window   */
                    gotoxy(1, 1);                /* goto top line ..          */
                    delline();                   /* delete top line           */
                    t = t->p_fwd;                /* get new top line pointer  */
                    p = b = p->p_fwd;            /* ..and bottom line ptr     */
                    gotoxy(1, max_lines - 2);    /* set up shop at bottom     */
                    }
                else
                    printf(bell);                /* else .. just ring bell    */
                }

            else
                {
                p = p->p_fwd;                    /* get next line pointer     */
                gotoxy(1, wherey() + 1);         /* ..move to next line       */
                }

            display_line(p, selected);           /* write new current line    */
            continue;                            /* ..and get next key        */

    case RETURN:                                 /* return key                */
            if ((phone = strchr(                 /* q. find a pound sign..    */
                p->p_buf, '#')) != 0)            /* ..on current line?        */
                {
                phone++;                         /* a. yes .. point at number*/
                close_down();                    /* ..clean up screen         */
                display_line(p,                  /* ..redisplay line          */
                    unselected_special);
                gotoxy(1, wherey() + 1);         /* ..and move to next line   */
                return;                          /* ..and go dial it          */
                }

            printf(bell);                        /* else .. ring bell         */
            continue;                            /* ..and try again           */

    case ESC:                                    /* escape key                */
            close_down();                        /* clean up screen..         */
            quit_with(no_request);               /* ..and exit w/o dialing    */

    default:                                     /* error case                */
            printf(bell);                        /* ..just ring bell          */
    }
}

}
```

```
/* ********************************************************************* *
 *       display_line() -- display one line from phone file            *
 * ********************************************************************* */

void    display_line(struct p_lines *p,     /* line to display        */
                      enum select_types s)   /* selected/unselected flag */
{

if (s != unselected_special)                /* q. need a spacer char?  */
    {
    color_set(unselected);                  /* a. yes .. select palette */
    cprintf(s ? " " : ">");                 /* ..put out spacer char   */
    }

color_set(s);                               /* choose proper colors    */
cprintf(line_fmt, p->p_buf);                /* ..and display line      */

}


/* ********************************************************************* *
 *       load_file() -- read PHONE.DAT into memory                     *
 * ********************************************************************* */

void    load_file(void)
{
char    *s;                                 /* string pointer          */
struct  p_lines *p = 0, *q;                 /* prev and current pointers*/

while (fgets(buf, sizeof(buf), fi))         /* read whole file         */
    {
    if ((s = strchr(buf, '\n')) != 0)       /* q. return in buffer?    */
        *s = '\0';                          /* a. yes .. end line there */

    if ((q = (struct p_lines *) malloc(     /* q. allocation of memory */
            sizeof(struct p_lines)          /* ..for another line ok?  */
            + strlen(buf))) == 0)
        quit_with(no_memory);               /* a. no .. give error/quit */

    strcpy(q->p_buf, buf);                  /* copy in current line    */

    if (NOT p)                              /* q. first cycle?         */
        {
        p_base = q;                         /* a. yes .. save first one */
        q->p_back = 0;                      /* ..clear backward pointer */
        }
     else
        {
        p->p_fwd = q;                       /* else.. chain previous to */
        q->p_back = p;                      /* ..current and vice-versa */
        }

    p = q;                                  /* current ptr becomes prev */

    }

if (p)                                      /* q. at least one line?   */
    p->p_fwd = 0;                           /* a. yes .. put in end mark*/
 else
    quit_with(no_lines);                    /* else .. quit w/error msg */

}
```

```c
/* ********************************************************************* *
 *       set_up_screen() -- set up screen, headers and footers         *
 * ********************************************************************* */

void    set_up_screen(void)
{

full_screen = 1;                              /* set up full screen flag   */

window(1, 1, 80, max_lines);                  /* define logical screen     */
color_set(unselected);                        /* set up standard colors    */
clrscr();                                     /* clear screen              */

gotoxy(11, max_lines);                        /* position at bottom        */
textcolor(hdr_fg);                            /* set up header and footer  */
textbackground(hdr_bg);                       /* ..fore/background colors  */
cprintf(footer);                              /* ..and display footer      */

gotoxy(1, 1);                                 /* goto top of screen        */
cprintf(header, "", "");                      /* ..display header          */

window(1, 2, 80, max_lines - 1);              /* define text window        */
color_set(unselected);                        /* set up standard colors    */

}


/* ********************************************************************* *
 *       color_set() -- select current foreground and background colors *
 * ********************************************************************* */

void    color_set(enum select_types s_flag) /* selected/unselected       */
{

switch (s_flag)                               /* based on flag ..          */
    {
    case selected:                            /* selected line             */
        textcolor(text_bg);                   /* set up the inverted..     */
        textbackground(text_fg);              /* ..color scheme            */
        break;                                /* ..then continue           */

    case unselected:                          /* unselected line           */
    case unselected_special:                  /* ..or special redisplay    */
        textcolor(text_fg);                   /* set up the normal..       */
        textbackground(text_bg);              /* ..color scheme            */
        break;                                /* ..then continue           */
    }

}


/* ********************************************************************* *
 *       close_down() -- close windows and quit to DOS                  *
 * ********************************************************************* */

void    close_down(void)
{


window(1, 1, 80, max_lines);                  /* define full screen window*/
color_set(unselected);                        /* set up normal colors      */
```

```
    clrscr();                               /* clear screen            */
    full_screen = 0;                        /* ..and full screen flag  */
    printf(copyright);                      /* redisplay program banner */

    }



/* ********************************************************************* *
 *       place_call() -- dial selected or entered phone number         *
 * ********************************************************************* */

void    place_call(char *dial)              /* phone number to dial    */
{
char    dial_buf[BUFSIZE+5];                /* dial buffer             */


    strcpy(dial_buf, "ATD");                /* copy in dial command    */
    strcat(dial_buf, dial);                 /* ..then phone number     */
    strcat(dial_buf, ";\r");                /* ..finally a ; and <cr>  */

    if (send_string(dial_buf))              /* q. send dial command ok? */
        quit_with(time_out);                /* a. no .. give error/quit */

    printf(wait_msg);                       /* give user wait message  */
    wait(3 * 18);                           /* ..then give modem time.. */
    printf(pick_up);                        /* ..then user instructions */

    while (NOT get_key())                   /* wait for a key to be hit */
        ;

    outp(mcr_port, inp(mcr_port) & ~DTR);   /* ..then hang up modem     */

    }



/* ********************************************************************* *
 *       find_file() -- find and open a file                           *
 * ********************************************************************* */

FILE    *find_file(char *s,                 /* file name to find       */
                   char *mode)              /* mode to open file in    */
{
char    *path, *m_path;                     /* path environment string */
FILE    *fi = 0;                            /* input file handle       */


    if ((fi = fopen(s, mode)) != 0)         /* q. find file?           */
        return(fi);                         /* a. yes .. return w/handle*/

    if (NOT (m_path = getenv("PATH")))      /* q. find path variable?  */
        quit_with(no_database);             /* a. no .. give error/quit */

    path = m_path = strdup(m_path);         /* get a copy of the string */

    for (; (path = strtok(path, ";")) != 0; /* using each path segment..*/
            path = 0)                       /* ..of the path variable  */
        {
        sprintf(buf, "%s%s%s", path,        /* build a filename from   */
            LAST(path) == '\\' ? "" : "\\", /* ..each path subdirectory */
            s);                             /* ..and base filename     */

        if ((fi = fopen(buf, mode)) != 0)   /* q. find file?           */
```

```
                break;                          /* a. yes .. exit loop       */
        }

    free(m_path);                               /* free copy of path string */

    if (NOT fi)                                 /* q. file found?           */
        quit_with(no_database);                 /* a. no .. give err/quit   */

    return(fi);                                 /* finally return w/handle  */

}


/* ****************************************************************** *
 *      validate_port() -- validate communications port parameter   *
 * ****************************************************************** */

void    validate_port(char *p)                  /* comm port string pointer */
{
int     far *port_table = MK_FP(0x40, 0);       /* BIOS serial port table   */

    touppers(p);                                /* make port name uppercase */

    if ((strlen(p) > 5) ||                      /* q. wrong length for name?*/
            strncmp("COM", p, 3) ||             /* ..or bad format?         */
            p[3] < '1' || p[3] > '4' ||         /* ..or invalid port number?*/
            (p[4] != '\0' && p[4] != ':'))      /* ..or bad string term?    */
        quit_with(bad_port, p);                 /* a. yes .. give error/quit*/

    port = p[3] - '1';                          /* get int 14h port number  */

    if (NOT (hw_port = port_table[port]))       /* q. port available?       */
        quit_with(no_port, port + 1);           /* a. no .. give error/quit */

    mcr_port = hw_port + 4;                      /* set up mcr i/o address   */

}



/* ****************************************************************** *
 *      send_string() -- send a string out the comm port            *
 * ****************************************************************** */

int     send_string(char *s)                    /* string to send out       */
{
int     rc = 0;                                 /* return code              */

    while (*s)                                  /* run thru whole string    */
        {
        while (NOT (_bios_serialcom(_COM_STATUS,/* while waiting for UART to*/
                port, 0) & SEND_READY))         /* ..finish w/last character*/
            kbhit();                            /* check keyboard           */

        if (((rc = _bios_serialcom(_COM_SEND,   /* q. send character ok     */
                port, *s++)) & COMM_ERROR) != 0)/* ..without a timeout?      */
            break;                              /* a. no .. stop loop here   */
        }

    return(rc & COMM_ERROR);                     /* return w/last status     */

}
```

```
/* ****************************************************************** *
 *       wait() -- wait n timer ticks                               *
 * ****************************************************************** */

void    wait(long n)                            /* time to wait in ticks   */
{
long    far *timer = MK_FP(0x40, 0x6c),         /* BIOS timer tick counter */
        start, work;                            /* start tick count        */

start = *timer;                                 /* get current time        */

while (n > 0)                                   /* loop 'til n ticks past   */
    {
    if ((work = *timer) != start)               /* q. time pass?            */
        {                                       /* a. yes .. see how much   */
        if (work < start)                       /* q. clock go past midnite?*/
            n--;                                /* a. yes .. count as 1 tick*/
         else
            n -= (UINT)(work - start);          /* else .. count everything */

        start = work;                           /* start again w/curr time  */
        }

     else
        kbhit();                                /* else .. check keyboard   */

    }
}


/* ****************************************************************** *
 *       get_key() -- get a key (including function keys)           *
 * ****************************************************************** */

int     get_key(void)
{
int     k = 0;                                  /* local key variable       */

if (kbhit())                                    /* q. key available?        */
    {                                           /* a. yes .. process it     */
    if (NOT (k = getch()))                      /* q. function key?         */
        k = 0x100 + getch();                    /* a. yes .. special key    */
    }

return(k);                                      /* return w/key if available*/

}


/* ****************************************************************** *
 *       touppers() -- uppercase a string                          *
 * ****************************************************************** */

void    touppers(char *s)                       /* string to uppercase      */
{

while (*s)                                       /* for the whole string..   */
    *s++ = toupper(*s);                         /* ..uppercase each char    */

}
```

```c
/* ******************************************************************* *
 *      quit_with() -- give an error message, then return to DOS       *
 * ******************************************************************* */

void    quit_with(char *msg, ...)           /* string to print         */
{
va_list list;                               /* variable list           */


if (mcr_port)                               /* q. valid port available? */
    outp(mcr_port, inp(mcr_port) & ~DTR);   /* a. yes .. hang up modem  */

va_start(list, msg);                        /* set up variable list     */
vprintf(msg, list);                         /* give error message ..    */
exit(rc);                                   /* ..and then quit          */

}



/* ******************************************************************* *
 *      control_break() -- control break intercept routine             *
 * ******************************************************************* */

int     control_break(void)
{


if (full_screen)                            /* q. full screen mode?     */
    close_down();                           /* a. yes .. clear screen   */

quit_with(stop_here);                       /* give error msg and quit  */
return(0);                                  /* ..and abort processing   */

}
```

CHAPTER

6

SYNCHRONIZING DIRECTORY CONTENTS WITH SYNC

SYNC displays a synchronized listing of two directories, graphically showing the difference between

the two. SYNC also provides keystroke commands that let you copy individual files between the

directories, or automatically copy all files necessary to make both directories equal.

DOS's directory structure provides a natural environment for maintaining copies or backups of important work. It's a simple matter to create a batch file that copies the contents of the current directory into a backup directory. However, if you've ever used multiple directories to maintain backups of programs or projects, then you've probably also enjoyed the task of searching and retrieving individual files from those directories.

SYNC helps you manage the contents of directories. It provides a synchronized display of two directories' contents, showing which files are more recent, which are equal (in size, date, and time), and which ones exist in only one of the directories displayed. SYNC also lets you copy a file at a time, or even synchronize the contents of both directories, so that both directories will contain the most recent version of every file displayed.

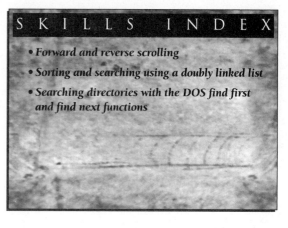

SKILLS INDEX

- *Forward and reverse scrolling*
- *Sorting and searching using a doubly linked list*
- *Searching directories with the DOS find first and find next functions*

■ USING SYNC

Start SYNC by entering the SYNC command followed by the names of the directories you wish to compare. SYNC's command syntax is

```
SYNC source1 source2
```

where *source1* and *source2* specify the directories to be compared.

The *source1* and *source2* arguments may be in any of the following formats:

- Drive only: *d:*

- Path only: *\path*

- Drive and path: *d:\path*

- Relative path: *path\dirname*

- Drive and relative path: *d:path\dirname*

- Current directory or parent directory: . or ..

The arguments may not contain file names or DOS wildcard characters. If either of the arguments contains wildcards or refers to a file, SYNC displays an error message and terminates. Of course, if you don't enter any arguments on the command line, SYNC displays a message describing the command syntax.

When started, SYNC displays the files found in the *source1* directory on the left side of the screen, and the files found in the *source2* directory on the right side of the screen. When a file exists in one directory but not the other, the file entry is displayed on one side, and the corresponding entry in the other directory is left blank. If both directories contain a particular file (the two files have the same name), the entry is displayed on both sides of the screen, each with its own size, time, and date. The entries are displayed in alphabetical order.

At the center of the screen is a vertical bar that contains an indicator of the relationship between the files on either side. SYNC notes four conditions when comparing the files: the left-hand file is more recent than the right-hand file (indicated by >>); the right-hand file is more recent than the left-hand file (<<); the two files are equal in size, date, and time (==); or one side has no matching file (blank). Should the dates and times of two files match, but the sizes differ, SYNC displays a ?? between the columns, indicating the size-only difference. Figure 6.1 shows an example of a screen produced by SYNC. The contents of the two directories (C:\DIR1 and C:\DIR2) are shown in Figure 6.2.

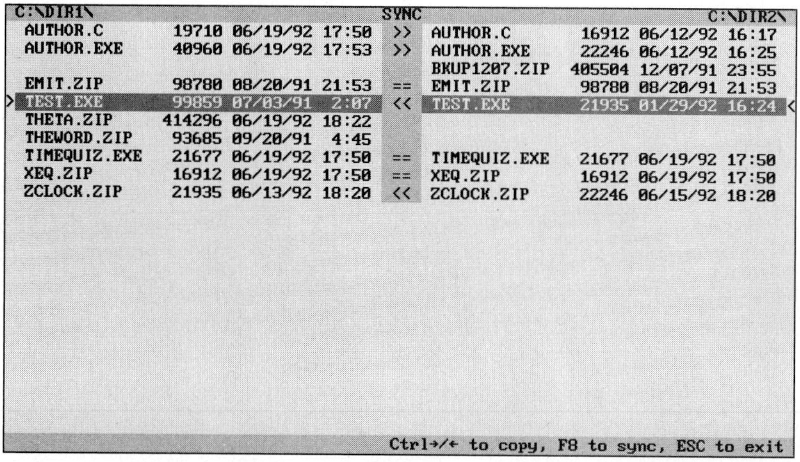

FIGURE 6.1

SYNC's screen format

```
C:\DIR1\                              SYNC                              C:\DIR2\
AUTHOR.C          19710 06/19/92 17:50  >>  AUTHOR.C        16912 06/12/92 16:17
AUTHOR.EXE        40960 06/19/92 17:53  >>  AUTHOR.EXE      22246 06/12/92 16:25
                                            BKUP1207.ZIP   405504 12/07/91 23:55
EMIT.ZIP          98780 08/20/91 21:53  ==  EMIT.ZIP        98780 08/20/91 21:53
TEST.EXE          99859 07/03/91  2:07  <<  TEST.EXE        21935 01/29/92 16:24
THETA.ZIP        414296 06/19/92 18:22
THEWORD.ZIP       93685 09/20/91  4:45
TIMEQUIZ.EXE      21677 06/19/92 17:50  ==  TIMEQUIZ.EXE    21677 06/19/92 17:50
XEQ.ZIP           16912 06/19/92 17:50  ==  XEQ.ZIP         16912 06/19/92 17:50
ZCLOCK.ZIP        21935 06/13/92 18:20  <<  ZCLOCK.ZIP      22246 06/15/92 18:20




                              Ctrl→/← to copy, F8 to sync, ESC to exit
```

FIGURE 6.2

Contents of sample directories C:\DIR1 and C:\DIR2

```
Directory of C:\DIR1               | Directory of C:\DIR2
                                   |
AUTHOR   C      19710 06-19-92  5:50p|AUTHOR   C      16912 06-12-92   4:17p
AUTHOR   EXE    40960 06-19-92  5:53p|AUTHOR   EXE    22246 06-12-92   4:25p
TEST     EXE    99859 07-03-91  2:07a|TEST     EXE    21935 01-29-92   4:24p
TIMEQUIZ EXE    21677 06-19-92  5:50p|TIMEQUIZ EXE    21677 06-19-92   5:50p
EMIT     ZIP    98780 08-20-91  9:53p|BKUP1207 ZIP   405504 12-07-91  11:55p
THETA    ZIP   414296 06-19-92  6:22p|EMIT     ZIP    98780 08-20-91   9:53p
THEWORD  ZIP    93685 09-20-91  4:45a|XEQ      ZIP    16912 06-19-92   5:50p
XEQ      ZIP    16912 06-19-92  5:50p|ZCLOCK   ZIP    22246 06-15-92   6:20p
ZCLOCK   ZIP    21935 06-13-92  6:20p|       8 file(s)
        9 file(s)                  |
```

Once the files are displayed, you have four options. You can scroll through the entries using the Down Arrow or Page Down, and Up Arrow or Page Up keys; or copy an entry using the Ctrl-Left Arrow or Ctrl-Right Arrow key-combination; or fully synchronize both directories using the F8 key; or exit to DOS using the Escape key or the Ctrl-Break key-combination.

At start up, SYNC highlights the first file entry (the entire line, across both sides) on the screen. You can move the highlight by using the Down Arrow, Up Arrow, Page Down, and Page Up keys.

If you press Down Arrow, the highlight moves toward the bottom of the screen until it reaches either the last entry in the list or the bottom of the screen. If there are more entries beyond the last one displayed, the highlight stops at the bottom line and the entries scroll upward on the screen. Up Arrow moves the highlight toward the top of the screen, stopping when it reaches the top line. As with Down Arrow, if more entries exist above the entry displayed at the top of the screen, the entries scroll downward until the highlight is positioned on the first entry.

The Page Down and Page Up keys also move the highlight, a screen at a time. If you press either of these keys, the highlight moves or the entries scroll in the appropriate direction until the first or last entry is displayed.

With both the arrow keys and the Page Up/Page Down keys, continuing to press a key after reaching the associated limit causes SYNC to sound an error tone.

Once you have selected a line by highlighting it, you can copy either file to the other directory, or if only one file is displayed, you can copy it to the other directory. To copy from the left-hand to the right-hand directory, press Ctrl-Right Arrow. To copy from the right-hand to the left-hand directory, press Ctrl-Left Arrow. (Press the arrow key that points in the direction of the copy.) Figure 6.3 shows SYNC's display while a file (in this case, THETA.ZIP) is being copied, and Figure 6.4 shows the display after the copy operation is completed. The copy of THETA.ZIP was initiated by pressing Ctrl-Right Arrow.

FIGURE 6.3

SYNC's display during a copy. Note the graph in the lower-left corner.

```
C:\DIR1\                                    SYNC                        C:\DIR2\
  AUTHOR.C        19710 06/19/92 17:50  >>   AUTHOR.C        16912 06/12/92 16:17
  AUTHOR.EXE      40960 06/19/92 17:53  >>   AUTHOR.EXE      22246 06/12/92 16:25
                                             BKUP1207.ZIP   405504 12/07/91 23:55
  EMIT.ZIP        98780 08/20/91 21:53  ==   EMIT.ZIP        98780 08/20/91 21:53
  TEST.EXE        99859 07/03/91  2:07  <<   TEST.EXE        21935 01/29/92 16:24
> THETA.ZIP      414296 06/19/92 18:22                                          <
  THEWORD.ZIP     93685 09/20/91  4:45
  TIMEQUIZ.EXE    21677 06/19/92 17:50  ==   TIMEQUIZ.EXE    21677 06/19/92 17:50
  XEQ.ZIP         16912 06/19/92 17:50  ==   XEQ.ZIP         16912 06/19/92 17:50
  ZCLOCK.ZIP      21935 06/13/92 18:20  <<   ZCLOCK.ZIP      22246 06/15/92 18:20




Copying: ███████        |  >>         Ctrl+/+ to copy, F8 to sync, ESC to exit
```

While SYNC is copying a file, a message is displayed in the lower-left corner of the screen (as shown in Figure 6.3). Accompanying the message is a bar that tracks the progress of the copy. Directly to the right of the progress bar is an indicator showing the direction selected for the copy (left-to-right or right-to-left).

To completely synchronize the two directories, press the F8 key. During the synchronization process, SYNC selects the most recent file from each line and copies it to the other directory, and copies files that exist only in one directory to the other directory. As the synchronization process progresses, SYNC highlights the line containing the file being copied, skipping those files that are already equal (in both directories). When the operation is completed, both directories contain the same files—the most recent copy of each file found when you started SYNC. After completing synchronization, SYNC returns to DOS.

FIGURE 6.4

SYNC's display after a copy is completed

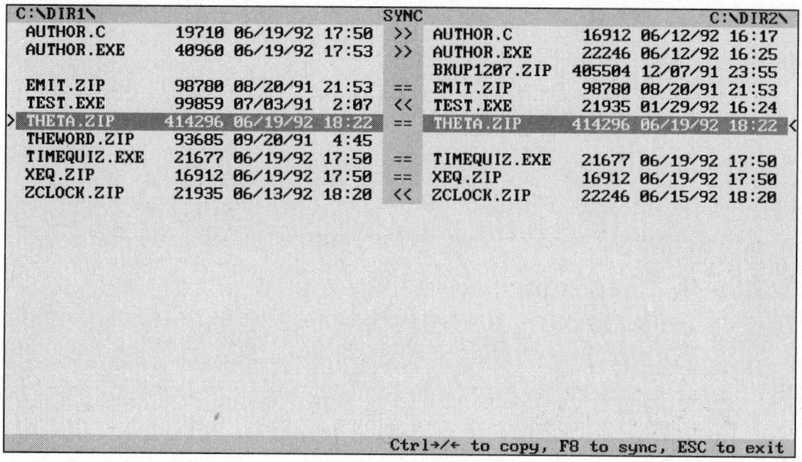

```
C:\DIR1\                              SYNC                                C:\DIR2\
    AUTHOR.C       19710 06/19/92 17:50  >>   AUTHOR.C       16912 06/12/92 16:17
    AUTHOR.EXE     40960 06/19/92 17:53  >>   AUTHOR.EXE     22246 06/12/92 16:25
                                              BKUP1207.ZIP  405504 12/07/91 23:55
    EMIT.ZIP       98780 08/20/91 21:53  ==   EMIT.ZIP       98780 08/20/91 21:53
    TEST.EXE       99859 07/03/91  2:07  <<   TEST.EXE       21935 01/29/92 16:24
>   THETA.ZIP     414296 06/19/92 18:22  ==   THETA.ZIP     414296 06/19/92 18:22  <
    THEWORD.ZIP    93685 09/20/91  4:45
    TIMEQUIZ.EXE   21677 06/19/92 17:50  ==   TIMEQUIZ.EXE   21677 06/19/92 17:50
    XEQ.ZIP        16912 06/19/92 17:50  ==   XEQ.ZIP        16912 06/19/92 17:50
    ZCLOCK.ZIP     21935 06/13/92 18:20  <<   ZCLOCK.ZIP     22246 06/15/92 18:20




                              Ctrl→/← to copy, F8 to sync, ESC to exit
```

To return to DOS manually, simply press Esc or Ctrl-Break. When you do so, SYNC issues the appropriate error messages and returns to DOS.

■ INSIDE SYNC

SYNC's simple external command structure belies its complex internal design. As we'll see, SYNC integrates ordinary programming techniques with unusual algorithms, forming a useful utility that you can easily upgrade into a powerful file management system.

When started, SYNC's main() routine displays the copyright notice and immediately calls the initialization() routine to set up SYNC's environment. Much of the work performed by initialization() is straightforward: checking the number of arguments, displaying help when it's requested or needed, saving the default drive and directory, setting up the control break routine, determining the size of the screen, and setting the display attributes for a monochrome monitor. There are, however, a few functions in initialization() that deserve more attention, and are described in the paragraphs that follow.

- ### Handling Critical DOS Errors

  Early in the routine, initialization() calls _dos_setvect(), thus setting interrupt vector 0x24 with the address of the critical_handler() routine. Anyone who has used DOS for any amount of time has probably encountered the infamous Abort, Retry, Ignore, or Fail (ARIorF) message at one time or another. The ARIorF message is produced by DOS's default critical error handler. When an error (such as a disk error) occurs, DOS calls the critical error handler using interrupt 0x24, and passes a value that indicates which of the abort, retry, ignore, or fail responses is allowed. SYNC's critical_handler() routine checks this value and determines if a fail response will be accepted by DOS, and if so, returns the fail response. The fail response causes DOS to return an error code to the application program. If DOS will not accept the fail response, critical_handler() returns the abort response, causing DOS to terminate SYNC.

- ### Validating the Arguments

  One of the initialization() routine's tasks is to check the arguments to verify that they do not contain wildcards, do not refer to files, and do not refer to the same directory. To do so, initialization() calls validate_name().

  The validate_name() routine is a general-purpose routine that performs a superset of the tests required by SYNC. (You may also find validate_name()'s capabilities useful when you enhance SYNC or reuse SYNC's code in other programs.)

  When calling validate_name(), initialization() passes the path specification to check, and the address of a return code to be filled in by validate_name(). After initializing some work areas, validate_name() determines if the drive letter was included in the path specification. If so, the drive variable is set to the number that corresponds to that drive letter. Otherwise, the drive is set to zero, representing the current drive.

  Next, validate_name() uses DOS function 0x4409, to determine if the drive is a local or remote (network) drive. This function is only available in DOS versions 3.1 and later, so validate_name() checks the DOS version before invoking this function. Although SYNC does not care if it is working with a remote drive, the return code from function 0x4409 tells validate_name() whether the drive letter is valid. If not, validate_name() sets the return code to −3 (invalid drive) and returns to initialization().

  Next, validate_name() attempts to retrieve the current directory for the drive. This test performs two functions: It verifies that the drive is ready and, if the DOS version is earlier than 3.1, returns an error if the drive letter is invalid. If the drive fails this test, validate_name() sets the return code to –2 (drive not ready), and returns to initialization().

- ### Testing for the Same Directory

An important test performed by SYNC determines whether the two command arguments refer to the same directory. Under DOS, you may refer to a directory in one of several ways. For example, assume the current directory is C:\SYNC\TEST. You can refer to the parent directory, C:\SYNC, as C:\SYNC, \SYNC, .., or even ..\..\SYNC. SYNC must therefore be able to determine that the two directory arguments in a command (such as the following) both refer to the same directory:

```
SYNC  ..  C:\SYNC
```

SYNC performs this test in validate_name() by simply changing the current directory to that specified in the argument, and then retrieving the name of the new current directory. When DOS returns the name of the current directory, the name is resolved and absolute, starting at the drive letter, and in uppercase.

After initialization() has tested both arguments with validate_name(), it compares the path names to verify that they do not point to the same directory. Before returning to main(), initialization() allocates a buffer for use during copy operations, and clears the whole_block string to the character used to display the copy progress bar.

- ### Building the File List

One of SYNC's more challenging techniques is building the file list. As shown earlier, SYNC place files with the same name and extension on the same line of the display. Internally, SYNC represents each pair of files with a single entry on a doubly linked list. (A doubly linked list is a list of entries, each of which contains a forward pointer to the next entry and a backward pointer to the previous entry.) Each entry is in the format of a lines structure that contains a forward and backward pointer, two directory entries, and a comparison indicator.

SYNC actually builds the linked list already sorted in memory, by calling build_files_list() to perform three functions: build the file list, exit if no files exist, and set the comparison indicators for each entry. To build the file list, build_files_list() enters a for loop and searches for every file in each of the two directories entered on the command line. When build_files_list() needs to add a new entry on the linked list, it calls add_entry(), described a bit later.

To search the directories, build_files_list() uses _dos_findfirst() and _dos_findnext(). The _dos_findfirst() routine searches a single directory for an entry that matches the supplied specification. After _dos_findfirst() returns the first matching entry,

*ote:
*lthough SYNC
*ly searches for
*rmal files,
*dos_findfirst()
*d _dos_find-
*xt() can also be
*ed to search for
*files (including
*ad-only,
*stem, and
*dden files),
*rectories, and
e volume label.

_dos_findnext() finds any subsequent matching entries. Each time _dos_findnext()
is called, it returns another entry from the directory specified in the _dos_findfirst()
call, until no more matching entries are found.

As SYNC loads the found entries into memory, it sorts them by inserting each
entry into the linked list in its appropriate place according to file name. The routines
add_entry() and new_entry() work cooperatively to build the list of files in memory.
The add_entry() routine's main job is to determine where the entry goes; new_entry()
allocates the memory and links the new structure into the list.

There are several algorithms that can be used to sort information. One common
method is to read the entire list of items, and then run a sort algorithm against them.
Another is to build a set of records in a disk file, and pass that file to a sort utility.
(This latter technique is a variation on reading the entire file into memory, and is
often used when the data will not fit into available RAM.) SYNC, however, uses a
third method: sorting the data as it is read into memory.

When called, add_entry() immediately enters a loop that searches through the list
of existing entries, looking for the proper place to insert the new entry. While SYNC
is processing the first directory, add_entry() simply checks the file name in existing
entries against the file name read from the first directory, inserting the new entry at
the appropriate place on the linked list. For example, when inserting entry *C* on a
linked list already containing entries *A*, *B*, and *D*, add_entry() would search the list,
and upon finding *D* (higher than *C*), would insert the entry *C* before *D*. Of course, if
add_entry() comes to the end of the list before finding a place to insert a new entry, it
adds the new entry to the end of the list.

Because SYNC has to synchronize the listing of the two directories, only one structure is used to represent both sides of the display. The definition of the d_entry and
lines structure is as follows:

```
struct  d_entry             /* directory entry           */
    {
    char d_name[13];        /* filename                  */
    UINT d_date,            /* file date                 */
         d_time;            /* ..time                    */
    unsigned
    long d_size,            /* ..and size                */
         d_compare;         /* ..date/time compare key   */
    char d_attrib,          /* file attribute            */
         d_display[24];     /* size, date, time display  */
    };

struct  lines               /* display lines linked list*/
    {
    struct lines    *l_fwd, *l_back;   /* forward and backward ptrs*/
    struct d_entry  l_dir[2];          /* directory entries         */
    enum    entry_types l_entry;       /* comparison char           */
    };
```

The d_entry structure describes the information returned by DOS from a find first or find next function call. Appended to the DOS information is information used by SYNC, including the compare results and a formatted string containing the size, date, and time.

In the lines structure, notice that room is reserved for two d_entry structures. The first d_entry—l_dir[0]—contains the directory entry for the left-hand column; the second d_entry—l_dir[1]—contains the directory entry for the right-hand column.

When SYNC processes the second directory, add_entry() must perform an additional check. Before determining if an entry should be inserted in the list, add_entry() looks for an entry of the same name already on the list. If one exists, SYNC simply moves the data contained in the directory entry into the corresponding entry (l_dir[1]). As before, if add_entry() encounters an entry with a name that is greater before it finds one that is equal, a new entry is created and inserted in the appropriate place.

When add_entry() needs to add an entry to the linked list, it calls new_entry(). Inserting a new entry into a doubly linked list is a rather tedious task. There are three starting conditions to be handled: inserting before the first entry, inserting in the middle, and inserting after the last entry.

When inserting an entry before the first entry, new_entry() must allocate the entry; set the new entry's forward pointer to point at the (old) first entry; set the new entry's backward pointer to zero; set the (old) first entry's backward pointer to the address of the new entry; and reset the base pointer to reference the new entry as the first on the chain. Figure 6.5 illustrates the process of inserting a new entry before the first entry in a linked list.

Inserting the entry into the middle of the linked list is somewhat more complicated. As before, the new entry must be created. After finding the proper insertion point, the new entry's backward and forward pointers are set to the address of the previous and next entries, respectively. Then the previous entry's forward pointer and the next entry's backward pointer are both set to address the new entry. When the operation is complete, the new entry, although possibly out of place physically, is logically inserted in its appropriate place on the linked list. Figure 6.6 illustrates the process of inserting a new entry on the linked list.

Of course, adding an entry to the end of a linked list is the easiest of all. Once the entry is allocated, new_entry() simply sets the backward pointer of the new entry to the address of the last entry on the list; sets the forward pointer of the new entry to zero; and places a pointer to the new entry in the forward pointer of the last entry on the list. Voilà—the new entry is now the last on the list.

te:

example of
entry added
the end of a
ibly linked list
resented in
apter 5,
HONE."

FIGURE 6.5

Inserting a new entry before the first one on a doubly linked list

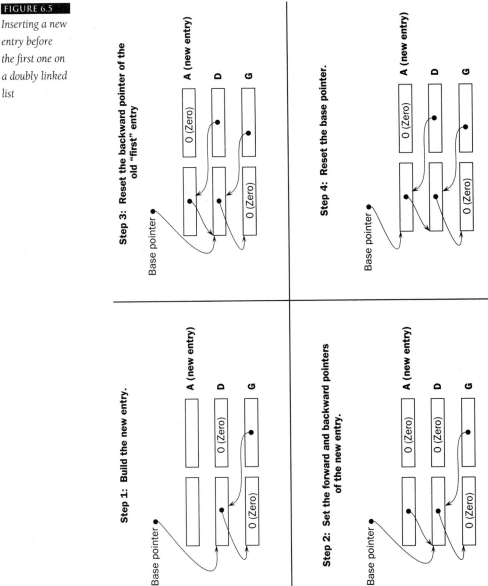

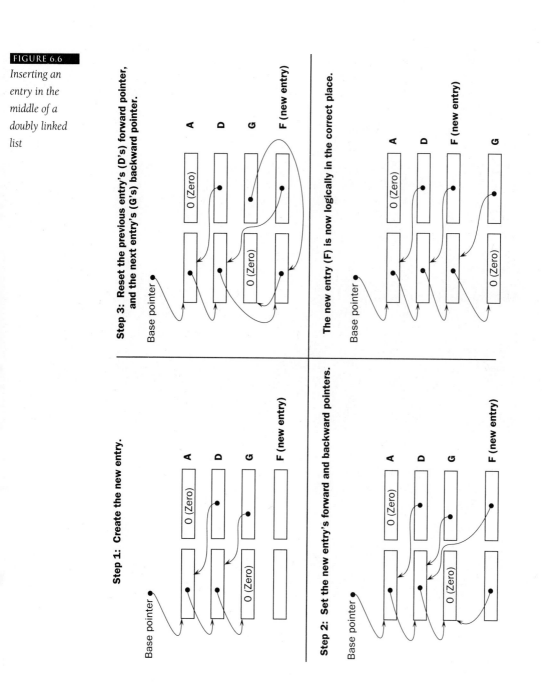

FIGURE 6.6

Inserting an entry in the middle of a doubly linked list

Step 1: Create the new entry.

Step 2: Set the new entry's forward and backward pointers.

Step 3: Reset the previous entry's (D's) forward pointer, and the next entry's (G's) backward pointer.

The new entry (F) is now logically in the correct place.

- ### Displaying the Entries

  When build_files_list() completes, it returns to main(). SYNC's next job is to display the first screenful of entries by calling display_files_list(). The first routines called by display_files_list() are set_up_screen() and home_screen(), which initialize the screen and display the first screenful of files, respectively.

  At the center of the display routines is display_line(). This routine goes to the line requested and displays the passed entry as either highlighted or unhighlighted. When an entry is highlighted, it is displayed in reverse video. Also, the line is preceded by a greater than (>) character and terminated with a less than (<) character. In Figure 6.1, for example, the line for TEST.EXE is selected. When the highlight is moved, the current entry is redisplayed as unhighlighted (normal video, with the > and < removed), the new line is selected (or the screen scrolled), and the new entry is highlighted.

- ### The Interactive Display

  After setting up the initial screen, display_files_list() enters a loop that waits for a keystroke. SYNC honors eight keystrokes: Up Arrow, Down Arrow, Page Up, Page Down, Ctrl-Left Arrow, Ctrl-Right Arrow, F8, and Esc.

  The four keys for movement (Up Arrow and Down Arrow, Page Up and Page Down) all use move_screen() to actually move the highlight. For the Up Arrow and Down Arrow keys, move_screen() is invoked one time and called along with the direction to move the highlight. Similarly, Page Up and Page Down invoke move_screen() the number of times necessary to move up or down a screenful of entries.

  As mentioned above, when move_screen() is called, it is passed the direction in which to move the highlight, up or down. If the highlight cannot be moved in the requested direction because it is already at the beginning or end of the list, move_screen() sounds an error tone, letting you know the limit has been reached.

- **Note.** *Since move_screen() is called iteratively to scroll the entries when Page Up or Page Down is pressed, you will actually see the entries scroll through the screen. This method demonstrates how code can be reused to build more complex functions. (This technique will also be demonstrated later, when the synchronization process is described.) An alternate implementation for Page Up and Page Down would be to clear the screen, reposition the cursor at a particular line, and display the appropriate entries.*

- ### Copying a File

  Once you have highlighted an entry, you can copy one of the highlighted files to the other directory by simply pressing the appropriate Ctrl-Left Arrow or Ctrl-Right

Arrow key-combination. The direction of the key you press is the direction in which the data is copied. In either case, display_files_list() calls copy_file() to actually copy the file from one directory to the other.

The copy_file() routine's first action is to call set_up_copy(), which tests the direction and ensures that the copy can be performed. (A copy cannot be performed if the source is blank.) If the source exists, set_up_copy() simply sets the passed to and passed from variables to the appropriate indices, and copy_file() performs the copy using those indices. Although somewhat lengthy, the copy_file() routine essentially just builds the file names, opens the files, copies the data, resets the output file's date and time, and closes the files. Two unusual routines used by copy_file() do bear closer examination, however.

Just before starting the copy, copy_file() calls check_file_dates() to determine if either entry has the year 1980 as part of the file date. Since PCs were not actually in use at that time, it is unlikely that a file would be marked with this date. (When a file is so marked, it usually indicates that the date on the PC was not set properly when the file was last modified.) When check_file_dates() encounters such a file, you are prompted to indicate if it is okay to overlay the file. Pressing Y (for Yes) overwrites the file; Esc returns to DOS; and any other key skips the copy.

As copy_file() copies the contents of the file, it calls update_progress(), which modifies the progress bar displayed at the bottom-left of the screen. As the copy progresses, update_progress() displays a small, animated graph showing the progress of the copy. Although only 16 characters are used for the progress bar, update_progress() uses both the half- and whole-box characters (ASCII hex codes 0xdd and 0xdb, respectively) when building the bar, resulting in a graph with 32 positions.

■ Synchronizing the Directories

If you press the F8 key while SYNC is active, it scans the list of files, selecting the most recent from each pair, and copies it to the other directory. SYNC also copies an existing file if the file has no corresponding file in the other directory. Of course, if the files are equal, the pair is skipped. This function is accomplished by sync_files(). A very simple function, sync_files() returns the highlight to the first file in the list, and moves through every entry in the list. As it does so, the highlight itself animates SYNC's operation.

As it highlights each entry, sync_files() calls copy_file(). Then copy_file() calls set_up_copy(), which selects the appropriate file from the pair and returns. Based on the return from set_up_copy(), copy_files() then either copies a file or returns to sync_files().

When every entry has been examined and, if necessary, copied, sync_files() returns to display_files_list(), which returns to DOS.

■ Exiting the Program

If you press the Escape key, display_files_list() calls close_down(). The close_down() routine clears the screen, redisplays the copyright notice, and returns to display_files_list(), which returns to main(). The main() routine then calls quit_with() to terminate SYNC and return to DOS.

■ SUMMARY

SYNC provides the basis for an interactive directory management program. Here are some enhancements you may wish to add to SYNC:

- Allow the deletion of one or both of the selected files.

- Display the current drive and subdirectory, and place an option in SYNC allowing the user to navigate between other drives and subdirectories.

- Allow the specification of files and wildcards on the command line.

LISTING

SYNC 1.00

```
/* ***************************************************************** *

    SYNC 1.00, Copyright (c) 1992, Michael Holmes and Bob Flanders
    PC Magazine C Lab Notes, Synchronize two directories

  * ***************************************************************** *

    This code for Borland C++ version 3.0. (MSC version on diskette)

        Compile with:  BCC -O2-i -mc sync.c

    To compile for Microsoft C, you need to change the following:
        - add a #include for sys\types.h
        - screen scrolling routines, insline() and delline()
        - screen color setting routines, textcolor() and textbackground()
        - logical screen definition routine, window()
        - change control break handling for ctrlbrk() and control_break()
        - change #pragma as necessary
        - change call for creatnew()

  * ***************************************************************** */


#pragma  pack(1)                        /* pack to byte alignment   */
#include <stdio.h>                      /* standard i/o library     */
#include <io.h>                         /* i/o routine headers      */
#include <stdlib.h>                     /* ANSI compatibility       */
#include <dos.h>                        /* DOS rtn definitions      */
#include <stdarg.h>                     /* argument functions       */
#include <direct.h>                     /* directory routines       */
#include <malloc.h>                     /* memory declarations      */
#include <string.h>                     /* string functions         */
#include <ctype.h>                      /* character functions      */
#include <conio.h>                      /* console i/o routines     */
#include <fcntl.h>                      /* file control header      */
#include <sys\stat.h>                   /* file status header       */

#define NOT !                           /* logical not              */
#define LAST(x) x[strlen(x) - 1]        /* get last char in string  */
#define UINT unsigned int               /* unsigned integer type    */
#define MAX_PATH  79                    /* max path length          */
#define BUF_SIZE  16384                 /* copy buffer size         */
#define FILE_ATTR _A_NORMAL | _A_RDONLY /* file attrib to search on */
#define KEY_1     p->l_dir[0].d_compare /* compare key for dir 1    */
#define KEY_2     p->l_dir[1].d_compare /* ..and dir 2              */

                                        /* key definitions          */
#define UP             0x100 + '\x48'   /* up key                   */
#define DOWN           0x100 + '\x50'   /* down key                 */
#define ESC            '\x1b'           /* escape key               */
#define F8             0x100 + '\x42'   /* F8 function key          */
#define CTRL_LEFT      0x100 + '\x73'   /* control left arrow key   */
#define CTRL_RIGHT     0x100 + '\x74'   /* control right arrow key  */
#define PAGE_UP        0x100 + '\x49'   /* page up key              */
```

```
#define PAGE_DOWN   0x100 + '\x51'              /* page down key              */


/* ********************************************************************* *
 *       routine definitions                                             *
 * ********************************************************************* */

void    initialization(int, char **),           /* arg check and setup        */
        build_files_list(void),                  /* build linked list          */
        display_files_list(void),                /* display linked list        */
        display_line(struct lines *, int,        /* display a directory pair   */
            enum select_types),
        add_file(int),                           /* add file to linked list    */
        new_entry(struct lines *,                /* add a new entry to ..      */
            enum add_types, int),                /* ..the linked list          */
        add_data(struct d_entry *d),             /* copy in directory entry    */
        sync_files(void),                        /* synchronize all files      */
        home_screen(void),                       /* display first screenful    */
        move_screen(int),                        /* scroll screen one line     */
        set_up_screen(void),                     /* set up base screen         */
        close_down(void),                        /* close down full screen     */
        color_set(enum select_types),            /* select color palette       */
        copy_file(int),                          /* copy one file              */
        update_progress(void),                   /* give progress bar          */
        wait(long),                              /* time to wait in ticks      */
        quit_with(char *, ...),                  /* quit with error message    */
        interrupt critical_handler(UINT,         /* critical error handler     */
            UINT, UINT, UINT, UINT, UINT,
            UINT, UINT, UINT, UINT, UINT,
            UINT);

int     check_file_dates(void),                  /* check for invalid dates    */
        delete_file(char *),                     /* delete file                */
        control_break(void),                     /* control break handler      */
        get_key(void);                           /* get any type of key        */

char    *validate_name(char *, char *),          /* validate file/dir name     */
        *translate_name(char *);                 /* get true name              */

enum    set_up_rtns set_up_copy(int,             /* determine source & dest..  */
            int *, int *);                       /* ..directories for copy     */


/* ********************************************************************* *
 *       globals                                                         *
 * ********************************************************************* */

int     rc = 1,                                  /* errorlevel return code     */
        full_screen,                             /* full screen mode active    */
        c_line,                                  /* current line               */
        text_fg = WHITE,                         /* default foreground color   */
        text_bg = BLUE,                          /* ..background color         */
        hdr_fg = YELLOW,                         /* header foreground color    */
        hdr_bg = CYAN,                           /* ..background color         */
        max_lines,                               /* screen size                */
        init_drive;                              /* initial drive setting      */

char    *args[2],                                /* directory arguments        */
        *paths[2],                               /* base file paths            */
        flags[2],                                /* ..and file/dir flags       */
        *buf,                                    /* disk read/write buffer     */
        direction,                               /* copy direction indicator   */
        *init_path,                              /* start up drive and path    */
        whole_blk[17],                           /* string of whole blocks     */
```

```
        *part_blk = "\xdd";                     /* ..string of a half blk   */

long    w_size,                                 /* working file size        */
        t_size;                                 /* total file size          */

extern
int     _wscroll = 0,                           /* disable screen scrolling */
        _fmode = O_BINARY;                      /* set global for bin files */


/* ***************************************************************** *
 *          structures                                              *
 * ***************************************************************** */

enum    select_types                            /* display line types       */
    {
    selected,                                   /* highlighted line         */
    unselected,                                 /* normal display line      */
    border                                      /* border lines             */
    };

enum    add_types                               /* add entry positions      */
    {
    before,                                     /* before current entry     */
    after                                       /* after current entry      */
    };

enum    entry_types                             /* directory entry types    */
    {
    one_sided = ' ',                            /* only one side used       */
    greater_than = '>',                         /* dir 1 > dir 2            */
    less_than = '<',                            /*          <               */
    equal_to = '=',                             /*          =               */
    almost_equal = '?'                          /* file date only matches   */
    };

enum    set_up_rtns                              /* set_up_copy() returns    */
    {
    set_up_ok,                                  /* set up completed ok      */
    no_file,                                    /* missing source file      */
    equal_files                                 /* equal timestamps         */
    };

struct  d_entry                                 /* directory entry          */
    {
    char d_name[13];                            /* filename                 */
    UINT d_date,                                /* file date                */
         d_time;                                /* ..time                   */
    unsigned
    long d_size,                                /* ..and size               */
         d_compare;                             /* ..date/time compare key  */
    char d_attrib,        ,                     /* file attribute           */
         d_display[24];                         /* size, date, time display */
    };

struct  lines                                   /* display lines linked list*/
    {
    struct lines    *l_fwd, *l_back;            /* forward and backward ptrs*/
    struct d_entry  l_dir[2];                   /* directory entries        */
    enum    entry_types l_entry;                /* comparison char          */
    } *l_base,                                  /* anchor to linked list    */
      *l_top,                                   /* ..current screen top     */
      *l_bottom,                                /* ..current screen bottom  */
      *p;                                       /* ..work pointer           */
```

```
union   REGS  r;                          /* cpu registers          */
struct  SREGS   s;                        /* segment registers      */
struct  find_t dos_entry;                 /* DOS directory entry     */


/* ********************************************************************** *
 *       messages and strings                                           *
 * ********************************************************************** */

char    copyright[]     = "SYNC 1.00 \xfe Copyright (c) 1992, "
                          "Michael Holmes and Bob Flanders\n"
                          "PC Magazine C Lab Notes \xfe "
                          "Synchronize two directories\n\n",
        *bad_drive[]  = { "Invalid drive %s\n",
                          "Drive not ready %s\n",
                          "Bad file specification %s\n" },
        empty_list[]    = "No files to process\n",
        only_dirs[]     = "%s is not a directory\n",
        same_path[]     = "Both arguments must not reference the "
                          "same directory\n",
        no_memory[]     = "Insufficient memory to continue processing\n",
        bell[]          = "\a",
        bad_width[]     = "Screen must be at least 80 columns wide\n",
        open_error[]    = "\nError opening file (%s)\n",
        read_error[]    = "\nError reading file (%s)\n",
        write_error[]   = "\nError writing file (%s)\n",
        stop_here[]     = "\nStopping at user's request\n",
        clear_error[]   = "\r%*s\r",
        bad_date[]      = "Invalid date detected, continue? ",
        ans_yes[]       = "Yes\r",
        ans_no[]        = "No\r",
        file_fmt[]      = "%8ld %02d/%02d/%2d %2d:%02d",
        line_fmt[]      = " %-12.12s%-24.24s",
        compare_fmt[]   = " %c%c ",
        header[]        = " %-37.37sSYNC%37.37s ",
        footer[]        = " Ctrl\x1a/\x1b to copy, F8 to sync, ESC to exit ",
        working[]       = "Copying: %-*.*s%-*.*s%*.*s\xb3 %c%c\r",
        done[]          = "SYNC completed normally\n",
        help[]          =
            "   Usage:   SYNC  source1 source2\n\n"
            "   Where:   source = d:\n"
            "                     [d:]path\n\n";


/* ********************************************************************** *
 *       main()                                                         *
 * ********************************************************************** */

void    main(int  ac,                     /* DOS cmd line token count */
             char *av[])                   /* ..token strings          */
{

printf(copyright);                         /* display copyright msg   */
initialization(ac, av);                    /* init and parse cmd line */

build_files_list();                        /* build list of files     */
display_files_list();                      /* ..then display them     */

rc = 0;                                    /* clear errorlevel and    */
quit_with(done);                           /* ..return to DOS         */

}
```

```
/* ****************************************************************** *
 *       initialization() -- init interrupts and parse command line   *
 * ****************************************************************** */

void    initialization(int  ac,            /* DOS cmd line token count */
                       char *av[])          /* ..token strings          */
{
int     i;                                 /* loop count               */
char    w_path[MAX_PATH],                  /* working path name        */
        *t_path[2];                        /* translated path          */
struct  text_info screen;                  /* screen info structure    */


if (ac != 3 ¦ ¦                            /* q. need help..           */
            NOT strcmp(av[1], "/?"))       /* ..or want help?          */
    quit_with(help);                       /* a. yes .. give help/quit */

_dos_getdrive((UINT *) &init_drive);       /* get the default drive    */
init_path = getcwd(NULL, MAX_PATH);        /* ..and current directory  */

ctrlbrk(control_break);                    /* set up ctrl break handler*/
_dos_setvect(0x24, critical_handler);      /* ..DOS critical handlers  */

gettextinfo(&screen);                      /* get current screen info  */
max_lines = screen.screenheight;           /* save maximum lines on scr*/

if (screen.screenwidth < 80)               /* q. less than 80 columns? */
    quit_with(bad_width);                  /* a. yes .. give error/quit*/

if (screen.currmode == BW80 ¦ ¦            /* q. black and white mode..*/
            screen.currmode == MONO)       /* ..or monochrome mode?    */
    {
    text_bg = hdr_bg = BLACK;              /* a. yes .. set up mono..   */
    text_fg = hdr_fg = LIGHTGRAY;          /* ..palette for text/hdrs   */
    }

for (i = 0; i < 2; i++)                     /* for each directory..      */
    {
    if (NOT (args[i] = validate_name(      /* q. valid file/directory?  */
            av[i + 1], &flags[i])))
        quit_with(bad_drive[flags[i]+3],   /* a. no .. give error msg   */
            av[i + 1]);                    /* ..and exit back to DOS    */

    if (flags[i])                          /* q. argument a filename?   */
        quit_with(only_dirs, args[i]);     /* a. yes .. give error/quit*/

    strcpy(w_path, args[i]);               /* copy in base path         */

    if (NOT flags[i])                      /* q. directory name?        */
        {                                  /* a. yes .. check format    */
        if (NOT (LAST(w_path) == '\\'))    /* q. dir end in backslash?  */
            strcat(w_path, "\\");          /* a. yes .. add the *.*      */
        }
      else
        *(strrchr(w_path, '\\') + 1) = 0;  /* end path after last \     */

    paths[i] = strdup(w_path);             /* save a copy of path       */
    t_path[i] = strdup(                    /* ..and translate path      */
            translate_name(w_path));       /* ..name for later          */

    if (LAST(t_path[i]) == '\\')           /* q. last char a backslash?*/
```

```
        LAST(t_path[i]) = 0;                    /* a. yes .. remove it      */
    }
if (NOT strcmp(t_path[0], t_path[1]))           /* q. same path?            */
    quit_with(same_path);                       /* a. yes .. give error/quit*/

for (i = 2; i; )                                /* for each translated name */
    free(t_path[--i]);                          /* ..free temporary memory  */

if ((buf = malloc(BUF_SIZE)) == 0)              /* q. short on memory?      */
    quit_with(no_memory);                       /* a. yes .. give error/quit*/

memset(whole_blk, 0xdb, 16);                    /* string of whole blocks   */
                                                /* ..for copy progress graph*/

}


/* ********************************************************************** *
 *      build_files_list() -- build linked list of files to display     *
 * ********************************************************************** */

void    build_files_list(void)
{
int     i, j,                                   /* loop controls            */
        rc;                                     /* find return code         */
char    w_path[MAX_PATH];                       /* path and files mask      */


for (i = 0; i < 2; i++)                         /* for both subdirectories  */
    {
    sprintf(w_path, "%s%s*.*",                  /* build findfirst mask     */
            paths[i],
            LAST(paths[i]) == '\\' ? "" : "\\");

    rc = _dos_findfirst(w_path,                 /* find first requested file*/
            FILE_ATTR, &dos_entry);

    for (j = 0; NOT rc; j++)                    /* find all requested files */
        {
        add_file(i);                            /* add entry to list        */
        rc = _dos_findnext(&dos_entry);         /* ..then try to find next  */
        }
    }

if (NOT l_base)                                 /* q. any files found?      */
    quit_with(empty_list);                      /* a. no .. give error/quit */

for (p = l_base; p; p = p->l_fwd)               /* run thru linked list     */
    {
    if (NOT p->l_dir[0].d_name[0] ||            /* q. only one side used..  */
            NOT p->l_dir[1].d_name[0])          /* ..by a dir entry?        */
        p->l_entry = one_sided;                 /* a. yes .. set to blank   */
    else if (KEY_1 == KEY_2)                    /* q. same date and time?   */
                                                /* a. yes .. now check size */
        {
        if (p->l_dir[0].d_size ==               /* q. both sizes same?      */
                p->l_dir[1].d_size)
            p->l_entry = equal_to;              /* a. yes .. set equal flag */
        else
            p->l_entry = almost_equal;          /* else .. show almost same */
        }
    else if (KEY_1 > KEY_2)                     /* q. dir 1 > dir 2?        */
        p->l_entry = greater_than;              /* a. yes .. set .gt. flag  */
    else
```

```
            p->l_entry = less_than;              /* else .. set less than flg*/
        }
}



/* ******************************************************************** *
 *          display_files_list() -- display file linked list            *
 * ******************************************************************** */
void    display_files_list(void)
{
int     key,                                /* key code                 */
        i;                                  /* loop control             */


set_up_screen();                            /* set up base screen       */
home_screen();                              /* display initial lines    */

for (;;)                                    /* loop 'til user quits     */
    {
    switch (key = get_key())                /* handle waiting character */
        {
        case 0:                             /* no key available         */
            continue;                       /* ..try again later        */

        case F8:                            /* F8 function key          */
            sync_files();                   /* syncronize all files     */
            close_down();                   /* clean up screen          */
            return;                         /* ..and return to caller   */

        case PAGE_UP:                       /* page up key              */
            move_screen(UP);                /* move the first line..    */

            for (i = max_lines - 3; i--;)   /* ..then loop for the rest */
                {
                if (p->l_back)              /* q. line available?       */
                    move_screen(UP);        /* a. yes .. scroll one line*/
                else
                    break;                  /* else .. exit loop        */
                }

            break;

        case PAGE_DOWN:                     /* up key                   */
            move_screen(DOWN);              /* move the first line..    */

            for (i = max_lines - 3; i--;)   /* ..then loop for the rest */
                {
                if (p->l_fwd)               /* q. line available?       */
                    move_screen(DOWN);      /* a. yes .. scroll one line*/
                else
                    break;                  /* else .. exit loop        */
                }

            break;                          /* ..wait for next key      */

        case UP:                            /* down key                 */
        case DOWN:                          /* up key                   */
            move_screen(key);               /* handle scrolling         */
            break;                          /* ..wait for next key      */

        case CTRL_RIGHT:                    /* ctrl right arrow         */
        case CTRL_LEFT:                     /* ctrl left arrow          */
```

```
        copy_file(key);                 /* copy one file           */
        break;                          /* ..then wait for next key */

    case ESC:                           /* escape key              */
        close_down();                   /* clean up screen..       */
        return;                         /* ..and exit gracefully   */

    default:                            /* error case              */
        printf(bell);                   /* ..just ring bell        */
    }
}

}


/* ******************************************************************** *
 *      display_line() -- display one directory pair                    *
 * ******************************************************************** */
void    display_line(struct lines *p,   /* line to display         */
                     int  line,         /* ..on which line         */
                     enum select_types s) /* selected/unselected flag */
{

gotoxy(1, line);                        /* move to proper line     */

color_set(unselected);                  /* use unselected palette  */
cprintf(s ? " " : ">");                 /* ..put out spacer char   */

color_set(s);                           /* choose proper colors    */
cprintf(line_fmt, p->l_dir[0].d_name,   /* display left side       */
        p->l_dir[0].d_display);

color_set(border);                      /* choose border colors    */
cprintf(compare_fmt, p->l_entry,        /* ..and display file..    */
        p->l_entry);                    /* ..relationships, if any */

color_set(s);                           /* choose colors, again    */
cprintf(line_fmt, p->l_dir[1].d_name,   /* ..then display right side*/
        p->l_dir[1].d_display);

color_set(unselected);                  /* use unselected palette  */
cprintf(s ? " " : "<");                 /* ..put out other side    */

gotoxy(1, line);                        /* position at start of line*/

}


/* ******************************************************************** *
 *      add_file() -- add file entry to linked list                     *
 * ******************************************************************** */
void    add_file(int d)                 /* directory number        */
{
int     rc;                             /* string compare rtn code */

for (p = l_base; p; )                   /* look down list of entries*/
    {
    if (NOT d)                          /* q. working on first dir? */
```

```
        {                               /* a. no .. do right side   */
    if ((strcmp(dos_entry.name,         /* q. find where to..       */
            p->l_dir[0].d_name)) < 0)   /* ..insert entry into list?*/
        {
        new_entry(p, before, 0);        /* a. yes .. before current */
        return;                         /* ..then return to caller  */
        }
    }
    else
        {
        if (p->l_dir[0].d_name[0])      /* q. left entry active?    */
            {                           /* a. yes .. process it     */
            if (NOT (rc = strcmp(       /* q. find a matching..     */
                dos_entry.name,         /* ..file in the other dir? */
                p->l_dir[0].d_name)))
                {
                add_data(&p->l_dir[1]); /* a. yes .. copy in entry  */
                return;                 /* ..and return to caller   */
                }
            }
        else
            {
            rc = strcmp(                /* else .. check and see..  */
            dos_entry.name,             /* ..where this entry..     */
            p->l_dir[1].d_name);        /* ..belongs in the list    */
            }

        if (rc < 0)                     /* q. fit in here?          */
            {
            new_entry(p, before, d);    /* a. yes .. add in before  */
            return;                     /* ..and return to caller   */
            }
        }

    if (p->l_fwd)                       /* q. find end of list?     */
        p = p->l_fwd;                   /* a. no .. continue looping*/

    else
        {
        new_entry(p, after, d);         /* else .. add to end       */
        return;                         /* ..and return to caller   */
        }
    }

new_entry(p, after, d);                 /* add the 1st entry to list*/

}


/* ******************************************************************* *
 *      new_entry() -- add a new entry to linked list                  *
 * ******************************************************************* */

void    new_entry(struct lines *p,      /* base entry               */
                    enum add_types bf,  /* before/after flag        */
                    int index)          /* index number for entry   */
{
struct  lines *n;                       /* work pointer             */

if ((n = (struct lines *) malloc(       /* q. get storage for a..   */
        sizeof (struct lines))) == 0)   /* ..new line entry?        */
    quit_with(no_memory);               /* a. no .. give error/quit */
```

```
        memset(n, 0, sizeof(struct lines));          /* clear entry to nulls    */

        if (NOT p)                                   /* q. adding first entry?  */
            {
            l_base = n;                              /* a. yes .. set up base ptr*/
            n->l_fwd = n->l_back = 0;                /* ..and clr both pointers  */
            }
         else
            {
            if (bf == before)                        /* q. before current entry? */
                {                                    /* a. yes .. chain into list*/
                if (p->l_back)                       /* q. previous entry exist? */
                    {
                    (p->l_back)->l_fwd = n;          /* a. yes .. patch fwd ptr  */
                    n->l_back = p->l_back;           /* ..and new backward ptr   */
                    }
                 else
                    {
                    l_base = n;                      /* else .. new one is first */
                    n->l_back = 0;                   /* ..and no backward pointer*/
                    }

                n->l_fwd = p;                        /* set up new's forward ptr */
                p->l_back = n;                       /* and next's backward ptr  */
                }

             else
                {
                if (p->l_fwd)                        /* q. next entry exist?     */
                    {
                    (p->l_fwd)->l_back = n;          /* a. yes .. patch to next..*/
                    n->l_fwd = p->l_fwd;             /* ..entry fwd and backward */
                    }
                 else
                    n->l_fwd = 0;                    /* ..and no more afterwards  */

                n->l_back = p;                       /* set up new's backward ptr*/
                p->l_fwd = n;                        /* and next's backward ptr  */
                }
            }

        add_data(&n->l_dir[index]);                  /* finally copy in dir entry*/

        }


        /* ********************************************************************** *
         *      add_data() -- add directory information to list entry            *
         * ********************************************************************** */

        void    add_data(struct d_entry *d)          /* directory entry          */
        {

        strncpy((char *) d->d_name,                  /* pick up filename         */
                dos_entry.name, 13);
        d->d_attrib = dos_entry.attrib;              /* ..and attribute          */
        d->d_date = dos_entry.wr_date;               /* .. file date             */
        d->d_time = dos_entry.wr_time;               /* ..time                   */
        d->d_size = dos_entry.size;                  /* ..and size               */

        d->d_compare = ((long) dos_entry.wr_date     /* build compare key..      */
```

```
                     << 16) + dos_entry.wr_time;   /* ..from date and time     */
        sprintf(d->d_display, file_fmt, d->d_size,  /* format size/date/time.. */
                    (d->d_date >> 5) & 0xf,            /* ..for screen display     */
                    d->d_date & 0x1f, ((d->d_date >> 9) & 0x7f)+ 80,
                    (d->d_time >> 11) & 0x1f, (d->d_time >> 5) & 0x3f);

        }


    /* ********************************************************************** *
     *       sync_files() -- synchronize all files in list                  *
     * ********************************************************************** */
    void    sync_files(void)
    {

    home_screen();                              /* display from top of list */

    for (;;)                                    /* loop thru linked list..  */
        {
        copy_file(F8);                          /* copy file..              */
        wait(5L);                               /* ..wait a quarter second  */

        if (p->l_fwd)                           /* q. more lines available? */
            move_screen(DOWN);                  /* a. yes .. move one line  */
         else
            break;                              /* else .. done loop        */
        }
    }



    /* ********************************************************************** *
     *       copy_file() -- copy one file                                   *
     * ********************************************************************** */
    void    copy_file(int key)                  /* key hit                  */
    {
    int     from, to,                           /* src/dest indices/handles */
            b_read;                             /* bytes read               */
    char    from_name[MAX_PATH],                /* from path and filename   */
            to_name[MAX_PATH];                  /* to path and filename     */
    enum    set_up_rtns rc;                     /* set up return code       */
    struct  d_entry *f;                         /* "from" directory entry   */


    if ((rc = set_up_copy(key, &from, &to))     /* q. request without a ..  */
            == no_file)                         /* ..source file?           */
        {
        printf(bell);                           /* a. yes .. no source avail*/
        return;                                 /* ..so just return now     */
        }
     else if (rc == equal_files)                /* q. files equal and sync  */
        return;                                 /* a. yes .. just return    */

    window(1, 1, 80, max_lines);                /* define window coordinates*/
    color_set(border);                          /* set up border colors     */
    gotoxy(1, max_lines);                        /* position at bottom       */

    if (check_file_dates())                     /* q. continue copy?        */
        {                                       /* a. yes .. process file   */
```

```
    direction = (from == 0) ?              /* copy direction indicator */
          greater_than : less_than;        /* ..for status display     */

    f = &p->l_dir[from];                   /* set up ptr to dir entry  */

    memcpy(&p->l_dir[to], f,               /* update directory entry.. */
          sizeof(struct d_entry));         /* ..for "to" size of fence */

    strcpy(from_name, paths[from]);        /* build fully qualified .. */
    strcat(from_name, f->d_name);          /* .."from" filename        */

    strcpy(to_name, paths[to]);            /* build fully qualified .. */
    strcat(to_name, f->d_name);            /* .."to" filename          */

    if ((from = open(from_name,            /* q. open input ok?        */
          O_BINARY |  O_RDONLY | S_IREAD)) == -1)
        quit_with(open_error, from_name);  /* a. no .. give error/quit */

    if ((to = creatnew(to_name,            /* q. create ok?            */
            f->d_attrib)) == -1)
        {                                  /* a. no .. handle error    */
        delete_file(to_name);              /* delete/unlink file       */

        if ((to = creatnew(to_name,        /* q. create this time?     */
                f->d_attrib)) == -1)
            quit_with(open_error, to_name); /* a. no .. give error/quit */
        }

    for (t_size = w_size = f->d_size;      /* loop reading/writing file*/
          ((b_read = read(from, buf, BUF_SIZE)) != -1);)
        {
        if (NOT b_read)                    /* q. at end of file?       */
            break;                         /* a. yes .. exit loop      */

        if (b_read != write(to, buf, b_read))   /* q. write ok?        */
            quit_with(write_error, to_name);     /* a. no .. give error */

        w_size -= b_read;                  /* subtract out amount read */
        update_progress();                 /* keep user informed       */
        }

    if (b_read == -1 || w_size)            /* q. err or didn't finish? */
        quit_with(read_error, from_name);  /* a. yes .. give error/quit*/

    _dos_setftime(to,                      /* set file's date and time */
          f->d_date, f->d_time);

    _dos_setfileattr(to_name,              /* ..and file's attributes  */
          f->d_attrib);

    close(to);                             /* close output file        */
    close(from);                           /* ..and input file         */

    p->l_entry = equal_to;                 /* show both files equal     */
    }

cprintf(clear_error,                       /* fix up display by        */
      81 - sizeof(footer), "");            /* ..clearing message area  */
window(1, 2, 80, max_lines - 1);           /* redefine text window     */
display_line(p, c_line, selected);         /* update line display      */

}
```

```c
/* ********************************************************************** *
 *        check_file_dates() -- check for invalid file dates            *
 * ********************************************************************** */

int     check_file_dates(void)
{
int     key;                                /* work and key variable    */

if (NOT ((p->l_dir[0].d_name[0] &&          /* q. dir 1 in use..        */
        NOT (p->l_dir[0].d_date & 0xfc00))  /* ..and year 1980          */
        || ((p->l_dir[1].d_name[0] &&       /* ..or dir 2 in use..      */
        NOT (p->l_dir[1].d_date & 0xfc00)))))/* ..and year 1980          */
    return(1);                              /* a. no .. just return     */

cprintf(bad_date);                          /* give notice of bad date  */

while(NOT (key = getch()))                  /* wait for a key to be hit */
    ;

if (key == ESC)                             /* q. user request cancel?  */
    quit_with(stop_here);                   /* a. yes .. give error/quit*/

key = (key == 'Y' || key == 'y' ||          /* change response to..     */
        key == '\r');                       /* ..a logical (true/false) */

cprintf(key ? ans_yes : ans_no);            /* show user's response     */
wait(9L);                                   /* ..wait a half-second     */
return(key);                                /* ..then return w/response */

}


/* ********************************************************************** *
 *        set_up_copy() -- determine source and destination files       *
 * ********************************************************************** */

enum    set_up_rtns set_up_copy(int  key,   /* key hit                  */
                        int *from,          /* source directory index   */
                        int *to)            /* destination dir index    */
{
int     name_index;                         /* dir entry with name      */


name_index = p->l_dir[0].d_name[0] ? 0 : 1; /* dir entry with filename  */

switch (key)
    {
    case CTRL_RIGHT:
        if (p->l_entry == one_sided &&      /* q. only in one dir..     */
                name_index)                 /* ..and not in dir 1?      */
            return(no_file);                /* a. yes .. return w/error */

        *from = 0;                          /* source is dir 1 ..       */
        *to = 1;                            /* ..and dest is dir 2      */
        break;                              /* ..continue with process  */

    case CTRL_LEFT:
        if (p->l_entry == one_sided &&      /* q. only in one dir..     */
                NOT name_index)             /* ..and not in dir 2?      */
            return(no_file);                /* a. yes .. return w/error */

        *from = 1;                          /* source is dir 2 ..       */
```

```
        *to = 0;                          /* ..and dest is dir 1        */
        break;                            /* ..continue with process    */

    case F8:                              /* F8 sync request            */
        switch (p->l_entry)               /* based on comparison char   */
            {
            case equal_to:                /* both files equal           */
            case almost_equal:            /* ..or almost equal          */
                return(equal_files);      /* ..no processing needed     */

            case greater_than:            /* dir 1 greater than dir 2   */
                *from = 0;                 /* from file is in dir 1      */
                *to = 1;                  /* ..and to file is in dir 2  */
                break;                    /* ..continue with process    */

            case less_than:               /* dir 1 is less than dir 2   */
                *from = 1;                 /* from file is in dir 2      */
                *to = 0;                  /* ..and to file is in dir 1  */
                break;                    /* ..continue with process    */

            case one_sided:               /* file only in one dir       */
                *from = name_index;        /* source entry has filename  */
                *to = name_index ? 0 : 1; /* dest is the other entry    */
                break;                    /* ..continue with process    */
            }

        break;                            /* ..continue some more       */
    }

    return(set_up_ok);                    /* rtn w/everything ok flag   */

}


/* *********************************************************************** *
 *      update_progress() -- update progress bar                          *
 * *********************************************************************** */

void    update_progress(void)
{
static
int     last_call = 0xff;                 /* value at last display      */
int     half,                             /* half unit flag             */
        skip;                             /* skip space                 */
long    whole;                            /* work number                */


whole = ((t_size - w_size) << 5) / t_size; /* scale up by nbr of units  */
                                          /* ..then divide to get nbr   */
half = (int) whole & 1;                    /* ..units and half units     */
                                          /* ..completed so far         */

if (last_call != whole)                   /* q. any change in graph..   */
    {                                     /* ..for this call?           */
    last_call = whole;                    /* a. yes .. save status      */

    whole >>= 1;                          /* get whole block count      */
    skip = 16 - (int) whole - half;       /* spaces to skip in bar      */

    cprintf(working, (int) whole,         /* display crude graph..      */
            (int) whole,  whole_blk,      /* ..using whole blocks..     */
            half, half, part_blk,         /* ..and partial units..      */
            skip, skip, "",               /* ..and skip to end of bar   */
```

```
              direction, direction);            /* ..& draw a direction flag*/
        }
}


/* ********************************************************************* *
 *      home_screen() -- display first group of lines                    *
 * ********************************************************************* */
void    home_screen(void)
{
int     i;                                       /* loop counter           */

for (i = 0, l_top = l_bottom = p = l_base;       /* loop thru building..    */
          i < (max_lines - 2); i++)              /* ..initial screen        */
    {
    display_line(l_bottom, i + 1,                /* ..and display one line  */
            i ? unselected : selected);

    if (l_bottom->l_fwd)                         /* q. something follows?   */
        l_bottom = l_bottom->l_fwd;              /* a. yes .. set up next one*/
     else
        break;                                   /* else .. exit loop       */
    }

if (i == (max_lines - 2))                        /* q. fill the screen?     */
    l_bottom = l_bottom->l_back;                 /* a. yes .. get last ptr  */

gotoxy(1, c_line = 1);                           /* position on first line  */

}


/* ********************************************************************* *
 *      move_screen() -- move scroll bar and redisplay lines             *
 * ********************************************************************* */
void    move_screen(int key)                     /* key code                */
{

switch (key)
    {
    case UP:                                     /* up key                  */
        display_line(p, c_line, unselected);/* unselect line              */

        if (p == l_top)                          /* q. cursor on top row?   */
            {                                    /* a. yes .. try moving up */
            if (p->l_back)                       /* q. any previous lines?  */
                {
                insline();                       /* a. yes .. make room     */
                l_top = p = p->l_back;           /* get top line's pointer  */
                l_bottom = l_bottom->l_back;/* ..and bottom line's ptr  */
                }
             else
                printf(bell);                    /* else .. just ring bell  */
            }

         else
            {
            p = p->l_back;                       /* get previous line pointer*/
```

```
            c_line--;                       /* move back one line      */
            }

        display_line(p, c_line, selected);  /* write new current line  */
        break;                              /* ..and continue process  */

    case DOWN:                              /* down key                */
        display_line(p, c_line, unselected);/* unselect line           */

        if (p == l_bottom)                  /* q. cursor on bottom row? */
            {                               /* a. yes .. try moving dwn */
            if (p->l_fwd)                   /* q. any more lines?      */
                {                           /* a. yes .. scroll window  */
                gotoxy(1, 1);               /* goto top line ..        */
                delline();                  /* delete top line         */
                l_top = l_top->l_fwd;       /* get new top line pointer */
                p = l_bottom = p->l_fwd;    /* ..and bottom line's ptr  */
                gotoxy(1, max_lines - 2);   /* set up shop at bottom    */
                }
            else
                printf(bell);               /* else .. just ring bell  */
            }

        else
            {
            p = p->l_fwd;                   /* get next line pointer    */
            c_line++;                       /* ..and move down one line */
            }

        display_line(p, c_line, selected);  /* write new current line  */
        break;                              /* ..and continue process  */
        }
    }


/* ******************************************************************** *
 *      set_up_screen() -- set up screen, headers and footers         *
 * ******************************************************************** */

void    set_up_screen(void)
{

full_screen = 1;                            /* set up full screen flag */

window(1, 1, 80, max_lines);                /* define window coordinates*/
color_set(unselected);                      /* set up standard colors  */
clrscr();                                   /* clear screen            */

color_set(border);                          /* set up border colors    */
gotoxy(1, 1);                               /* goto top of screen      */
cprintf(header, paths[0], paths[1]);        /* ..display header        */

gotoxy(82 - sizeof(footer), max_lines);     /* position at bottom right */
cprintf(footer);                            /* ..and display footer    */

gotoxy(1, max_lines);                       /* goto bottom left corner */
cprintf(clear_error,                        /* fix up error area by    */
        81 - sizeof(footer), "");           /* ..clearing to blanks    */

window(1, 2, 80, max_lines - 1);            /* define text window      */
```

```
        }


/* ********************************************************************* *
 *      color_set() -- select current foreground and background colors   *
 * ********************************************************************* */

void    color_set(enum select_types s_flag) /* selected/unselected      */
{

switch (s_flag)                              /* based on flag ..        */
    {
    case selected:                           /* selected line           */
        textcolor(text_bg);                  /* set up the inverted..   */
        textbackground(text_fg);             /* ..color scheme          */
        break;                               /* ..then continue         */

    case unselected:                         /* unselected line         */
        textcolor(text_fg);                  /* set up the normal..     */
        textbackground(text_bg);             /* ..color scheme          */
        break;                               /* ..then continue         */

    case border:                             /* border lines            */
        textcolor(hdr_fg);                   /* set up the border..     */
        textbackground(hdr_bg);              /* ..color scheme          */
        break;                               /* ..then continue         */
    }

}



/* ********************************************************************* *
 *      close_down() -- close windows and quit to DOS                     *
 * ********************************************************************* */

void    close_down(void)
{

window(1, 1, 80, max_lines);                 /* define full screen window*/
color_set(unselected);                       /* set up normal colors    */
clrscr();                                    /* clear screen            */
full_screen = 0;                             /* ..and full screen flag  */
printf(copyright);                           /* redisplay program banner */

}



/* ********************************************************************* *
 *      get_key() -- get a key (including function keys)                  *
 * ********************************************************************* */

int     get_key(void)
{
int     k = 0;                               /* local key variable      */

if (kbhit())                                 /* q. key available?       */
    {                                        /* a. yes .. process it    */
    if (NOT (k = getch()))                   /* q. function key?        */
```

```
            k = 0x100 + getch();            /* a. yes .. special key    */
        }

    return(k);                              /* return w/key if available*/

    }



/* ***************************************************************** *
 *        validate_name() -- validate file/dir name                  *
 * ***************************************************************** */

char    *validate_name(char *name,          /* source file/dir name      */
                       char *rc)            /* return code               */
                                            /*  -3 = invalid drive       */
                                            /*  -2 = drive not ready     */
                                            /*  -1 = invalid name        */
                                            /*   0 = directory           */
                                            /*   1 = filespec            */
{
int     i,                                  /* work variable             */
        drive;                              /* drive number              */
static
char    full[MAX_PATH];                     /* normalized full name      */
char    *p,                                 /* work pointer              */
        c,                                  /* character holder          */
        work[MAX_PATH],                     /* work field                */
        current_path[MAX_PATH];             /* current path              */


full[0] = 0;                                /* initialize return string */
memset(work, 0, sizeof(work));              /* clear to nulls            */
strcpy(work, name);                         /* copy source local         */
i = strlen(work) - 1;                       /* ..and pick up length      */

if (work[i] == '\\' && i                    /* q. more than drive:\?    */
        && (i > 2 | | work[1] != ':'))      /* ..or other trailing \?   */
    work[i] = 0;                            /* a. yes .. remove last \   */

drive = (work[1] == ':') ?                  /* get name's drive number   */
        toupper(work[0]) - 'A' + 1 : 0;

if ((_osmajor == 3 && _osminor >= 1) | |    /* q. DOS 3.1 or higher?    */
        (_osmajor > 3))
    {
    r.x.ax = 0x4409;                        /* a. yes .. do local test   */
    r.h.bl = drive;                         /* bl = drive to test        */
    int86(0x21, &r, &r);                    /* test drive validity       */

    if (r.x.cflag)                          /* q. bad drive?             */
        {
        *rc = -3;                           /* a. yes .. set return code*/
        return(0);                          /* ..and return to caller    */
        }
    }

if (NOT (_getdcwd(drive, current_path,      /* q. accessible drive?      */
        MAX_PATH)))
    {
    *rc = -2;                               /* a. no .. set error return*/
    return(0);                              /* ..and return to caller    */
    }
```

```
*rc = -1;                                      /* set up for error return */

if (chdir(work))                               /* q. a directory?          */
    {                                          /* a. no .. backup one \    */
    if ((p = strrchr(work, '\\')) != 0)        /* q. find a backslash?     */
        {                                      /* a. yes .. check it out   */
        if ((p - work) > 2 ¦ ¦                 /* q. more than just d:\?   */
                work[1] != ':' ¦ ¦             /* ..or no colon anyway..   */
                work[0] == '.')                /* ..or some .\ or ..\?     */
            {
            *p++ = 0;                          /* a. yes .. backoff filenm */
            c = 0;                             /* ..and clear char holder  */
            }
        else
            {
            c = *(++p);                        /* get 1st char after \     */
            *p++ = 0;                          /* ..and make into new path */
            }

        if (NOT chdir(work))                   /* q. find the directory?   */
            {
            *rc = 1;                           /* a. yes .. show filename   */
            _getdcwd(drive, full, MAX_PATH);   /* ..then get path           */

            if (LAST(full) != '\\')            /* q. last char a \?        */
                strcat(full, "\\");            /* a. no .. put in path sep */

            if (c)                             /* q. filespec need help?   */
                strncat(full, &c, 1);          /* a. yes .. add saved char */

            strcat(full, p);                   /* ..and add filename       */
            }
        }

    else
        {
        _getdcwd(drive, full, MAX_PATH);       /* else ..then get path     */

        p = &work[work[1] == ':' ? 2 : 0];     /* get start of filespec    */
        i = strlen(p);                         /* ..and length of remainder*/

        if (LAST(full) != '\\' && i)           /* q. do we need a \ ?      */
            strcat(full, "\\");                /* a. yes .. put in path sep*/

        if (i)                                 /* q. filename given?       */
            {
            *rc = 1;                           /* a. yes .. return filespec*/
            strcat(full, p);                   /* ..and copy in filename   */
            }

        else
            *rc = 0;                           /* else .. show as dir      */
        }
    }

else
    {
    *rc = 0;                                   /* show directory was found */
    _getdcwd(drive, full, MAX_PATH);           /* ..then get path          */
    }

chdir(current_path);                           /* reset original directory */

return(*rc >= 0 ? strdup(full) : 0);           /* rtn normalized path\name */
```

```
}


/* **********************************************************************  *
 *        translate_name() -- translate a DOS directory name            *
 * **********************************************************************  */

char    *translate_name(char *name)           /* name to translate         */
{
static
char    work[65];                             /* work/return area          */

if (_osmajor == 2)                            /* q. translate available?   */
    return(name);                             /* a. no .. rtn with source  */

r.h.ah = 0x60;                                /* ah = translate            */
r.x.si = FP_OFF(name);                        /* set ptr to input name     */
s.ds = FP_SEG(name);                          /* ..and segment             */
r.x.di = FP_OFF(work);                        /* set ptr to output area    */
s.es = FP_SEG(work);                          /* ..and segment             */
int86x(0x21, &r, &r, &s);                     /* translate the name        */

return(r.x.cflag ? NULL : work);              /* return workarea or null   */

}



/* **********************************************************************  *
 *        quit_with() -- give an error message, then return to DOS      *
 * **********************************************************************  */

void    quit_with(char *msg, ...)             /* string to print           */
{
UINT    i;                                    /* work parm for set drive   */
va_list list;                                 /* variable list             */


_dos_setdrive(init_drive, &i);                /* reset the default drive   */
chdir(init_path);                             /* ..and the start up path   */

if (full_screen)                              /* q. full screen mode?      */
    close_down();                             /* a. yes .. clear screen    */

va_start(list, msg);                          /* set up variable list      */
vprintf(msg, list);                           /* give error message ..     */
exit(rc);                                     /* ..and then quit           */

}



/* **********************************************************************  *
 *        wait() -- wait n timer ticks                                  *
 * **********************************************************************  */

void    wait(long n)                          /* time to wait in ticks     */
{
long    far *timer = MK_FP(0x40, 0x6c),       /* BIOS timer tick counter   */
        start, work;                          /* start tick count          */
```

```
    start = *timer;                          /* get current time        */

    while (n > 0)                            /* loop 'til n ticks past   */
        {
        if ((work = *timer) != start)        /* q. time pass?           */
            {                                /* a. yes .. see how much   */
            if (work < start)                /* q. clock go past midnite?*/
                n--;                         /* a. yes .. count as 1 tick*/
            else
                n -= (UINT)(work - start);    /* else .. count everything */

            start = work;                    /* start again w/curr time  */
            }

        else
            kbhit();                         /* else .. check keyboard   */

        }
    }




/* *********************************************************************** *
 *      delete_file() -- delete file any way necessary                   *
 * *********************************************************************** */

int     delete_file(char *s)                 /* filename to delete      */
{
int     rc;                                  /* return code, 0=ok       */

if ((rc = unlink(s)) != 0)                   /* q. regular file unlink? */
    if (NOT (rc = chmod(s, S_IWRITE)))       /* a. no .. q. change ok?  */
        rc = unlink(s);                      /* a. yes .. try again     */

return(rc);                                  /* return w/final status   */

}




/* *********************************************************************** *
 *      control_break() -- control break intercept routine               *
 * *********************************************************************** */

int     control_break(void)
{

quit_with(stop_here);                        /* give error msg and quit */
return(0);                                    /* ..and abort processing  */

}
```

```
/* *********************************************************************** *
 *       critical_handler() -- DOS critical error handler                  *
 * *********************************************************************** */

#pragma argsused                        /* hold unused argument messages  */
#pragma option -O2-b-e                   /* no global register allocation  */
                                         /* ..or dead code elimination     */

void    interrupt critical_handler(UINT bp,
        UINT di, UINT si, UINT ds, UINT es,
        UINT dx, UINT cx, UINT bx, UINT ax,
        UINT cs, UINT ip, UINT flags)
{

if (ax & 0x800)                          /* q. fail allowed?               */
    ax = (ax & 0xff00) | 3;              /* a. yes .. fail request         */
else
    ax = (ax & 0xff00) | 2;              /* else .. abort request          */

}
```

7

RETRIEVING THE LATEST FILES WITH UP2DATE

UP2DATE compares the contents of multiple directories and subsequently copies the most up-to-

date files to a target directory. Optionally, you can select automatic overwrite of existing files, limit

selection of files to those that match files already existing in the target directory, and set up a test

mode to process files without actually copying them.

In the early days of DOS—before the word *subdirectory* had been coined, and when the alternative question to "Should I buy a hard disk?" was, "Should I buy a house?"—the art of managing disk files consisted of determining which floppy contained the desired version of your files. Life was simpler back then, and all of the files lived in what we now call the root directory.

Then came DOS 2.0, with its added support for hard disks and subdirectories. DOS 2.0 no longer limited you to a single copy of a file on a disk. Rather, you could have many copies of a file, each in a different directory representing various versions or intermediate revisions of the files. Should disaster strike, you would simply copy the most recent files from the backup directories into the current directory. But sometimes this is not as easy as it seems.

S K I L L S   I N D E X

• *Intelligent directory processing*
• *Matching record processing*
• *Using huge arrays*

If you have ever had the misfortune of having to search through several directories looking for the most recent copy of one or more files, you have probably discovered that DOS's tools are woefully inadequate for the job. When challenged with this duty, you probably combine the listings of the directories to search, sort the combined listing according to file name, search the listing for the most recent files, and issue DOS commands to copy them to the desired directory.

When this task next confronts you, try using UP2DATE. UP2DATE automates the procedure by searching a set of source directories and copying the files with the most recent time- and datestamps to a target directory.

■ USING UP2DATE

In its simplest form, UP2DATE examines the files in a source directory and, as required, copies them to a target directory according to the following rules: A file that exists in the source directory but not in the target directory is always copied. A file that exists in both the source and target directories is copied *only* if the file in the source directory has a more recent date than the file in the target directory. For example, if you have two directories on drive C named \BACKUP and \CURRENT, and you want to copy the most recent files from \BACKUP and place them in \CURRENT, you can issue this command:

```
UP2DATE C:\BACKUP C:\CURRENT
```

UP2DATE will compare the contents of the \BACKUP directory to the contents of the \CURRENT directory, and copy to \CURRENT any files that exist in \BACKUP but not in \CURRENT. If \BACKUP contains files that are younger (more recent, according to the file's time and date) than the same files in \CURRENT, then UP2DATE displays the entries from both directories and prompts you with, "File exists in target directory, overwrite? (Y/N/ESC)." Press Y, and the file will be overwritten; press N, and UP2DATE will skip the file and continue processing. Pressing Esc immediately halts UP2DATE and returns control to DOS. Of course, if \BACKUP contains files older than those in \CURRENT, no files are copied.

If you enter the command UP2DATE with no arguments, you receive a series of messages describing the full syntax for UP2DATE, as follows:

```
UP2DATE source1 [source2 [...]] target [options]
where:   source = d:
                  [d:]path
                  [d:]filename.ext
                  [d:]path\filename.ext
         target = d:
                  [d:]path
        options:  /T  Shows files that would be copied; no files are actually copied
                  /F  Only copies files that already exist in the target directory
                  /O  Overwrites older files in target without prompting
```

When you invoke UP2DATE, you must specify at least one source argument and a target argument. Sources come in three categories: a directory, a set of files, or a specific file.

When you specify a directory, you tell UP2DATE to test all of the files contained within that directory. There are two formats you can use to specify a directory: drive letter and colon (D:), or a path name optionally preceded by a drive letter and colon (D:\SRC1). When you specify a drive letter only, UP2DATE searches the current directory on that drive.

To specify a set of files, simply use the DOS wildcard characters ? and *. For example, you can select all of the files in the current directory starting with the character *T* by specifying T*.* as a source.

The last option for the source argument is a specific file that matches a specific, unambiguous name. You can select a specific file name by specifying the complete file name and extension, such as TEST.OBJ. When you specify either a set of files or a specific file, you can precede the specification with a drive, path, or both, as in D:\SRC1\TEST.OBJ. When you specify the drive, path, file name, and extension, the specification is called a *fully qualified* file name.

The target argument must specify a directory, either by a drive letter and colon (D:), or a path optionally preceded by a drive letter and colon (D:\TGT). As with the source arguments, if you specify a drive only, UP2DATE assumes the current directory on that drive. In any case, the target directory must exist before you execute UP2DATE.

UP2DATE's power is evident when you use it to scan more than one source directory. Assume your hard disk has the subdirectories and files shown in Figure 7.1.

```
\SRC1
TEST.H         504    03-04-92  02:13pm
TEST.C        8304    03-15-92  04:52pm
TEST.OBJ      1207    03-15-92  04:54pm
TEST.EXE     12231    03-15-92  04:54pm
\SRC2
TEST.C        6241    03-14-92  11:52am
TEST.H         504    03-04-92  02:13pm
\SRC3
TEST.C        5226    03-12-92  09:54pm
TEST.H         527    03-15-92  03:22pm
\TGT
TEST.EXE     11704    03-12-92  10:02pm
```

Now, to copy the most recent files from \SRC1, \SRC2, and \SRC3 into the directory \TGT, simply issue this command:

```
UP2DATE \SRC1 \SRC2 \SRC3 \TGT
```

First, UP2DATE verifies the arguments passed to it on the command line. Each source specification is examined to determine if it is a file or a directory, and the target is checked to ensure it is a directory. In this example, because all of the arguments refer to directories, UP2DATE builds a file list by searching for all of the files contained in each directory, including the target directory, and loading into memory the appropriate information about each file found.

Next, UP2DATE sorts the file list by file name, extension, date, and time, and then scans the list, noting the most recent entry among those with the same file name and extension. If the most recent entry does not already reside in the target directory, it is copied to the target. For the files listed in Figure 7.1, UP2DATE would copy TEST.OBJ in \SRC1 to \TGT because it is the only file of that name in any of the directories. The file TEST.C in \SRC1 is copied to \TGT because it is the most recent of all the TEST.C files found. Similarly, UP2DATE copies TEST.H in \SRC3 to \TGT because its date and time indicate it is more recent than TEST.H in either \SRC1 or \SRC2. Finally, before UP2DATE copies TEST.EXE in \SRC1 to \TGT, UP2DATE tells you that TEST.EXE already exists in \TGT, and asks you if it's OK to overwrite it.

Though the overwrite question can save you from a disaster when UP2DATE is about to overwrite an important file, it can also be tedious if you are already certain that the files in the target need to be overwritten. If you use the /O option, UP2DATE will overwrite older existing files in the target directory without asking you for confirmation. For example, to copy files from \SRC1 to \TGT, overwriting existing files without confirmation, you can enter the command

```
UP2DATE \SRC1 \TGT /O
```

UP2DATE lets you copy a specific set of files by specifying file names with or without wildcards. For example, to copy the latest .C and .H files from the SRC1, \SRC2, and \SRC3 directories to the \TGT directory, use the following command:

```
UP2DATE SRC1\*.C \SRC1\*.H \SRC2\*.C \SRC2\*.H \SRC3\*.C
    \SRC3\*.H \TGT
```

Compare the contents of \SRC1 and \TGT, and you will see that the only file they have in common is TEST.EXE, and \SRC1 contains the most recent version. Though you could use the command

```
UP2DATE \SRC1\TEST.EXE \TGT
```

to update the TEST.EXE file, when you specify the /F option, UP2DATE only copies files that already exist in the target directory. Consider the command

```
UP2DATE \SRC1 \TGT /F
```

In response to this command, UP2DATE will copy files from \SRC1 that have the same file name and extension as those in \TGT, but are more recent. Among the files in Figure 7.1, only TEST.EXE meets these criteria. UP2DATE will then ask if you want to overwrite the file, and will do so if you respond with a Y.

If you want to see what UP2DATE is going to do without actually copying any files, use the /T option. UP2DATE will then perform all processing and issue all associated messages (except the overlay prompt), but no files are copied to the target directory. This option lets you make certain UP2DATE is going to perform as you expect.

■ INSIDE UP2DATE

The UP2DATE program automates the same series of steps you would take to accomplish the task manually. To analyze how UP2DATE works, we can identify the steps as follows: initialization to get ready for the task, building the list of files that may be copied, selecting the files to copy, and copying the selected files to the target directory.

- **Initializing UP2DATE**

  When UP2DATE starts, it first prints the copyright message. Interrupt service routines are then installed to intercept the control break keystroke (interrupt 0x23) and the DOS critical error interrupt (0x24). The control_break() and critical_handler() routines let UP2DATE shut down gracefully should you choose to interrupt its processing via the Ctrl-Break key, or if a DOS error occurs, such as Drive Not Ready. After setting up these interrupt service routines, UP2DATE saves the default drive so it can be restored when processing is complete. If no arguments were specified on the command line, a command line syntax message is displayed.

- **Validating the Arguments**

  UP2DATE validates the command line arguments for consistency and accuracy by calling the parse_parms() routine, which performs two functions. First, it examines each argument from the command line to see if any options were specified. An option always starts with a forward slash character and is followed by a single letter. UP2DATE recognizes three options: /T, /F, and /O.

  When parse_parms() finds a forward slash anywhere within the command line, it checks the character that follows against the entries in the cmd_parm table passed by the caller. Each cmd_parm entry consists of two fields. The first field is the character that defines the option, and the second is the address of a flag that parse_parms() should set if it finds the option. If parse_parms() searches the entire cmd_parm table without finding the option, it prints an error message and returns to DOS.

  The second function parse_parms() performs is to build the pos_parms array. The pos_parms array contains a pointer to each directory or file argument specified on the command line. When parse_parms() determines that an argument does not represent an option, it adds the argument to the pos_parms array, which tracks arguments that are not options. UP2DATE can then process source and target arguments without using special-purpose logic to skip over an argument that specifies an option.

  When a program written in C executes, the C startup code parses the command line, builds an array of char pointers, and passes that array to main(). Each element of the array points to one command line argument, where a command line argument is defined as a group of characters separated by one or more blanks. Though convenient, this can cause problems. For example, if you enter the command

  ```
  UP2DATE \SRC1 \TGT/F
  ```

  the C startup code will report that there are two command line arguments, \SRC1 and \TGT/F. When parse_parms() scans the arguments, it creates an entry for \SRC1 in pos_parms. When parse_parms() scans \TGT/F, it notes that you specified /F, strips it from the argument (leaving \TGT), and places a pointer to \TGT in the pos_parms array.

UP2DATE tests the validity of the arguments returned by parse_parms() by invoking check_dirs(). The check_dirs() routine verifies each argument in the pos_parms array, ensuring that the entry refers to a valid drive; that the drive is ready (a floppy drive has a disk in it, for example); and that a path, if specified, exists. The validate_name() function performs the mechanics of these tests.

If an argument is valid, validate_name() returns a code indicating whether the argument represents a directory or a file name, along with a fully qualified name representing the argument. For example, assuming the directory structure shown in Figure 7.1, if you enter the command

```
UP2DATE \SRC1\TEST.C \TGT
```

then validate_name() will return a value indicating that the \SRC1\TEST.C argument refers to a file and the \TGT refers to a directory. On the other hand, if you enter

```
UP2DATE A: \TGT
```

and drive A contains no disk, validate_name() will indicate that the drive is not ready, and UP2DATE will terminate with an error message.

After check_dirs() determines that all arguments refer to valid drives and/or directories, it also verifies that the last argument, the target, names a directory and not a specific file.

■ BUILDING THE LIST OF FILES

As mentioned, UP2DATE simply automates the steps you would take to accomplish the task manually. Nowhere is that more evident than when UP2DATE builds the list of files to be copied, and this action is implemented as a set of discrete steps.

■ Getting the Memory

The number of files UP2DATE can process is limited only by the amount of memory it has available in which to build a list of those files. UP2DATE calls max_d_entries() to determine the maximum number of files that can be accommodated. This function retrieves the amount of memory available, subtracts 25k to allow for buffers, and divides it by the size of D_ENTRY, the structure that holds the file information. Figure 7.2 shows the format of a D_ENTRY. UP2DATE sets the max_cnt variable to the number of entries memory can hold.

FIGURE 7.2

Format of a
D_ENTRY

UP2DATE builds an array where each member is in the following format:

File Name	File Date	File Time	File Size	Dir Index	Attr

Size in bytes ⟶   13   2   2   4   1   1

File Name: Contains a left-justified file name and extension separated by a period. The remaining bytes are set to zero.

File Date and   Contain the date and time of the last update to the file. The fields are
File Time: in DOS format, as recorded in the directory entry for the file represented. UP2DATE swaps the bytes in these fields before sorting the entries.

File Size: Contains the four-byte file size field from the directory entry for the file represented.

Dir Index: Contains an index that denotes the directory in which this file was found.

Attr: Contains the value of the attributes field in the directory entry for the file represented.

UP2DATE calls cln_malloc(), allocating the memory to hold the number of D_ENTRY structures found in max_cnt. The cln_malloc() function ensures that the required memory is available, terminating the program if memory is insufficient. The address returned by cln_malloc() points to the area in memory that UP2DATE will use to build the list of files. UP2DATE saves this address in the file_list variable.

■ **Reading the Directories**

After allocating sufficient memory, UP2DATE calls read_list() to load directory information for files that match the command line arguments. UP2DATE passes to read_list() the index number of a pos_parms entry to process. If the entry refers to a directory, read_list() invokes join_path() to add *.* to the directory specification.

Then read_list() uses _dos_findfirst() and _dos_findnext() to retrieve the directory entries that match the argument. For every entry retrieved, read_list() calls the build_entry() routine to fill in a D_ENTRY structure representing the file found. The build_entry() function accepts three arguments: the address of the new D_ENTRY; the index (passed to read_list() as the first argument) that signifies the directory containing the entry; and a flag that controls whether build_entry() rearranges the bytes of the date, time, and size fields. The sort routine does not compare the individual fields of each D_ENTRY entry; instead, it compares the entries as though they were strings. So that the sort step can properly compare and order the entries, the bytes must be rearranged. (See the Endnote, "Sorting Directory Entries" for more information on this procedure.)

If the number of files exceeds the capacity of the memory array, read_list() prints a message indicating that there is insufficient memory to continue processing and returns to DOS.

■ Making an Ordered Array from Disarray

Once all of the required directory entries are in memory, UP2DATE calls sort() to order them by file name, extension, and date and time. There are four routines that perform the sorting function, sort(), sort_subfile(), sort_exchange(), and sort_compare(). As the interface to the actual sorting algorithm, sort() prepares to sort the array by presetting certain sort-specific variables, finding the lowest and highest values in the array, placing them first and last in the array, respectively, and invoking the sort algorithm, sort_subfile().

The sort_subfile() function is recursive, that is, it calls itself. It employs two sort algorithms, shellsort and quicksort, to perform the actual sort. Shellsort is used when less than 50 entries are being sorted or when more than one hundred recursions of sort_subfile() have occurred; otherwise, quicksort is used.

There are many sort algorithms available, and they vary widely in their performance. Often, the number of elements or initial order of the elements will drastically affect the performance of one algorithm, but have little impact on another. Normally, a single sort algorithm will suffice when sorting a list of files, but UP2DATE can process over 20,000 files if you have 500k of free memory. When considering which algorithm to use, you must examine the positive and negative aspects of each algorithm.

Shellsort is a fairly simple algorithm and is easy to implement, but takes a relatively long time to sort a large number of elements. Quicksort sorts a large number of elements much more quickly, but since the algorithm is recursive, it potentially requires an immense amount of memory to execute.

The sort_subfile() function tries to take advantage of the positive aspects of each algorithm while minimizing the negative. As noted earlier, quicksort sorts a large number of elements more quickly than shellsort. Generally, quicksort selects an arbitrary element from the list, and places that element so that all elements of lower value come before it, and all elements of higher value come after it. In other words, it places the selected element in its final location, never to be moved again. Having done this, it calls itself twice, first to sort the lower elements, and then to sort the higher elements. When quicksort is the only algorithm used, it calls itself until all of the elements in the list are in order. The sort_subfile() function limits quicksort to

100 recursions, thereby limiting the amount of necessary stack space to approximately 1k. After this, sort_subfile() uses shellsort until the recursion level drops below 100. In any case, if sort_subfile() is asked to sort 50 or fewer elements, it uses shellsort to sort them.

A common operation used by most sort algorithms is exchanging two elements. The sort_exchange() routine exchanges the contents of two elements in the array of D_ENTRYs byte by byte. As the sort algorithm progresses, sort_exchange() rearranges the D_ENTRYs into the order needed to process the list.

Finally, the sort_compare() routine compares the contents of two D_ENTRY array elements, returning a −1 if the first is less than the second, 0 if they are the same, and 1 if the first is greater than the second. The sort algorithm uses the value returned by sort_compare() to determine the relative value of two items and if they must be exchanged. After the sort has completed, the D_ENTRYs are ordered by name, extension, and date and time. UP2DATE can now search the list and keep only the entries that need to be copied to the target directory.

■ Selecting the Files to Copy

UP2DATE determines which files to copy by applying three tests to an entry. First, the entry must be the most recent entry among all entries with the same file name. Second, the entry selected must reside in a directory other than the target. Third, if the /F option was specified, the entry's file name must match a file in the target directory.

UP2DATE applies these tests to each entry by calling merge_list(). The merge_list() function loops through the list of files, comparing entries with the same name and extension. When the sort completes, if several entries have the same name and extension, the youngest entry will always be last among the group of entries with the same name, and merge_list() discards the older entries, keeping only the youngest.

Once merge_list() finds the youngest entry, it determines if that entry represents a file in the target directory. If so, the file does not need to be copied since it is already in the target. Otherwise, merge_list() checks to see if the /F option was specified on the command line. If so, the youngest entry's name and extension must match the name and extension of a file that already exists in the target directory. If it does not, merge_list() skips the entry without copying the file to the target directory.

As merge_list() qualifies entries, the entries are copied to consecutive elements at the top of the array, effectively packing the array. When all entries have been checked, the number of selected entries is displayed, and the list of files to copy is complete.

■ **Copying the Files to the Target**

As part of its preparation for copying the selected files to the target directory, UP2DATE calls normalize_list() to return the date and time fields in the D_ENTRY to DOS format.

Finally, UP2DATE actually copies the selected files to the target directory via execute_list(). Upon entry, execute_list() allocates memory for a buffer used to copy the data from the source files to files in the target directory. After this, execute_list() enters a loop, processing each entry remaining in the D_ENTRY array.

For each entry, execute_list() creates a fully qualified file name for the input and output files. It then displays the file being copied and opens the input and output files. Before copying a file, execute_list() checks to see if the /T option was specified. If so, it does not open the file and performs no file I/O. Following this, a simple loop is used to copy the data from the input to the output file. After finishing the copy, execute_list() sets the output file's date, time, and attributes to match those of the source file, by invoking _dos_setftime() and _dos_setfileattr(). Then execute_list() closes the files.

Before opening the output file, execute_list() uses _dos_findfirst() to determine if the file already exists in the target directory. If so, it asks you if you want to overwrite the existing file. If you specified the /O option on the command line, execute_list() bypasses this prompt.

After all of the files have been processed, execute_list() displays a final summary message stating the number of files copied.

■ **SUMMARY**

UP2DATE is a fairly versatile utility that uses several standard programming techniques and algorithms. Not only does it make up for shortcomings in DOS utilities, it also automates what would otherwise be a fairly tedious manual procedure. The next time you have to gather the most recent files from a set of directories, UP2DATE will be there to help.

As written, UP2DATE can be told which files to include in its search for the most recent files, but there isn't any way to tell it which files to exclude from this search. You might wish to add a feature that would allow the exclusion of files. You might implement this by building a second list of files matching the exclusion criteria. When read_list() reads the files from the source directory, each file name would be checked against the exclude list before being moved into the array.

A more robust implementation would be a routine to parse a DOS wildcard against a file name and see if the file name qualifies against the exclude specification. If so, it would not be added to the array.

Another feature to add to UP2DATE is a date/time limit. As presented, UP2DATE processes all files without regard to the date and time of the files. With a date/time limit feature, you can eliminate files from the process based on their age. For instance, you might add the /D switch to specify the date of the oldest files UP2DATE may process, as shown in this command:

```
UP2DATE \SRC1 \TGT /D03-14-92
```

In this example, the oldest file that UP2DATE would consider would have the date March 14, 1992.

Finally, the overwrite feature could optionally back up the existing file. You could modify the Y/N/ESC prompt to accept Y/N/B/ESC, where B would simply rename the existing file before copying the newer file.

SORTING DIRECTORY ENTRIES

UP2DATE builds and sorts in memory an array of all the directory entries that match the arguments specified on the command line. During the build process, UP2DATE calls swap_formats(), which reorders bytes in the date and time fields.

Directory entries contain date and time fields that are each two bytes (sixteen bits) long. When you look at the bit layout, the date field has this format:

```
Bits 15............9  8.....5  4.......0
      y y y y y y y  m m m m  d d d d
```

where *yyyyyyy* is the year, and may contain the value 0-119,
     representing 1980 through 2099
        mmmm is the month and may contain the value 1-12
        ddddd is the day and may contain the value 1-31

Similarly, the time field has this format:

```
Bits 15.....11  10.....5  4.....0
      h h h h h   m m m m  s s s s
```

where *hhhhh* is the hour and may contain the value 0-23
        mmmmmm is the minute and may contain the value 0-59
        sssss is the seconds and may contain the value 0-29

The seconds value is unusual because it must be multiplied by two to get the actual seconds.

The bytes of the data and time fields appear in memory with the least significant bytes in the lower address. When read as a series of bytes, however, the most significant appears (in our left-to-right orientation) to come after the least significant. If you were to view a dump of a directory entry, the bit layout of the date field appears as

```
mmmddddd yyyyyyym
```

and the time as

```
mmmsssss hhhhhmmm
```

Unfortunately, when the bytes are in this order in memory, a string compare cannot be used to compare the contents of the fields. Normally, string compare functions compare two strings, starting at the leftmost byte (the byte at the lowest address in each string) and proceeding to the rightmost byte (the byte at the highest address in each string). The compare proceeds from left to right, comparing corresponding bytes in the two strings until a mismatch is detected or the end of the string is encountered. If there are no mismatches, the strings are equal. Otherwise, the first mismatch determines which string has the greater value. Since the high-order bytes in the date and time fields are to the right of the low-order bytes, the low-order bytes will take precedence, causing the entries to be incorrectly sorted. UP2DATE solves the translation problem by reversing the order of the bytes in the time and date fields before the sort begins.   ■

E N D N O T E

QUALIFYING DOS FILE NAMES

Many times, a utility may accept only an argument that refers to a specific file, and the sum total of the argument checking is to call the open file routine. If the user enters the name of a directory, for example, open returns an error. Or, if the drive letter refers to a floppy drive that contains no disk, the user sees the familiar "Abort, Retry or Fail" message.

UP2DATE circumvents these problems by checking the arguments before putting them to use, using the following steps:

1 *Check if the drive was specified.* Compare the second character in the specification to a colon. If the second character in an argument is a colon, the first must be a drive letter.

When a drive is specified, check the DOS version. DOS versions 3.10 and later have a function (0x4409) that checks if the drive letter is a local or network drive. A side effect of this function sets an error code if the drive specified is invalid. If this function returns a carry flag, the drive is bad, and you can stop here. (If you are using a version of DOS earlier than 3.10, step two will also check that the specified drive is valid, but your program won't be able to distinguish it from a Drive Not Ready error.)

When no drive is specified, assume the current drive.

2 *Check that the drive is ready.* After determining that the drive letter is valid, the drive may not be ready, such as when a floppy drive has no disk inserted. Testing for this requires that you install a DOS critical error handler, as shown in the code. Next, use the _getcwd() function to retrieve the working directory from the drive. If the function fails, something is significantly wrong with the drive; again, you can stop and issue an error message.

3 *Test if a directory was specified.* You can test if an argument refers to a directory by trying to change to the directory with the chdir() function. If chdir() succeeds, you know you've got a directory. If it fails, however, you may still be unsure if the argument is formed properly.

Consider the specification \PGM\TSET\DATA, where the user inadvertently misspelled TEST. When chdir() fails, you might assume that the specification refers to a file, but then the file open would fail because the path \PGM\TSET does not exist. You can check for this condition by removing the part of the specification after the final backslash, and attempting to chdir() to the remaining portion. In the above example, you would remove \DATA, leaving \PGM\TSET. When you attempt to chdir() to this directory, it too will fail, and you will know you have a bad path. If the entry is specified properly (\PGM\TEST\DATA), and the first chdir() fails, but the chdir() to \PGM\TEST succeeds, you can assume that DATA is a file (or will be a file) in the \PGM\TEST directory.

Another test you can apply to an operand when testing for a directory is to scan the argument for the wildcard characters ? and *. If either of these wildcard characters appears anywhere in the argument, it is unlikely that the argument is a directory specification. Of course, wildcard characters can be used when specifying directories, but the use and effect of such arguments will vary with the functions of the utility. In this case, you may still want to check the path preceding the wildcard specification.

■

UP2DATE 1.00

```
/* ********************************************************************* *

   UP2DATE 1.00, Copyright (c) 1992, Michael Holmes and Bob Flanders
   PC Magazine C Lab Notes, Update a target directory from many sources

 * ********************************************************************* */

This code is for Borland C++ version 3.0. (MSC version on diskette)

Compile with: BCC -O2-i -mc -N up2date.c

To compile for Microsoft C, you need to change the following:

        - add a #include for sys\types.h
        - change memory allocation scheme for _fmalloc(), farrealloc()
           and coreleft() routines
        - change call for creatnew()
        - change control break handling for ctrlbrk() and control_break()
        - remove #pragma statements preceding critical_handler()

 * ********************************************************************* */

#include <stdio.h>                      /* standard i/o library      */
#include <io.h>                         /* i/o routine headers       */
#include <stdlib.h>                     /* ANSI compatibility        */
#include <dos.h>                        /* DOS rtn definitions       */
#include <direct.h>                     /* directory routines        */
#include <malloc.h>                     /* memory declarations       */
#include <string.h>                     /* string functions          */
#include <ctype.h>                      /* character functions       */
#include <conio.h>                      /* console i/o routines      */
#include <fcntl.h>                      /* file control header       */
#include <sys\stat.h>                   /* file status header        */

#define NOT !                           /* logical not               */
#define ANY(x,y) strcspn(x,y) != strlen(x) /* any matching characters? */
#define CLEAR(s,c) memset(s,c,sizeof(s))   /* string clear            */
#define LAST(x) x[strlen(x) - 1]        /* get last char in string   */
#define UINT unsigned int               /* unsigned integer type     */
#define D_ENTRY  struct directory_entry /* shorthand for dir entry   */
#define MAX_PATH 79                     /* max path length           */
#define BUF_SIZE 16384                  /* copy buffer size          */
#define RESERVED 25000                  /* reserved memory from top  */
#define FILE_ATTR _A_NORMAL | _A_RDONLY /* file attrib to search on  */


/* ********************************************************************* *
 *        routine definitions
 * ********************************************************************* */

void    quit_with(int, char *),         /* quit with error message   */
        file_error(char *, char *),     /* file error terminations   */
        check_dirs(void),               /* check for directories     */
```

```
        *cln_malloc(long),                      /* allocate memory            */
        keepalive(int),                         /* give keepalive blips       */
        keep_level(int),                        /* handle keepalive levels    */
        merge_list(void),                       /* merge directories          */
        normalize_list(void),                   /* convert back to intel fmt*/
        execute_list(void),                     /* copy files on list         */
        build_entry(D_ENTRY *, int, int),       /* build internal dir entry */
        give_file_info(D_ENTRY huge *,          /* display file information */
            char *, int),
        fix_up_dirs(void),                      /* fix up directory lists     */
        swap_formats(char huge *),              /* swap internal formats      */
        interrupt critical_handler(UINT,        /* critical error handler     */
            UINT, UINT, UINT, UINT, UINT,
            UINT, UINT, UINT, UINT, UINT,
            UINT),
        sort(char huge *, long, int,            /* sort an array of elements*/
            int (*)(char huge *, char huge *)),
        sort_subfile(char huge *,               /* sort a subfile             */
            char huge *),
        sort_exchange(char huge *,              /* exchange table elements    */
            char huge *);
int     sort_d_entry(char huge *,               /* compare an element         */
            char huge *),
        (*sort_fcompare)(char huge *,           /* sort's compare routine     */
            char huge *),
        parse_parms(int, char **, int,          /* parse command line         */
            struct cmd_parm *, char ***),
        delete_file(char *),                    /* delete a file              */
        overwrite_prompt(void),                 /* prompt for overwrite       */
        control_break(void);                    /* control break handler      */
char    *join_path(char *, char *),             /* join a path and filespec */
        *format_list(D_ENTRY *),                /* format a dir entry         */
        *validate_name(char *, char *);         /* validate file/dir name     */
long    max_d_entrys(void),                     /* max memory for d_entry's */
        read_list(int, D_ENTRY huge *);         /* read a directory           */


/* ******************************************************************** *
 *      command line parms and switches                                 *
 * ******************************************************************** */

char    sw_test,                                /* switch parameters          */
        sw_freshen,
        sw_owrite;

struct  cmd_parm                                /* command line parm          */
    {
    char cp_ltr,                                /* switch letter              */
        *cp_entry;                              /* pointer to data            */
    };

struct  cmd_parm parm_table[] =                 /* UP2DATE's cmd line parms */
    {
    { 'T', &sw_test },                          /* T - test option            */
    { 'F', &sw_freshen },                       /* F - freshen option         */
    { 'O', &sw_owrite },                        /* O - overwrite option       */
    };

                                                /* number of table entries    */
#define PARM_TABLE_CNT  sizeof(parm_table) / sizeof(struct cmd_parm)
```

```
/* **************************************************************** *
 *      globals                                                     *
 * **************************************************************** */

int     pos_found,                          /* number positionals found */
        target_dir,                         /* target dir index         */
        init_drive,                         /* startup drive            */
        blip_freq = 50,                     /* frequency of keepalives  */
        sort_width,                         /* sort record size         */
        sort_level = 0;                     /* current recursion level  */

char    **pos_parms,                        /* positional parms array   */
        *dir_flags,                         /* directory/filemask flags */
        *init_path;                         /* startup drive and path   */

long    files_cnt,                          /* number in files_list     */
        max_cnt,                            /* available entries in tbl */
        sort_threshold;                     /* shellsort threshold      */

long    shell_cyc,                          /* entries per pass         */
        shell_adj;                          /* pointer adj amount       */
char    huge *shell_i, huge *shell_j,       /* sort work pointers       */
        huge *shell_limit;                  /* loop limit register      */

union   REGS r;                             /* cpu registers            */
struct  find_t dos_entry;                   /* DOS directory entry      */


/* **************************************************************** *
 *      messages and strings                                        *
 * **************************************************************** */

char    copyright[]     = "UP2DATE 1.00 \xfe Copyright (c) 1992, "
                          "Michael Holmes and Bob Flanders\n"
                          "PC Magazine C Lab Notes \xfe "
                          "Update a target directory from many "
                          "sources\n\n",
        *bad_drive[]    = { "Invalid drive %s\n",
                          "Drive not ready %s\n",
                          "Bad file specification %s\n" },
        no_target[]     = "No target directory specified\n",
        bad_op[]        = "Invalid parameter %s\n",
        must_be[]       = " must be a directory\n",
        empty_list[]    = "No files to process\n",
        all_current[]   = "Target is up to date\n",
        no_mem[]        = "Insufficient memory to continue processing\n",
        no_source[]     = "\b-- No source files found\n",
        no_freshens[]   = "\b-- No target files to freshen\n",
        file_exists[]   = "\nFile exists in target directory, "
                          "overwrite? (Y/N/Esc)  ",
        stop_here[]     = "\nStopping at user's request\n",
        test_mode[]     = "Test mode in effect, no files copied\n",
        totals[]        = "Completed: %ld file%s copied to %s\n",
        reading[]       = "  Reading: %s  ",
        sorting[]       = "  Sorting:  ",
        merging[]       = "  Merging:  ",
        copying[]       = "  Copying",
        over_writing[]  = "\nOverwrite",
        sort_done[]     = "\b%lu entries sorted\n",
        merge_done[]    = "\b%lu files selected\n",
        open_error[]    = "\nError opening file (%s)\n",
        read_error[]    = "\nError reading file (%s)\n",
        write_error[]   = "\nError writing file (%s)\n",
```

```
    format[]        = "%-35.35s%10ld   %02d/%02d/%04d   %02d:%02d",
    info_msg[]      = "%s: %s   ",
    new_line[]      = "\n",
    null_line[]     = "",
    help[]          =
      "  Usage:  UP2DATE source1 [source2 [...]] target [options]"
      "\n\n"
      "  Where:   source = d:\n"
      "                    [d:]path\n"
      "                    [d:]filename.ext\n"
      "                    [d:]path\\filename.ext\n\n"
      "           target = d:\n"
      "                    [d:]path\n\n"
      "Options: /T  shows files that would be copied; no files "
      "are actually copied\n"
      "         /F  only copies files that already exist in the "
      "target directory\n"
      "             /O  overwrites older files in target without "
      "prompting\n";


/* ********************************************************************* *
 *      structures                                                      *
 * ********************************************************************* */

D_ENTRY                                 /* directory entry          */
    {
    char file_name[13];                 /* filename                 */
    UINT fdate,                         /* file date                */
         ftime;                         /* ..time                   */
    long fsize;                         /* ..and size               */
    char pf_index;                      /* directory index nbr      */
    char file_attrib;                   /* file attribute           */
    } huge *files_list;                 /* final list               */


/* ********************************************************************* *
 *      main()                                                          *
 * ********************************************************************* */

int     main(int  ac,                   /* DOS cmd line token count */
             char *av[])                /* ..token strings          */
{
int     i;                              /* loop counter             */


printf(copyright);                      /* display copyright msg    */

ctrlbrk(control_break);                 /* set up ctrl break and    */
_dos_setvect(0x24, critical_handler);   /* ..DOS critical handlers  */
_dos_getdrive((UINT *) &init_drive);    /* get the default drive    */

if (ac == 1)                            /* q. need help?            */
    quit_with(0, help);                 /* a. yes .. give help msg  */


/* ********************** *
 *  validate parameters   *
 * ********************** */

pos_found = parse_parms(ac, av,         /* parse switches and       */
        PARM_TABLE_CNT, parm_table,     /* ..positional parameters  */
        &pos_parms);
```

```c
    if (pos_found < 2)                        /* q. no target directory?  */
        quit_with(0, no_target);              /* a. yes .. give err/quit  */

    check_dirs();                             /* check accessibility ..   */
                                              /* ..to directories         */


/* *********************** *
 *  build the list of files  *
 * *********************** */

    max_cnt = max_d_entrys();                 /* get max nbr of entries   */
    files_list = (D_ENTRY *) cln_malloc(      /* build a big array of ..  */
            sizeof(D_ENTRY) * max_cnt);       /* ..file entries to start  */

    for (i = 0; i < pos_found; i++)           /* for each directory ..    */
        files_cnt += read_list(i,             /* build part of the list   */
                &files_list[files_cnt]);      /* ..and tally files count  */

    sort((char *) files_list, files_cnt,      /* sort into filename order */
            sizeof(D_ENTRY), sort_d_entry);

    merge_list();                             /* select files to process  */


/* ***************** *
 *  process the list  *
 * ***************** */

    normalize_list();                         /* convert nbrs to intel fmt*/
    fix_up_dirs();                            /* fix up directory names   */
    execute_list();                           /* process files in list    */

    return(0);                                /* rtn with errorlevel = 0  */

    }



/* ********************************************************************* *
 *        check_dirs() -- check availability of directory              *
 * ********************************************************************* */

void    check_dirs()
{
int     i;                                    /* loop count               */
char    *p;                                   /* work pointer             */


    dir_flags = (char *) malloc(pos_found);   /* allocate for flag array  */

    for (i = 0; i < pos_found; i++)           /* for each directory       */
        if ((p = validate_name(pos_parms[i],  /* q. valid file/directory? */
                &dir_flags[i])) != 0)
            pos_parms[i] = strdup(p);         /* a. yes .. save for later */
        else
            {
            printf(bad_drive[dir_flags[i]+3], /* else .. give error msg   */
                pos_parms[i]);
            quit_with(0, null_line);          /* ..and gracefully quit    */
            }

    target_dir = pos_found - 1;               /* set up target index nbr  */
```

```
    if (dir_flags[target_dir])                  /* q. last one a directory? */
        {
        printf(pos_parms[target_dir]);          /* a. no .. give dir name   */
        quit_with(0, must_be);                  /* ..and error message      */
        }
    }


/* ********************************************************************** *
 *       read_list() -- read and build a directory list                 *
 * ********************************************************************** */

long    read_list(int pf_nbr,                   /* index of dir to search   */
                  D_ENTRY huge *w)              /* where to put next entry  */
{
long    i = 0;                                  /* loop count / nbr entries */
int     rc;                                     /* return code              */
char    working_path[MAX_PATH];                 /* path and files mask      */


strcpy(working_path, pos_parms[pf_nbr]);        /* copy in base path        */

if (NOT dir_flags[pf_nbr])                      /* q. directory?            */
    strcpy(working_path,                        /* a. yes .. add the *.*    */
           join_path(working_path, "*.*"));

printf(reading, working_path);                  /* inform the user          */

for (rc = _dos_findfirst(working_path,          /* find first and next file */
            FILE_ATTR, &dos_entry);             /* ..'til done all done     */
            NOT rc && max_cnt;                  /* ..or out of space        */
            i++, max_cnt--, w++)                /* keep track of ptr & cnts */
    {
    build_entry((D_ENTRY *) w, pf_nbr, 1);      /* build internal fmt entry */
    keepalive(0);                               /* do keepalive messages    */
    rc = _dos_findnext(&dos_entry);             /* ..then try to find next  */
    }

if (NOT i)                                       /* q. empty directory?      */
    {                                           /* a. yes .. determine msg  */
    if (pf_nbr != target_dir)                   /* q. target directory?     */
        printf(no_source);                      /* a. no .. print msg       */

    else if (sw_freshen)                        /* q. freshen target empty? */
        printf(no_freshens);                    /* a. yes .. give msg       */

    else                                        /* if it's ok to be empty.. */
        keepalive(1);                           /* ..just clean up k/a msgs */
    }
 else
    keepalive(1);                               /* clean up user display    */

if (NOT max_cnt)                                /* q. run out of space?     */
    quit_with(0, no_mem);                       /* a. yes .. give error msg */

return(i);                                      /* send back nbr of files   */

}
```

```
/* ********************************************************************** *
 *      merge_list -- weed out dupes and older versions of files        *
 * ********************************************************************** */
void    merge_list(void)
{
int     fresh_flag = 0;                     /* freshen selected file    */
long    i;                                  /* loop control             */
D_ENTRY huge *from,                         /* source pointer           */
        huge *to,                           /* destination pointer      */
        huge *work;                         /* match pointer            */

if (NOT (i = files_cnt))                    /* q. no files at all?      */
    quit_with(0, empty_list);               /* a. yes .. give err/quit  */

work = to = from = files_list;              /* set up pointers          */

printf(merging);                            /* tell user where we are   */

for (work++, files_cnt = 0; --i;)           /* loop thru files array    */
    {
    if (strncmp((char *) work,              /* q. different filename?   */
        (char *) from,
        sizeof(work->file_name)))
        {                                   /* a. yes .. process "from" */
        if (from->pf_index != target_dir)   /* q. from source directory?*/
            {                               /* a. yes .. check usability*/
            if ((sw_freshen && fresh_flag)  /* q. satisfy freshen?      */
                || NOT sw_freshen)          /* ..or just in add mode    */
                {
                files_cnt++;                /* a. yes .. bump final cnt */
                memcpy((char *) to++,       /* ..and move entry to top  */
                    (char *) from, sizeof(D_ENTRY));
                }
            }

        fresh_flag = 0;                     /* clear fnd on target flag */
        from = work++;                      /* set up for next entry    */
        }

    else
        {
        if (from->pf_index == target_dir)   /* q. target directory?     */
            fresh_flag = 1;                 /* a. yes .. set flag       */

        from = work++;                      /* set up for next compare  */
        }
    }

if (from->pf_index != target_dir)           /* q. last a source file?   */
    {                                       /* a. yes .. process it     */
    if ((sw_freshen && fresh_flag)          /* q. satisfy freshen?      */
        || NOT sw_freshen)                  /* ..or just in add mode    */
        {
        files_cnt++;                        /* a. yes .. bump final cnt */
        memcpy((char *) to, (char *) from,  /* ..and move last entry .. */
            sizeof(D_ENTRY));               /* ..to top of files_list   */
        }
    }

printf(merge_done, files_cnt);              /* give completion stats    */
```

```
    if (NOT files_cnt)                      /* q. any files left?       */
        quit_with(0, all_current);          /* a. no .. give msg/quit   */

    }


/* ******************************************************************** *
 *      execute_list() -- copy files based on file list                 *
 * ******************************************************************** */

void    execute_list(void)
{
long    i, j = 0,                           /* loop counter             */
        f_size;                             /* filesize downcounter     */
D_ENTRY huge *w,                            /* work pointer             */
        ow_entry;                           /* overwrite entry          */
int     i_file,                             /* input file handle        */
        o_file,                             /* output file handle       */
        b_read;                             /* bytes read               */
char    from_string[MAX_PATH],              /* from filename            */
        to_string[MAX_PATH],                /* to filename              */
        *buf;                               /* i/o buffer               */


blip_freq = 1;                              /* change blip frequency    */
buf = (char *) cln_malloc(BUF_SIZE);        /* get i/o buffer           */
_fmode = O_BINARY;                          /* set global for bin files */

for (w = files_list, i = 0;                 /* loop thru list           */
        i < files_cnt; i++, w++)
    {
    if (i != 0)                             /* q. not 1st cycle?        */
        keepalive(1);                       /* a. yes .. clear k/a msg  */

    strcpy(from_string, join_path(          /* build fully qualified .. */
            pos_parms[w->pf_index],         /* ..from filename          */
            w->file_name));

    strcpy(to_string, join_path(            /* build fully qualified .. */
            pos_parms[target_dir],          /* ..to filename            */
            w->file_name));

    give_file_info(w, copying, 1);          /* put out info on file     */

    if (sw_test)                            /* q. test mode?            */
        continue;                           /* a. yes .. continue       */

    if ((i_file = open(from_string,         /* q. open input ok?        */
            O_BINARY | O_RDONLY | S_IREAD)) == -1)
        file_error(read_error, from_string);/* a. no .. give error/quit */

    if ((o_file = creatnew(to_string,       /* q. create ok?            */
            w->file_attrib)) == -1)
        {                                   /* a. no .. handle error    */
        if (NOT sw_owrite)                  /* q. overwrite enabled?    */
            {                               /* a. no .. give user info  */
            if (NOT _dos_findfirst(         /* q. can we get file info? */
                    to_string, FILE_ATTR,
                    &dos_entry))
                {
                build_entry(&ow_entry,      /* a. yes .. build std form */
                    target_dir, 0);
```

```
                    give_file_info(&ow_entry,     /* ..tell about target file */
                        over_writing, 1);
                    }

            if (overwrite_prompt())               /* q. bypass this file?    */
                {
                close(i_file);                    /* a. yes .. close file    */
                continue;                         /* ..then continue         */
                }
            }

        delete_file(to_string);                   /* delete/unlink file      */

        if ((o_file = creatnew(to_string,         /* q. create this time?    */
                w->file_attrib)) == -1)
            file_error(open_error,                /* a. no .. give error msg */
                to_string);
            }

    for (f_size = w->fsize;                        /* loop reading/writing file*/
            ((b_read = read(i_file, buf, BUF_SIZE)) != -1);
            f_size -= b_read)
        {
        if (NOT b_read)                           /* q. at end of file?      */
            break;                                /* a. yes .. exit loop     */

        if (b_read != write(o_file, buf, b_read))   /* q. write ok?        */
            file_error(write_error, from_string);   /* a. no .. give err*/

        keepalive(0);                             /* keep user informed      */
        }

    if (b_read == -1 || f_size)                    /* q. error|didn't finish? */
        file_error(read_error, to_string);        /* a. yes .. give err/quit */

    _dos_setftime(o_file,                         /* set file's date and time */
        w->fdate, w->ftime);

    _dos_setfileattr(to_string,                   /* ..and file's attributes */
        w->file_attrib);

    close(o_file);                                /* close output file       */
    close(i_file);                                /* ..and input file        */

    j++;                                          /* count as processed file */
    }

keepalive(1);                                     /* clean up keepalive msgs */

printf(totals, j, j == 1 ? "" : "s",              /* give totals and counts  */
    pos_parms[target_dir]);

if (sw_test)                                      /* q. test mode?           */
    printf(test_mode);                            /* a. yes .. give disclaimer*/

}


/* ****************************************************************** *
 *      overwrite_prompt() -- give overwrite prompt; wait for response  *
 * ****************************************************************** */

int     overwrite_prompt()                        /* 0 = ok to overwrite     */
```

```
{
int     reply;                              /* reply to prompt          */

printf(file_exists);                        /* give request to overwrite*/

while (1)                                   /* loop 'til good answer    */
    {
    reply = getch();                        /* get a good response      */

    switch (toupper(reply))                 /* handle user's response   */
        {
        case 'Y':                           /* Y = yes                  */
            printf("Yes  ");                /* show user's response     */
            return(0);                      /* overwrite file on return */

        case 0x1b:                          /* ESC = escape             */
            quit_with(0, stop_here);        /* give msg and quit        */

        default:                            /* all else, assume no      */
            printf("No  ");                 /* show user's response     */
            return(1);                      /* do not overwrite on rtn  */
        }
    }
}


/* ********************************************************************* *
 *      build_entry() -- build internal directory entry                *
 * ********************************************************************* */

void    build_entry(D_ENTRY *w,             /* target directory entry   */
                    int    dir_nbr,         /* ..and directory index    */
                    int    flag)            /* swap bytes into high/low */
{
strncpy((char *)w->file_name,               /* pick up filename         */
            dos_entry.name, 13);
w->pf_index = dir_nbr;                       /* ..directory nbr          */
w->file_attrib = dos_entry.attrib;          /* ..and attribute          */
w->fdate = dos_entry.wr_date;               /* .. file date             */
w->ftime = dos_entry.wr_time;               /* ..time                   */
w->fsize = dos_entry.size;                  /* ..and size               */

if (flag)
    swap_formats((char huge *) &w->fdate);  /* swap formats for sorting */

}



/* ********************************************************************* *
 *      give_file_info() -- tell how file is processed                 *
 * ********************************************************************* */

void    give_file_info(D_ENTRY huge *w,     /* entry to display         */
                       char *s,             /* status string            */
                       int  flag)           /* flag, 0=fmt swap needed  */
{

if (flag)                                   /* q. need info lines?      */
```

```
      printf(info_msg,                        /* a. yes .. display numbers*/
              s, format_list((D_ENTRY *) w));

else
      keepalive(0);                           /* else .. give k/a msgs    */

}



/* ****************************************************************** *
 *      format_list() -- format a directory entry for display        *
 * ****************************************************************** */

char    *format_list(D_ENTRY *d)              /* directory entry pointer  */
{
static
char    f_string[80];                         /* formatted string         */

sprintf(f_string, format,
          join_path(pos_parms[d->pf_index], d->file_name),
          d->fsize, (d->fdate >> 5) & 0xf, d->fdate & 0x1f,
          ((d->fdate >> 9) & 0x7f)+ 1980,
          (d->ftime >> 11) & 0x1f, (d->ftime >> 5) & 0x3f);

return(f_string);

}



/* ****************************************************************** *
 *      normalize_list() -- change back to Intel formatted nbrs      *
 * ****************************************************************** */

void    normalize_list(void)
{
long    i;                                    /* loop counter             */
D_ENTRY huge *w;                              /* directory entry work ptr */

for (w = files_list, i = 0;                   /* do each remaining entry  */
            i < files_cnt; i++, w++)          /* ..on the list            */
    swap_formats((char *) &w->fdate);         /* swap the nbrs back ar'nd */

}



/* ****************************************************************** *
 *      fix_up_dirs() -- fix up directory lists                      *
 * ****************************************************************** */

void    fix_up_dirs(void)
{
int     i;                                    /* loop counter             */
char    *p, *q;                               /* string pointers          */

for (i = 0; i < pos_found; i++)               /* check each positional    */
    {
    p = pos_parms[i];                         /* get a positional parm    */
```

```
        if ((dir_flags[i] == 1) &&          /* q. filename entry?      */
              ((q = strrchr(p, '\\')) != 0))  /* ..and find the last '\'? */
          *++q = 0;                          /* a. yes .. kill path there*/
        }
    }


/* ********************************************************************* *
 *       sort() -- Hoare's Quicksort                                     *
 * ********************************************************************* */

void    sort(char huge *m,                   /* array to be sorted      */
            long nbr_recs,                   /* number of records       */
            int  width,                      /* size of one element     */
            int  (*fcompare)(char huge *,    /* comparison routine      */
                  char huge *))
{
long    i;                                   /* loop counter            */
char    huge *n,                             /* ptr to end of array     */
        huge *smallest, huge *largest,       /* pointers to min and max */
        huge *p;                             /* work pointer            */

if (nbr_recs < 2)                            /* q. enough to work with? */
    return;                                  /* a. no .. just return    */

printf(sorting);                             /* put out header message  */
blip_freq = 1000;                            /* keepalive frequency     */

n = m + (nbr_recs - 1) * width;              /* find last record in array*/

sort_width = width;                          /* save record size        */
sort_fcompare = fcompare;                    /* ..and compare routine   */
sort_threshold = sort_width * 50;            /* ..shellsort threshold   */

smallest = m;                                /* set up for min key      */
largest  = n;                                /* ..and max key           */

for (p = m, i = nbr_recs; i;                 /* loop thru to find the.. */
          i--, p += sort_width)              /* ..min and max keys      */
    {
    if ((*sort_fcompare)(p, largest) > 0)    /* q. work > largest?      */
        largest = p;                         /* a. yes .. save pointer  */

    if ((*sort_fcompare)(p, smallest) < 0)   /* q. work < smallest?     */
        smallest = p;                        /* a. yes .. save pointer  */
    }

sort_exchange(m, smallest);                  /* move smallest to front*/
sort_exchange(n, m == largest ?              /* ..and largest to end    */
          smallest : largest);

sort_subfile(m, n);                          /* sort whole array..      */
printf(sort_done, nbr_recs);                 /* ..tell how big it is     */

}


/* ********************************************************************* *
 *       sort_subfile() -- sort a group of items                         *
 * ********************************************************************* */

void    sort_subfile(char huge *m,           /* array to be sorted      */
                    char huge *n)            /* last record in array    */
```

```
{
char    huge *i, huge *j;                        /* work pointers           */

if (m >= n)                                      /* q. anything to sort?    */
    return;                                      /* a. no .. return         */

keep_level(++sort_level / 16);                   /* handle recursion display */

if ((n - m) < sort_threshold ||                  /* q. only bunch of entries?*/
        sort_level > 100)                        /* ..or we're in too deep? */
    {                                            /* a. yes .. do a shellsort */
    shell_cyc = (n - m) / sort_width + 1;        /* number of recs in subfile*/

    while (shell_cyc /= 2)                        /* do half per pass        */
        {
        shell_adj = shell_cyc * sort_width;      /* compute skip amount     */
        shell_limit = n - shell_adj;             /* ..determine limit pointer*/

        for (shell_j = m;                        /* move down array one     */
            shell_j <= shell_limit;              /* ..record at a time      */
            shell_j += sort_width)
            {
            for (shell_i = shell_j;              /* and start compares by   */
                shell_i >= m;                    /* ..working backwards     */
                shell_i -= shell_adj)
                {
                keepalive(0);                    /* give keepalive msg      */

                if ((*sort_fcompare)             /* q. in order?            */
                        (shell_i + shell_adj,
                        shell_i) >= 0)
                    break;                       /* a. yes .. exit loop     */

                  else
                    sort_exchange(               /* else .. swap entries    */
                        shell_i + shell_adj,
                        shell_i);
                }
            }
        }
    }

  else
    {
    i = m + (((n - m) / sort_width) / 2)         /* pick a pivot point      */
                * sort_width;                    /* ..for "median of 3"     */

    if ((*sort_fcompare)(m, i) > 0)              /* q. left end > pivot?    */
        sort_exchange(m, i);                     /* a. yes .. swap elements */

    if ((*sort_fcompare)(m, n) > 0)              /* q. left end > right end? */
        sort_exchange(m, n);                     /* a. yes .. swap around   */

    if ((*sort_fcompare)(i, n) > 0)              /* q. pivot > right end?   */
        sort_exchange(i, n);                     /* a. yes .. swap elements */

    i = m;                                       /* set up quicksort's      */
    j = n + sort_width;                          /* ..work pointers         */

    while(1)
        {
        for (i += sort_width;                    /* walk down from ..       */
```

```
                    (*sort_fcompare)(i, m) < 0;      /* ..left side of array     */
                    i += sort_width)
                    keepalive(0);                    /* give keepalive msg       */

              for (j -= sort_width;                  /* walk up from right ..    */
                    (*sort_fcompare)(j, m) > 0;      /* ..side of array          */
                    j -= sort_width)
                    keepalive(0);                    /* give keepalive msg       */

              if (j <= i)                            /* q. loop thru again?      */
                    break;                           /* a. no .. exit loop       */
                else
                    sort_exchange(i, j);             /* exchange end points      */
                }

          sort_exchange(m, j);                       /* place partition element  */
          sort_subfile(m, j - sort_width);           /* sort left half subfile   */
          sort_subfile(j + sort_width, n);           /* ..and right half subfile */
          }

    keep_level(--sort_level / 16);                   /* clean up keep alive msgs */

    }


/* ****************************************************************** *
 *        sort_exchange() -- swap two sort records                  *
 * ****************************************************************** */

void    sort_exchange(char huge *a,                  /* memory to be swapped     */
                      char huge *b)                  /* ..byte at a time         */
{
int     count;                                       /* loop counter             */
char    temp;                                        /* hold area                */

for (count = sort_width; count--; )                  /* do until count exhausted */
    {
    temp = *a;                                       /* save 1st byte            */
    *a++ = *b;                                        /* move 2nd to 1st          */
    *b++ = temp;                                      /* ..then move 1st to 2nd   */
    }

}


/* ****************************************************************** *
 *        sort_compare() -- helper routine for sort                 *
 * ****************************************************************** */

int     sort_d_entry(char huge *s1, char huge *s2)
{

return(_fmemcmp((const void *) s1,              /* compare entries in array */
        (const void *) s2, sizeof(D_ENTRY)));

}


/* ****************************************************************** *
 *        parse_parms() -- parse command line parms                 *
 * ****************************************************************** */

int     parse_parms(int  ac,                         /* argument count           */
```

```
                        char *av[],             /* command line arguments  */
                        int  n,                 /* parse table entries     */
                        struct cmd_parm *t,     /* cmd line parse table     */
                        char ***parms_array)    /* positional parms array   */
{
int     i, j,                                   /* loop counter             */
        parms_fnd = 0,                          /* positional parms found   */
        slash_fnd = 0;                          /* slash found in token     */
char    *p, *q,                                 /* character pointers       */
        c;                                      /* work character           */


*parms_array = (char **) cln_malloc(           /* set up for max nbr tokens*/
        sizeof(char *) * ac);

for (i = 1; i < ac; i++)                        /* for each cmd line token  */
    {
    p = av[i];                                  /* set up pointer to token  */

    while (*p)                                  /* process token            */
        {
        if (*p == '/' || slash_fnd)             /* q. option?               */
            {
            if (NOT slash_fnd)                  /* q. embedded slash?       */
                p++;                            /* a. no .. bump past slash */

            c = toupper(*p);                    /* get char and upcase it   */
            slash_fnd = 0;                      /* reset switch             */

            if (c == '?')                       /* q. help request?         */
                quit_with(0, help);             /* a. yes .. give help ..   */

            for (j = 0; j < n; j++)             /* check each table entry   */
                if (c == t[j].cp_ltr)           /* q. find match?           */
                    break;                      /* a. yes .. exit loop      */

            if (j == n)                         /* q. no matches?           */
                {                               /* a. no .. process error   */
                if ((q = strchr(p, '/'))        /* q. any more switches?    */
                        != 0)
                    *q = 0;                     /* a. yes .. isolate bad one*/

                printf(bad_op, --p);            /* ..give error message     */
                quit_with(0, null_line);        /* ..and exit w/errorlevel  */
                }

            (*t[j].cp_entry)++;                 /* show slash parm used     */
            p++;                                /* ..and point at next one  */
            }

        else
            {
            (*parms_array)[parms_fnd++] = p;/* save positional string   */

            if (*(p += strcspn(p, "/")))        /* q. any switches left?    */
                {
                *p++ = 0;                       /* a. yes .. make a string  */
                slash_fnd = 1;                  /* ..show nxt char a switch */
                }
            }
        }

    }
```

```
*parms_array = (char **) farrealloc(          /* readjust array size   */
              *parms_array,                   /* ..for what was found   */
              sizeof(char *) * parms_fnd);

return(parms_fnd);                            /* rtn w/nbr of positionals */

}



/* ******************************************************************** *
 *        cln_malloc() -- local malloc w/error handling               *
 * ******************************************************************** */

void    *cln_malloc(long size)                /* amount of memory to get  */
{
void    *p;                                   /* temporary pointer        */

if (NOT (p = (void *) _fmalloc(size)))        /* q. enough memory?        */
    {
    printf(no_mem);                           /* a. no .. give error msg  */
    exit(1);                                  /* ..and quit               */
    }

return(p);                                    /* else .. return w/address */

}



/* ******************************************************************** *
 *        max_d_entrys() -- compute max available memory for d_entry's *
 * ******************************************************************** */

long    max_d_entrys()
{

return((coreleft() - RESERVED)                /* rtn nbr of entries   */
       / sizeof(D_ENTRY));

}



/* ******************************************************************** *
 *        file_error() -- give file related error message then quit   *
 * ******************************************************************** */

void    file_error(char *msg,                 /* message format       */
               char *filename)                /* filename argument    */
{

printf(msg, filename);                        /* give error message .. */
exit(1);                                      /* ..and then quit       */

}



/* ******************************************************************** *
 *        quit_with() -- give an error message, then return to DOS    *
 * ******************************************************************** */

void    quit_with(int ka_flag,                /* give keepalive message */
               char *msg)                     /* string to print        */
```

```
{

if (ka_flag)                                /* q. need to clean up?      */
    keepalive(1);                           /* a. yes .. clear k/a msg   */

printf(msg);                                /* give error message ..     */
exit(1);                                    /* ..and then quit           */

}



/* ****************************************************************** *
 *        keepalive() -- put out a keepalive blip to the user       *
 * ****************************************************************** */

void    keepalive(int flag)                 /* 0=next blip, 1=clean up   */
{
static
int     b_cnt = 0,                          /* blip counter              */
        b_call = 0;                         /* raw counter               */
static
char    blips[] = "|/-\\",                  /* progress blips            */
        blip_fmt[]    = "\b%c",             /* message format            */
        blip_clean[]  = "\b ";              /* clean up message          */

if (flag)                                   /* q. clean up call?         */
    {
    fprintf(stderr, blip_clean);            /* a. yes .. erase blip..    */
    printf(new_line);                       /* ..force a new line        */
    b_call = 0;                             /* ..and reset counter       */
    }

 else
    if (NOT (b_call++ % blip_freq))         /* q. called enough times?   */
        fprintf(stderr, blip_fmt,           /* a. yes .. put next spoke  */
            blips[b_cnt++ & 3]);            /* ..to simulate a wheel     */

}



/* ****************************************************************** *
 *        keep_level() -- keep track of levels for keepalive msgs    *
 * ****************************************************************** */

void    keep_level(int new_level)           /* new level                 */
{
static
int     level = 0;                          /* last level known          */

for(; new_level < level; level--)           /* back up as many levels..  */
    printf("\b \b");                        /* ..by blanking old chars   */

for(; new_level > level; level++)           /* move over for new levels  */
    printf("-");

}
```

```
/* ********************************************************************** *
 *        swap_formats() -- swap between normal and intel integer format  *
 * ********************************************************************** */

void     swap_formats(char huge *p)            /* area to be converted    */
{
int      work;                                 /* work variable           */

swab((char *) p, (char *) p, 8);               /* swap bytes around       */

work = *(int *)(p + 4);                        /* then swap high ..       */
*(int *)(p + 4) = *(int *)(p + 6);             /* ..and low words of ..   */
*(int *)(p + 6) = work;                        /* ..file size around      */

}



/* ********************************************************************** *
 *        delete_file() -- delete file any way necessary                  *
 * ********************************************************************** */

int      delete_file(char *s)                  /* filename to delete      */
{
int      rc;                                   /* return code, 0=ok       */

if ((rc = unlink(s)) != 0)                     /* q. regular file unlink? */
    if (NOT (rc = chmod(s, S_IWRITE)))         /* a. no .. q. change ok?  */
        rc = unlink(s);                        /* a. yes .. try again     */

return(rc);                                    /* return w/final status   */

}



/* ********************************************************************** *
 *        validate_name() -- validate file/dir name                       *
 * ********************************************************************** */

char     *validate_name(char *name,            /* source file/dir name    */
                        char *rc)              /* return code             */
                                               /*  -3 = invalid drive     */
                                               /*  -2 = drive not ready   */
                                               /*  -1 = invalid name      */
                                               /*   0 = directory         */
                                               /*   1 = filespec          */
{
int      i,                                    /* work variable           */
         drive;                                /* drive number            */
static
char     full[MAX_PATH];                       /* normalized full name    */
char     *p,                                   /* work pointer            */
         c,                                    /* character holder        */
         work[MAX_PATH],                       /* work field              */
         current_path[MAX_PATH];               /* current path            */

full[0] = 0;                                   /* initialize return string */
CLEAR(work, 0);                                /* clear to nulls          */
```

```
strcpy(work, name);                          /* copy source local       */
i = strlen(work) - 1;                         /* ..and pick up length    */

if (work[i] == '\\' && i                      /* q. more than drive:\?   */
        && (i > 2 || work[1] != ':'))         /* ..or other trailing \?  */
    work[i] = 0;                              /* a. yes .. remove last \  */

drive = (work[1] == ':') ?                    /* get name's drive number */
            toupper(work[0]) - 'A' + 1 : 0;

if ((_osmajor == 3 && _osminor >= 1) ||       /* q. DOS 3.1 or higher?   */
        (_osmajor > 3))
    {
    r.x.ax = 0x4409;                          /* a. yes .. do local test */
    r.h.bl = drive;                           /* bl = drive to test      */
    int86(0x21, &r, &r);                      /* test drive validity     */

    if (r.x.cflag)                            /* q. bad drive?           */
        {
        *rc = -3;                             /* a. yes .. set return code*/
        return(0);                            /* ..and return to caller  */
        }
    }

if (NOT (_getdcwd(drive, current_path,        /* q. accessible drive?    */
        MAX_PATH)))
    {
    *rc = -2;                                 /* a. no .. set error return*/
    return(0);                                /* ..and return to caller  */
    }

*rc = -1;                                     /* set up for error return */

if (chdir(work))                              /* q. a directory?         */
    {   if ((p = strrchr(work, '\\')) != 0)   /* a. no .. backup one \   */
                                              /* q. find a backslash?    */
        {
        if ((p - work) > 2 ||                 /* q. more than just d:\   */
                work[1] != ':' ||             /* ..or no colon anyway..  */
                work[0] == '.')               /* ..or some .\ or ..\?    */
            {
            *p++ = 0;                         /* a. yes .. backoff filenm */
            c = 0;                            /* ..and clear char holder */
            }
        else
            {
            c = *(++p);                       /* get 1st char after \    */
            *p++ = 0;                         /* ..and make into new path */
            }

        if (NOT chdir(work))                  /* q. find the directory?  */
            {
            *rc = 1;                          /* a. yes .. show filename  */
            _getdcwd(drive, full, MAX_PATH);  /* ..then get path         */

            if (LAST(full) != '\\')           /* q. last char a '\'?     */
                strcat(full, "\\");           /* a. no .. put in path sep */

            if (c)                            /* q. filespec need help?  */
                strncat(full, &c, 1);         /* a. yes .. add saved char */

            strcat(full, p);                  /* ..and add filename      */
            }
        }
    }
```

```
        else
            {
            _getdcwd(drive, full, MAX_PATH);      /* a. yes ..then get path   */

            p = &work[work[1] == ':' ? 2 : 0];    /* get start of filespec    */
            i = strlen(p);                        /* ..and length of remainder*/

            if (LAST(full) != '\\' && i)          /* q. do we need a '\' ?    */
                strcat(full, "\\");               /* a. yes .. put in path sep*/

            if (i)                                /* q. filename given?       */
                {
                *rc = 1;                          /* a. yes .. return filespec*/
                strcat(full, p);                  /* ..and copy in filename   */
                }

            else
                *rc = 0;                          /* else .. show as dir      */
            }
        }

    else
        {
        *rc = 0;                                  /* show directory was found */
        _getdcwd(drive, full, MAX_PATH);          /* ..then get path          */
        }

    chdir(current_path);                          /* reset original directory */

    return(*rc >= 0 ? full : 0);                  /* rtn normalized path\name */

}


/* ******************************************************************** *
 *      join_path() -- join a path and filespec together                *
 * ******************************************************************** */

char    *join_path(char *path,                    /* path name                */
                   char *filespec)                /* ..and filespec           */
{
static
char    out_string[MAX_PATH];                     /* output string            */

sprintf(out_string, "%s%s%s", path,               /* format output string     */
        LAST(path) == '\\' ? "" : "\\",
        filespec);

return(out_string);                               /* return w/concat'd string */

}


/* ******************************************************************** *
 *      control_break() -- control break intercept routine              *
 * ******************************************************************** */

int     control_break(void)
{
UINT    i;                                        /* work parm for set drive  */
```

```
    _dos_setdrive(init_drive, &i);            /* reset the default drive  */

    if (init_path)                            /* q. valid path?        */
        chdir(init_path);                     /* a. yes .. then restore it*/

    printf(stop_here);                        /* give error message ..    */

    return(0);

}



/* ********************************************************************** *
 *        critical_handler() -- DOS critical error handler              *
 * ********************************************************************** */

#pragma argsused                             /* hold unused argument messages  */
#pragma option -O2-b-e                        /* no global register allocation  */
                                             /* ..or dead code elimination     */

void    interrupt critical_handler(UINT bp,
            UINT di, UINT si, UINT ds, UINT es,
            UINT dx, UINT cx, UINT bx, UINT ax,
            UINT cs, UINT ip, UINT flags)
{

    if (ax & 0x800)                          /* q. fail allowed?      */
        ax = (ax & 0xff00) | 3;              /* a. yes .. fail request   */
    else
        ax = (ax & 0xff00) | 2;              /* else .. abort request    */

}
```

8

ANALYZING YOUR DISK STRUCTURE WITH CHKSTRUC

CHKSTRUC analyzes a DOS drive, reporting any problems found in the logical structure of that drive. CHKSTRUC can detect lost clusters, cross-linked clusters, file fragmentation, and other drive problems. If a problem is discovered, CHKSTRUC will make recommendations on how to repair it.

I t's almost inevitable that minor flaws will occur in a drive's logical structure during the course of normal operation. Sometimes you'll find the flaws during disk maintenance. At other times you find them indirectly, through poor system performance or incorrect system operation.

For example, suppose DOS notifies you that the disk is full when you are copying a file, but you know the space should be available. As a result, you run the DOS utility CHKDSK and find that there are "598 lost allocation units found in 23 chains." Certainly CHKDSK can correct this condition, but there are other errors that CHKDSK will report but not correct (such as the unhelpful "Probable non-DOS disk" message) and a few that CHKDSK does not detect at all (such as conflicting copies of the File Allocation Table or FAT).

All in all, it's really up to you to find errors and determine the appropriate corrective action

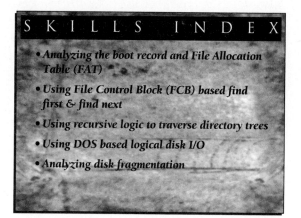

SKILLS INDEX

- *Analyzing the boot record and File Allocation Table (FAT)*
- *Using File Control Block (FCB) based find first & find next*
- *Using recursive logic to traverse directory trees*
- *Using DOS based logical disk I/O*
- *Analyzing disk fragmentation*

CHKSTRUC helps you do this by scanning a disk's structure and reporting the errors found. CHKSTRUC also suggests steps that you should take to correct the problem. Most important, however, CHKSTRUC shows you how to read a disk and detect problems before it's too late.

■ HOW TO USE CHKSTRUC

CHKSTRUC is easy to use. To check the current disk's structure, simply type the command CHKSTRUC. The full syntax for CHKSTRUC is

```
CHKSTRUC [d:] [/V]
```

The *d:* argument tells CHKSTRUC what disk you want to analyze. If you omit this argument, CHKSTRUC will analyze the current default drive. For example, to analyze the disk in drive B, enter this command:

```
CHKSTRUC B:
```

As CHKSTRUC runs, it informs you of general flaws that it encounters. The /V switch sets the *verbose mode*, causing CHKSTRUC to display more information as analysis proceeds.

When you start CHKSTRUC, it displays a copyright notice and vital statistics about the disk, and then begins analyzing the disk's structure. As analysis progresses, and because analysis can take some time, CHKSTRUC displays a rotating bar that tells you the program is working while it checks for errors in the disk's structure. As CHKSTRUC runs, it produces a report describing the errors found on the drive.

■ DIAGNOSING DISK ERRORS

There are several problems that CHKSTRUC detects when analyzing a drive's structure, the first of which is a mismatched media descriptor byte. The boot record and all copies of a drive's FAT contain a byte, called the media descriptor, that describes the type of media in the drive. Normally, the media descriptor in the boot record will match the first byte in the FATs. If not, you can fix this error by running a commercially available disk-repair program (such as Norton Disk Doctor by Symantec Corporation).

In and of itself, the mismatched media-descriptor error is a trivial one and is unlikely to cause problems; however, the error may indicate that a more serious underlying problem exists. For example, you may have a program that is somehow corrupting data in the boot record or FAT.

■ All FATs Are Created Equal

All standard DOS disk formats contain two copies of the FAT. (RAM disks are one exception, typically using only one copy of the FAT.) DOS uses the first FAT to determine the current allocation status of the disk, and ensures the other versions match the first. Under normal conditions, the contents of all FATs should be the same.

CHKSTRUC compares subsequent FATs to the first FAT. If CHKSTRUC detects a difference between the FATs, it displays a message indicating the number of the FAT that does not match the first one. You can remedy this condition by running DOS CHKDSK against that drive, using the /F switch.

Unequal FATs will not affect your system operation, as long as the first one is accurate; however, this condition may indicate an underlying problem, such as a program erroneously writing over the FAT.

■ CHKDSK Recovery Files

When you invoke the DOS CHKDSK utility with the /F switch and CHKSTRUC finds a set of unlinked, allocated clusters, it gives you the option of building a file in the root directory for each set found. CHKDSK names these recovery files FILE*nnnn*.CHK, where the *nnnn* is replaced with a number from 0000 to 9999. If CHKSTRUC spots these files in the root directory of the specified drive, it displays a message reminding you that they exist and that you can delete them when they are no longer needed.

The presence of CHKDSK recovery files is not a flaw in the file system, but these recovery files may be using large amounts of disk space that could be used for other purposes.

■ Allocation Errors

Inconsistencies or errors in the information that tracks a file's size or location on disk are known as *allocation errors*. These errors can occur in the file's directory entry, FAT entries, or both. CHKSTRUC detects five of these errors, which are described in the paragraphs that follow: invalid file size, invalid cluster number, cross-linked files, a free cluster in the allocation chain, and a bad (unusable) cluster in the allocation chain.

■ FILE SIZE ERROR

An *invalid file size* occurs when the number of clusters allocated to a file does not match the file size field found in the directory entry. A file should have only enough clusters allocated to hold the data indicated by the file size. CHKSTRUC informs you if the FAT indicates that a file owns too many or too few clusters.

When a file has too many clusters, it is using more disk space than necessary. Although it is relatively easy to resolve this problem by using the DOS CHKDSK program, the problem itself may be the result of another program corrupting the FAT or directory entry. In either case, there is a possibility that the file with the error may be damaged.

Conversely, when a file has too few clusters, there is not enough disk space allocated to the file to hold the amount of data indicated by the file size field in the directory entry. Unless the directory entry is in error, the file is most likely damaged and may have to be restored from a backup. In this case, CHKDSK will repair the problem by adjusting the file size field in the directory entry. As an alternative to CHKDSK, you can attempt to recover the data with a commercial disk editor.

- **INVALID CLUSTER NUMBER**
  CHKSTRUC detects an *invalid cluster number* when the value of a FAT entry falls outside the range of cluster numbers for that drive. The size of a DOS drive and that drive's cluster size determine the number of clusters available on that drive, and limit cluster numbers to a specific range. When DOS encounters an invalid cluster number in the allocation chain for a file, there is no way DOS can determine the location of the next cluster in the file. Again, you can use CHKDSK to repair this problem, but the file will be truncated at the invalid cluster.

- **CROSS-LINKED FILES**
  If the allocation chains of two or more files intersect, the files are cross-linked. CHKSTRUC detects cross-linked files, but does not report the name of the first file involved in the error. In many cases, one of the files involved in a cross-link contains accurate information, but the other files will be corrupt. This occurs when one file's allocation chain is intact, but an entry in the second file's chain erroneously references a cluster belonging to the first file. The DOS CHKDSK utility reports cross-linked files, but it will not repair them. Most commercial disk-repair utilities can fix the problem, but you will likely lose data from at least one of the files involved in the cross-link.

- **FREE CLUSTER OR CHAIN**
  FAT entries that contain a zero value represent free clusters. Free clusters are available and are not in use by any file. When CHKSTRUC examines the allocation chain belonging to a file and finds that one of the entries points to a free cluster, CHKSTRUC displays an error message. This problem may be significant or trivial, based on the number of clusters found in the allocation chain. If the clusters in the allocation chain contain

enough space to hold the entire file, it may turn out that the file is intact. But if the free cluster falls in the "middle" of the file (as determined by the file size in the directory entry), the remainder of the data may be irretrievable. CHKDSK can repair the free-cluster problem, but it usually results in damage to the affected files.

■ **Note.** *If a file references a free cluster, and that free cluster is subsequently allocated to a second file, the files will then be cross-linked.*

■ **Bad Cluster**
Finally, when you format a drive with DOS, it checks the disk space for *unusable* (or bad) *clusters*. A bad cluster contains one or more sectors that cannot be reliably read. DOS places a special value in the FAT for a bad cluster so the space will never be allocated. A file's allocation chain should never contain a reference to a bad cluster. The consequences of and solutions to this problem are similar to those for the free-cluster problem, except that a bad cluster does not cause a cross-link as a side effect.

■ **Lost Clusters**
A *lost cluster* is an allocation unit that the FAT entry notes as in use, but that is not allocated to a file. When CHKSTRUC finds this problem, it displays an error showing the number of lost clusters on the disk. If you see this message, you can easily correct the condition by running the CHKDSK/F command.

■ **Directory Structure Errors**
All directories, except the root, must contain the entries named . and .., and they must appear in order as the first two entries in the directory. If CHKSTRUC does not locate these entries, it displays an error message. You can use CHKDSK/F to repair this problem, but CHKDSK changes the directory into a normal file, and all files contained in that directory are lost.

A fully qualified file name contains four sections: the drive, the path, a file name, and an extension. For example, in the name C:\CLABNOTE\CHKSTRUC.C, C: is the drive, \CLABNOTE\ is the path, CHKSTRUC is the file name, and .C is the extension. DOS effectively limits the maximum size of the path portion of a fully qualified file name to 65 characters (63 plus the opening and closing backslashes). When CHKSTRUC finds a path name requiring more than 65 characters, it reports that the directories are nested too deeply and terminates. This error frequently occurs when a subdirectory entry erroneously references one of its parent directories in the directory tree structure. When a directory entry references a parent directory, it causes a "loop" in the structure.

CHKSTRUC does not attempt to bypass this error, because it does not know where the loop started. The best method for correcting the problem is to use a commercial disk editor to find and manually repair the directory entry referencing the parent. Although DOS CHKDSK displays several error messages when it encounters this condition, it does not effectively repair the problem and can cause loss of data in its attempts.

■ File and Directory Fragmentation

When DOS allocates clusters to files, the clusters may be anywhere on the drive, but the best possible allocation is a set of clusters that are contiguous; otherwise, the file is fragmented. If a drive contains many fragmented files and directories, or if the fragmented files are broken into many groups of clusters, it does not affect proper operation of the system, but it can severely impact system performance.

CHKSTRUC checks for fragmented files and directories, and recommends defragmentation when more than ten percent of the files on a drive are fragmented. If you specify the /V switch, CHKSTRUC also displays the names of fragmented files. Many methods and utilities exist for correcting fragmentation. They range from backing up, formatting, and restoring the disk, to running a commercial defragmentation utility.

■ CHKSTRUC's Report

CHKSTRUC issues many messages during execution, informing you of errors and giving you general information about your drive's structure. Figure 8.1 shows the CHKSTRUC report produced for a drive that had a significant number of problems. Also, see the Endnote, "CHKSTRUC Messages," for a complete listing.

FIGURE 8.1

CHKSTRUC's report for a drive with many errors

```
CHKSTRUC 1.00 ■ Copyright (c) 1992, Bob Flanders and Michael Holmes
PC Magazine C Lab Notes ■ Check disk and directory structure

        Drive A: TEST DISK
      Disk Info: 2400 Sectors, 2371 Clusters, 512 Clustersize
       Capacity: 1.2mb, 1.1mb available

 Recovery Files: CHKDSK recovery files found in root directory
     Allocation: A:\INVALIDC.LST has an invalid cluster
     Allocation: A:\FREECLUS.TER has a free cluster in the chain
     Allocation: A:\BAD-CLUS.TER has a bad cluster in the chain
     Allocation: A:\SIZE-PRO.BLM directory and FAT sizes differ
     Allocation: A:\CROSSLIN.KED is cross-linked
   Lost Cluster: 2 allocated but not part of any file
        Summary: 8 files and 1 directories processed
                 8 unfragmented (89%), 1 fragmented (11%), 2 free spaces
     Suggestion: First, run CHKDSK supplied with DOS using the /F
                 parameter. Next, check and delete any files named
                 FILEnnnn.CHK found in the root directory. Finally, use
                 a disk defragmentation utility to re-organize the disk
                 space.
```

■ Other Considerations

CHKSTRUC will not work on a network drive, or a drive created with the DOS SUBST command. If you specify an invalid drive letter or a drive that is not ready, CHKSTRUC will display an appropriate message and return to DOS. Also, if there is insufficient memory to complete any operation, CHKSTRUC will tell you and exit to DOS.

■ Using CHKSTRUC's Return Code

If you want to run CHKSTRUC from a batch program, you can test CHKSTRUC's findings by its return code. CHKSTRUC returns a value from 0 to 5, where a higher value represents a more severe error. Table 8.1 is a list of the possible return codes and their meanings.

TABLE 8.1
CHKSTRUC
Return Codes

Code	Definition
0	**No error**
1	**Fragmented files**
2	**\FILE*nnn*.CHK found**
3	**Run CHKDSK/F**
4	**Run a commercial repair utility**
5	**Drive not ready, bad drive, etc.**

■ INSIDE CHKSTRUC

CHKSTRUC.EXE is a compact memory-model program that consists of a main() routine that performs initialization, and a series of function calls that perform the analysis of the disk structure. CHKSTRUC.EXE is only 18k long, but the actual amount of memory required by CHKSTRUC varies with the size of the FAT on the disk being checked.

■ Initialization

When the program starts, CHKSTRUC displays the copyright message using printf() and sets up a routine to intercept control break and DOS critical errors. If you press Ctrl-Break during CHKSTRUC's execution, DOS invokes the control_break() function, which resets the default drive and directory, displays a message that you requested the abort, and exits to DOS.

If a DOS critical error (such as drive not ready, for example) occurs, DOS passes control to the critical_handler(). The Borland C++ interface to an interrupt routine presents the CPU registers to the handler as a set of parameters passed on the stack. Additionally, the interface sets up access to the program's data areas so the interrupt handler can update global variables.

When DOS calls the critical error handler, it sets bit 3 in the AH register to specify whether the handler may return a fail code in response to the error. Since the interrupt interface presents the registers as 16-bit values, the eight high-order bits in the AX register represent the AH register. Therefore, critical_handler() checks bit 11 in the AX parameter, and if it is on, returns a fail code (AL=3), or otherwise returns an abort code (AL=2).

■ **Note.** *There is no standard method used by C compilers to implement an interface to interrupts. Be sure to check your compiler's documentation before writing such a function.*

Next, CHKSTRUC saves the current drive and Disk Transfer Area (DTA) so they can be restored before CHKSTRUC returns to DOS. The DOS find-first and find-next file functions return information via the DTA. CHKSTRUC sets the DTA address to point at the structure dir_entry. Later, when CHKSTRUC calls _dos_findfirst() or _dos_findnext(), DOS fills dir_entry with information from matching directory entries, giving CHKSTRUC easy access to directory information. When CHKSTRUC saves the current drive, it places it in both the init_drive variable and the drive[] string. Since the drive[] string contains the disk name that CHKSTRUC checks, if you do not specify another drive on the command line, CHKSTRUC checks the default drive.

CHKSTRUC then checks the arguments passed on the command line by calling the parse_parms() function, which determines the validity of command line arguments by checking them against the entries in parm_table[]. If the command line arguments pass the tests imposed by parse_parms(), then CHKSTRUC checks to see if you specified a drive, and if so, that the argument was in the d: format. If you specified a drive, CHKSTRUC then makes it the current drive. Otherwise, CHKSTRUC analyzes the logical structure of the current drive.

When CHKSTRUC completes checking of the command line arguments, it then retrieves the current working directory, using the getcwd() function. Next, CHKSTRUC calls the drive_check() function to ensure that the drive is not a network drive or the result of a DOS SUBST or ASSIGN command. If the drive is a network drive, an ASSIGN drive, or a SUBST drive, CHKSTRUC displays an error message and returns to DOS.

The drive_check() function starts by checking the version of DOS. If the DOS version is 3.1 or later, drive_check() calls DOS function 0x4409 to ensure that the drive is not a network drive, or a pseudodrive resulting from the DOS SUBST command. In versions of DOS earlier than 3.1, there was no support for the SUBST command, nor was there any intrinsic support for networks. If CHKSTRUC determines that the DOS version is pre-3.1, it assumes that the drive is a local drive.

Finally, if the version of DOS is 3.31 or later, check_drive() sets the global switch sw_dos4. Starting with version 3.31, DOS provided a new interface to interrupt 0x25 (read logical sector), required to access drives larger than 32 megabytes. The sw_dos4 switch tells CHKSTRUC which interface to use later in the program.

■ The Real Work Begins

When CHKSTRUC analyzes a drive's structure, it examines three areas of the disk: the boot record, the FAT, and all directories on that disk. The boot record is contained in the first sector of a DOS disk and describes the overall layout of the disk. CHKSTRUC uses the boot sector when determining the location and size of the FATs and the highest valid cluster number. See Figure 8.2 for an overall layout of a disk and Figure 8.3 for a layout of the boot record.

The File Allocation Table (FAT) is the structure DOS uses to allocate disk space to files and directories. Each entry in the FAT is a 12- or 16-bit value that maps to a disk cluster. Table 8.2 shows the possible values that FAT entries may contain. All values are shown in hexadecimal, and, where needed, the leading digit is enclosed in parentheses to denote the 16-bit vs. 12-bit value. For example, the value (F)FF8 represents the value FFF8 for a 16-bit FAT, and the value FF8 for a 12-bit FAT. Figure 8.4 shows how an allocation chain is traced through the FAT.

For every file on the disk there is a single directory entry. A directory entry contains the name and extension of the file; date and time the file was last updated; file size; attribute byte; and starting cluster. CHKSTRUC verifies every entry in every directory on the disk. Figure 8.5 illustrates the relationship between a directory entry and the FAT chain.

CHKSTRUC invokes six functions to analyze the structure of the disk: get_fat(), fat_check(), free_check(), chkdsk_files(), dir_search(), and unlinked_check(). Each checks for a certain set of problems with the disk structure, as described in the following paragraphs.

■ Reading the FAT

The function get_fat() starts by invoking DOS function 0x36: get disk free space. This function returns four values: the number of sectors per cluster, the number of unallocated clusters on the disk, the number of bytes per sector (sector size), and the total number of clusters on the disk. CHKSTRUC uses the sector size to allocate memory for the boot record and reads the boot record into the allocated memory. If an error occurs while reading the boot record, CHKSTRUC displays an error message and returns to DOS.

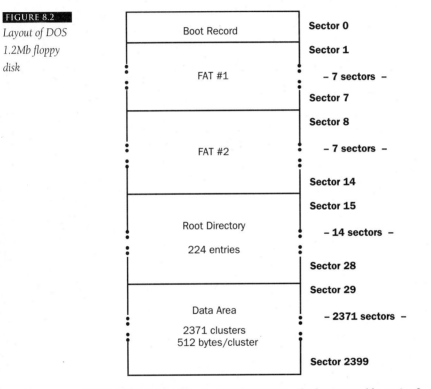

FIGURE 8.2

Layout of DOS 1.2Mb floppy disk

A DOS 1.2Mb floppy disk contains four areas: the boot record in sector 0, two FATs starting in sector 1, the root directory after the last copy of the FAT, and the data area directly following the root directory. The diagram shows the starting sectors for each area.

The get_fat() function calculates the drive capacity and space available, and then prints the drive information message. Then get_fat() calculates the amount of memory needed to contain the FAT and the associated fat_bits array, and allocates memory for these structures. To calculate the FAT size, the function multiplies sector size by number of FAT sectors. The memory required for the fat_bits array is determined by adding 7 to max_cluster and dividing the total by 8 (the number of bits per byte). After allocating the memory, CHKSTRUC reads the entire FAT from the drive being analyzed by calling get_fat(). The get_fat() function calls read_disk(), which actually loads the FAT into memory.

Layout of boot record from 1.2Mb floppy disk

Offset	Value	Declaration	Description
+0	EB 3C 90	char jmp[3],	Jump instruction to boot program
+3	M S D O S 5 . 0	char oem[8];	OEM name
+11	0200 (512)	unsigned int bytes;	Bytes per sector
+13	01	char cluster;	Sectors per cluster
+14	0001	unsigned int res_sectors;	Reserved sectors
+16	02	char FATs;	Number of FATs
+17	00E0 (224)	unsigned int roots;	Number of root directory entries
+19	0960 (2400)	unsigned int sectors;	Total sectors
+21	F9	char media;	Media descriptor
+22	0007	unsigned int fatsize;	Sectors per FAT
+24	000F (15)	unsigned int tracksize;	Sectors per track
+26	0002	unsigned int heads;	Number of heads
+28	00000000	long hidden;	Hidden sectors
+32	00000000	long sectors_32;	Sectors if above 32Mb

The diagram shows a boot record from a DOS 1.2Mb floppy disk formatted with DOS 5.0. The contents of the fields will vary based on the DOS version, the software used to format the disk, and the size of the disk being formatted. The numbers are shown in hex. Where relevant, the decimal equivalent is also shown.

As analysis proceeds, CHKSTRUC checks for allocation errors by examining the FAT. When CHKSTRUC checks for cross-links, it uses the fat_bits array to track clusters that have already been checked. The array contains one bit per cluster, and the bit is optionally set to 1 by the walk_fat() function discussed later. Once the bit is set for a cluster, if any other file references that cluster, CHKSTRUC displays a message showing the file as cross-linked.

TABLE 8.2
Possible Values in a FAT Entry

Value	Definition
Zero (0)	**The cluster is not allocated to any file.**
One (1)	**Invalid. If this value is ever seen in a FAT entry, it is an error.**
2 through max_cluster	**A pointer to the NEXT cluster in the chain. The max_cluster value is calculated from values found in the boot sector.**
max_cluster+1 through (F)FEF	**Invalid for the drive being checked.**
(F)FF0 through (F)FF6	**Reserved cluster. The DOS *Programmer's Reference* marks this entry with "Reserved; Do not use." It is not clear whether Microsoft intended the values (F)FF0 through (F)FF6 to be reserved or that the clusters represented by these values are reserved. Experimentation reveals that DOS does not treat these values differently from other valid cluster numbers.**
(F)FF7	**The cluster contains one or more bad sectors and cannot reliably contain data.**
(F)FF8 through (F)FFF	**End of chain. There are no more clusters for this file or directory. In practice, we find that DOS always marks the last cluster with (F)FFF.**

The read_disk() function selects the proper interface for DOS interrupt 0x25 (read logical sector) and breaks the read into manageable portions. The DOS documentation contains no explicit limitation on the number of sectors that can be read with a single invocation of interrupt 0x25; however, there is an implied limit of 64k imposed by the nature of segmented addressing. The read_disk() function avoids the 64k limit by breaking a single request that is longer than 64k into a series of reads, each with a maximum length of 64k.

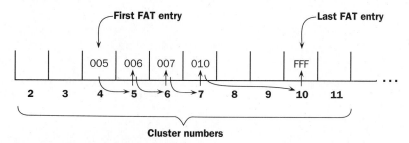

FIGURE 8.4

FAT layout

The FAT is essentially an array of integer values that describe the order of the clusters contained in files. FAT entries are 12 or 16 bits wide, depending on the disk capacity. Assume that you have a file whose first cluster is number 4 followed by clusters 5, 6, 7, and 10. This chain would indicate that the file is fragmented with one extra segment. If these entries were in a 12-bit FAT, they would appear as follows:

Note that the entry for cluster 4 points to entry 5; entry for cluster 5 points to entry 6, and so on. The last entry for cluster 10 is FFF, which indicates end of file.

If read_disk() completes with no errors, get_fat() checks the media descriptor in the FAT against that found in the boot record, reporting an error if they do not match.

- ## Checking the FAT

  In many cases, DOS maintains more than one copy of the FAT on a disk. The additional FATs are nothing more than copies of the first, or primary, FAT and theoretically can be used should the primary FAT become unreadable. If a disk contains more than one FAT, all of them should contain precisely the same information. To determine if this is so, the fat_check() routine reads each sector in the secondary FATs and compares them to the corresponding information in the primary FAT. If any FAT does not match the primary one, fat_check() displays a message identifying the FAT in error.

- ## Counting the Free Areas

  A set of contiguous, unallocated clusters is a *free area*. The free_check() routine calls walk_fat() for every valid cluster number, counting the number of free areas by searching the FAT for sets of adjacent zero entries. Walk_fat() performs three functions: It retrieves the value stored in the requested entry, checks the validity of the value for the disk being analyzed, and, optionally, notes that the cluster has been retrieved in the fat_bits array.

FIGURE 8.5

Directory:FAT
relationship

The following illustrates the interaction between a directory entry, the FAT, and clusters of a file. Assume the boot record for a given drive shows the following:

> 512 bytes per sector
> 2 sectors per cluster

This indicates that the cluster size for the disk is 1024.

Consider the following directory entry:

> DATA.FIL Size: 4250 First Cluster: 12
>   Additional Clusters: 13, 14, 17, 19

DATA.FIL thus consists of 5 clusters, and the file is fragmented with two extra segments. Here is a graphic illustration representing the relationship between the directory entry, its associated FAT entries, and the data on the disk.

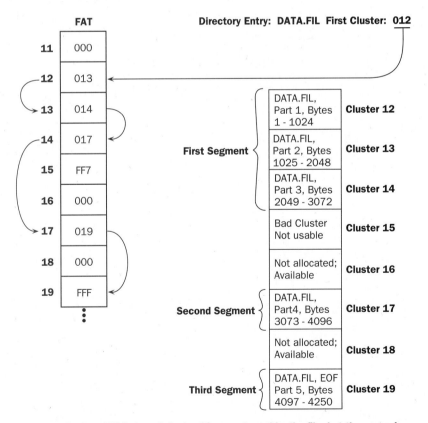

Note that the last 870 bytes of cluster 19 are not used by the file, but the space is allocated to DATA.FIL. There is no (standard) way for this space to be used by another file.

When walk_fat() retrieves a 16-bit FAT entry, it treats the FAT as an unsigned integer array and retrieves the requested entry. When dealing with a 12-bit FAT, retrieving the value becomes a bit more complicated. In this case, each entry is 1.5 bytes wide, and must be retrieved by calculating the offset, retrieving the 16-bit value at that location, and isolating the upper or lower 12 bits retrieved, depending on the offset into the FAT.

The walk_fat() function performs two validity checks. First, it checks to see if the cluster has been previously processed, by checking the corresponding bit in the fat_bits array. If the bit is on, the cluster being processed is cross-linked. Then walk_fat() determines if the FAT entry marks the cluster as free, allocated, bad (unusable disk sector), or end of file. Then, if requested by the caller, walk_fat() sets the bit in fat_bits that represents the requested cluster number, and returns a value indicating the cluster's status.

■ Finding CHKDSK Recovery Files

When you execute the DOS CHKDSK command with the /F parameter, and CHKDSK finds allocated clusters that are not a part of a file, it displays a message like "15 lost allocation units found in 2 chains," followed by "Convert lost chains to files (Y/N)?" If you answer yes, CHKDSK places a file called FILE*nnnn*.CHK in the root directory for each lost chain. The *nnnn* is replaced by a number from 0000 to 9999. In most cases, after retrieving any valuable information needed from these files, you delete them so the disk space can be reused. CHKSTRUC informs you if any of these files are found in the root directory.

The chkdsk_files() routine uses the _dos_findfirst() and _dos_findnext() routines to search for these files. For each entry found using the mask \FILE????.CHK, chkdsk_files() checks that the characters in the ???? portion are numbers. If even one of these files exists, CHKSTRUC prints a message telling you of its findings and then returns to main().

■ Checking Out the Files

On the surface, the DOS file system seems rather simple. There are two types of entries: files and directories. Directories may contain other directories, and files contain data. Supporting this system, however, is an intricate network of directory entries and file allocation chains that form the file structure. Checking the file structure is the most complex operation CHKSTRUC performs, and the function dir_search() does most of the work.

The dir_search() function is a recursive routine that accepts a single argument named base_dir, which is a pointer to a string naming a directory. The directory named by base_dir, and all files and subdirectories contained directly and indirectly in base_dir, are examined by dir_search(). When main() invokes dir_search(), it passes a pointer to a string naming the root directory of the drive being examined, causing dir_search() to examine all files and directories on that drive.

The dir_search() function starts by allocating space for a path name and an FCB used for directory searches. Although at first glance it appears easier to use the newer DOS find-first/find-next functions (0x4e and 0x4f), rather than FCB style functions (0x11 and 0x12), you later find that only the FCB functions return the first cluster number from the matching directory entries. Since the first cluster number is required in a program such as CHKSTRUC, you must use the FCB functions.

After this, dir_search() calls translate_name(), which retrieves the "true" name of the directory via the undocumented DOS function 0x60. Since function 0x60 did not exist before DOS version 3, translate_name() checks the DOS version number before invoking this function.

Four conditions cause the true name of a directory to differ from the name passed to dir_search(): if the drive is a network drive, if the drive was created with the SUBST command, if the drive was altered with the ASSIGN command, or if a directory was the target of a JOIN command. CHKSTRUC checks for network, ASSIGN, and SUBST drives soon after it starts running. Having checked these three, the only possible cause for a mismatch is when the directory is the result of a DOS JOIN command. In this case, the directory name passed to dir_search() represents another drive. If dir_search() detects that a directory is the result of a JOIN command, it does not attempt to check that directory's contents. Otherwise, dir_search() enters a loop, checking the entries in that directory.

The dir_search() function checks the length of a fully qualified DOS file name. The maximum length of the path portion is 63 characters. If you add to this the drive (2 characters), the opening and closing backslashes (2 characters), the file name (8 characters), and the extension (4 characters, including the .), you get a total length of 79. These restrictions arise from limitations in DOS's internal structures.

For each entry found, dir_search() assembles a fully qualified file name and checks the length. If the length is greater than 79, dir_search() prints the "nested too deep" error message and immediately exits the program. CHKSTRUC does not attempt to recover from this error because it is likely that at some previous level, a directory entry has become corrupt and refers to itself or some parent directory. Under normal circumstances, DOS will not create a directory that refers to a parent directory. When this occurs, you get an endless loop of directories that appear to be cross-linked.

Every directory, excluding the root directory, must contain the . and .. entries. The
. is a directory's pointer to itself and can be used to force a reference to a file in the
current directory. The .. refers to the parent directory and is handy for use when
changing to the parent directory. The dir_search() function ensures that the . and ..
entries exist in every directory except the root. If not, the function prints an error
message describing the condition.

When processing a drive's directory structure using recursive functions, it is important to keep in mind the amount of stack space needed to support the recursions. In CHKSTRUC's case, if the directory entry being processed refers to another
directory, dir_search() calls itself to check the entry, making dir_search() a recursive function. Because a path may be up to 65 characters long (including backslashes), and a subdirectory name can be a single letter, it is possible for
dir_search() to call itself up to 32 times. Since each entry requires approximately
52 bytes of stack space, CHKSTRUC could use up to 1,664 bytes of stack space, depending on the structure being analyzed.

To test for fragmentation of space allocated to a file, dir_search() calls frag_check().
The frag_check() function calls walk_fat() (discussed earlier) to check the FAT chain
associated with the file. When calling walk_fat(), frag_check() passes an argument requesting that the bit corresponding to the requested cluster in the fat_bits array be set.
As noted before, when walk_fat() checks an entry that already has the corresponding
bit set in the fat_bits array, it returns a value indicating that the cluster is cross-linked.
When frag_check() processes the FAT chain for a directory entry, each allocated cluster should be accessed once, and only once.

The frag_check() routine ensures that the cluster numbers associated with a file
are valid and contiguous. The one exception that frag_check() specifically skips is
when an entry's clusters surround a bad spot on the disk. In this case, frag_check()
does not mark the file as fragmented, since the bad clusters cannot be moved to a different spot on the disk.

Next, dir_search() checks if the entry being processed represents a file (as opposed
to a directory). If so, dir_search() tests whether the file size in the directory entry cor-
relates with the number of clusters allocated. If it does not, CHKSTRUC displays an
appropriate error message.

When all of the entries in the directory have been processed, dir_search() frees the
memory allocated for the path name and the FCB, and returns the number of entries
found in the directory processed.

▪ Are There Any Unlinked Clusters Out There?

CHKSTRUC's last test determines if there are any lost clusters. It does this by calling unlinked_check(). The unlinked_check() function uses walk_fat() to check every FAT entry and determine if any allocated entries were not processed.

When a drive's file structure has no errors, each allocated cluster (except for bad clusters) on that drive should be associated with one, and only one file. If this is true, then dir_search() has examined every file on the drive, and every allocated cluster has been retrieved via walk_fat() once, and only once. As noted earlier, walk_fat() optionally notes when a cluster has been accessed by making an entry in the fat_bits array. When testing for lost clusters, unlinked_check() asks walk_fat() to check each FAT entry. If walk_fat() returns a code indicating that an entry has not been processed, then the entry was not associated with a file, and therefore represents a lost cluster. Then unlinked_check() tallies the number of entries that are allocated but not in use by any file. If all is well, the result is zero.

▪ Final Reporting

When CHKSTRUC finishes analyzing the structure, it displays the totals and suggestions via the user_report() function, which calculates the percentages of fragmented files and displays the final report.

During analysis, CHKSTRUC modifies the variable named repair, which is used by user_report() when determining which suggestions to print. The four low-order bits of the repair variable control what suggestions are displayed at the end of the CHKSTRUC report. The user_report() function counts the number of suggestions needed, allocates memory to hold the suggestions, and concatenates them together, inserting the appropriate adverbs to make the suggestions somewhat friendlier. For example, "Run CHKDSK/F. Run a disk defragmentation utility." sounds less friendly than "First, run CHKDSK supplied with DOS using the /F parameter. Then, use a disk defragmentation utility to reorganize the disk space." Remember, the suggestions CHKSTRUC gives you may vary.

▪ SUMMARY

CHKSTRUC demonstrates several techniques needed to analyze the DOS disk structure, but there are a few items you could add to increase CHKSTRUC's functionality.

First, you might implement functions to read all files and verify their accessibility. This test can be further enhanced by reading the files first through DOS open/read/close functions, then using DOS interrupt 0x25, and then comparing the data to ensure it matches. Assuming your algorithms for accessing the data are correct, this sequence would test the validity of the disk structure.

In another similar function, you might read (or even write, then read) all of the unused disk space to verify its integrity. Finding bad disk space before using it for live data can avert disaster before it happens.

Finally, for the more adventurous, consider implementing routines that fix problems found during the analysis, and then find a different use for the space that CHKDSK formerly occupied!

CHKSTRUC MESSAGES

CHKSTRUC produces messages in this format:

message prefix: description

where the *message prefix* classifies the message, and the *description* gives more detailed information. Here's a list of the message classifications and descriptions, along with the meanings of the various messages CHKSTRUC produces.

Drive X: label serial

CHKSTRUC's drive message (the first message after the copyright) tells you the letter of the drive being analyzed. CHKSTRUC also displays the disk's volume label and serial number, if they are available.

Disk Info: *n* Sectors, *n* Clusters, *n* Clustersize

This message shows you general information about the drive, and contains the number of sectors and clusters, along with the disk's cluster size.

Capacity: capacity, available

This message shows the capacity and available space on the disk. The values are rounded to kilobytes, megabytes, or gigabytes, if appropriate.

Media Descriptor: FAT and boot record do not match

The media descriptor bytes in the boot record and primary FAT did not match.

FAT Mismatch: FAT *n* does not match the first FAT

In most cases, DOS drives contain more than one FAT. Under normal conditions, the contents of all FATs should be exactly the same. CHKSTRUC compares additional

FATs to the primary FAT. If CHKSTRUC detects a difference, it displays a message indicating the number of the FAT that does not match.

Recovery Files: CHKDSK recovery files found in root directory

CHKDSK names recovery files FILE*nnnn*.CHK, where *nnnn* is a number from 0000 to 9999. If CHKSTRUC spots these files in the root directory of the drive, it displays this message to remind you that they exist and that you can delete them when they are no longer needed.

Allocation: *filename* has an invalid cluster

The FAT entries for a given drive may only contain certain values, based on the number of clusters available. CHKSTRUC has found an invalid FAT entry on the allocation chain of the file shown.

Allocation: *filename* has a free cluster in the chain

When a FAT entry contains a zero, it represents a free cluster that may be allocated to a file as needed. CHKSTRUC displays this message if it finds that a file's allocation chain references a free cluster.

Allocation: *filename* has a bad cluster in the chain

When DOS formats a drive, it checks to assure that it can write to and read from every sector on the drive. If any sector fails this test, the cluster containing that sector is marked as a bad cluster. CHKSTRUC displays this message if it finds that a file's allocation chain references a bad cluster.

Allocation: *filename* directory and FAT sizes differ

A file's directory entry contains a file size field showing the number of bytes in that file. The allocation chain of that file should reference *only* the number of clusters necessary to contain the number of bytes shown in the directory entry. CHKSTRUC displays this message if it finds a file that owns a number of clusters different from that required by the file size.

Allocation: *filename* **is cross-linked**

Each allocated cluster should be owned by one and only one file. CHKSTRUC displays this message if it finds that a file references a cluster owned by another file.

Lost Cluster: *n* **allocated but not part of any file**

A lost cluster is an allocation unit that the FAT indicates is in use, but is owned by no existing file. This message shows how many lost clusters are on the disk.

Structure: *dirname* **is missing the . and/or .. files**

All directories except the root directory must contain the . and .. entries. If CHKSTRUC does not locate these entries, it displays this error message.

Structure: Run Aborted. Directories nested too deep in *dirname*

The maximum length of a path is 63 characters (excluding the opening and closing backslashes). If CHKSTRUC finds a path longer than this, it displays this message and aborts the run.

Fragmented File: *filename*
Fragmented Dir: *dirname*

If you specify the /V switch, CHKSTRUC displays these messages when it encounters a file or directory that does not occupy contiguous space on the disk.

Checking FATs: All FATs match the first FAT

This is a simple progress message displayed if the /V switch has been specified, and CHKSTRUC displays it when comparing the contents of FATs on disks that contain multiple FATs. If secondary FATs do not match the primary FAT, this message is overwritten with the "FAT Mismatch" message.

Free Areas: *n*

CHKSTRUC displays this after it has counted the number of contiguous free areas on the disk. This condition has no direct impact on system operation, but it can cause fragmentation in new files, especially if a large number of free areas exist on the disk.

Summary: *n* files and *n* directories processed
**   *n* unfragmented (*n*%), *n* fragmented (*n*%), *n* free**
**   spaces**

This message lists statistics about the disk scanned and includes the number of files and directories found, the number and percentage fragmented and unfragmented, and the number of free spaces found.

Suggestion:

This section lists the steps you can take to repair the problems on the disk. If no errors exist, CHKSTRUC displays "No service needed." ∎

LISTING

CHKSTRUC 1.00

```
/* ****************************************************************** *

    CHKSTRUC 1.00, Copyright (c) 1992, Bob Flanders and Michael Holmes
    PC Magazine C Lab Notes, Check disk and directory structure

 * ****************************************************************** *

    This code is for Borland C++ version 3.0. (MSC version on diskette)

            Compile with: BCC -2 -mc -N chkstruc.c

    To compile for Microsoft C, you need to change the following:

            - handle MK_FP(), FP_SEG(), and FP_OFF() differences
            - change memory allocation scheme for _fmalloc(), farrealloc()
              and farfree() routines
            - change control break handling for ctrlbrk() and control_break()
            - remove #pragma statements preceding critical_handler()

 * ****************************************************************** */


#pragma  pack(1)                        /* pack to byte alignment   */
#include <stdio.h>                      /* standard i/o library     */
#include <io.h>                         /* i/o routine headers      */
#include <stdlib.h>                     /* ANSI compatibility       */
#include <direct.h>                     /* directory functions      */
#include <dos.h>                        /* DOS rtn definitions      */
#include <malloc.h>                     /* memory declarations      */
#include <string.h>                     /* string functions         */
#include <ctype.h>                      /* character functions      */
#include <conio.h>                      /* console i/o routines     */
#include <fcntl.h>                      /* file control header      */
#include <memory.h>                     /* memory functions         */

#define NOT !                           /* logical not              */
#define ANY(x,y) strcspn(x,y) != strlen(x)  /* any matching characters? */
#define CLEAR(s,c) memset(s,c,sizeof(s))    /* string clear             */
#define LAST(x) x[strlen(x) - 1]        /* get last char in string  */
#define D_ENTRY  struct directory_entry /* shorthand for dir entry  */
#define UINT unsigned int               /* unsigned integer type    */
#define NOT !                           /* logical not              */
#define HUGE  char huge                 /* shorthand                */
#define BOOT  boot_record               /* boot record shorthand    */
#define FILES (_A_SYSTEM | _A_HIDDEN | _A_SUBDIR)   /* files type   */
#define LABEL (_A_VOLID)                            /* label type   */
#define MAX_PATH 79                     /* max path length          */


/* ****************************************************************** *
 *          routine definitions                                       *
 * ****************************************************************** */

void    quit_with(int, char *),         /* quit with error message  */
```

```
        keepalive(int),                  /* keepalive messages     */
        get_fat(void),                   /* read FAT into memory   */
        fat_check(void),                 /* check multiple FAT copies*/
        free_check(void),                /* check nbr of freespaces  */
        unlinked_check(void),            /* unlinked clusters check  */
        drive_check(void),               /* check for local drive    */
        dir_search(char *),              /* search directory         */
        chkdsk_files(void),              /* check chkdsk leftovers   */
        user_report(int),                /* give closing user report */
        set_bit(char *, UINT, int),      /* set bit in bit array     */
       *cln_malloc(long),                /* amount of memory to get   */
        interrupt critical_handler(UINT, /* critical error handler   */
            UINT, UINT, UINT, UINT, UINT,
            UINT, UINT, UINT, UINT, UINT,
            UINT);
int     local_check(char),               /* local drive check        */
        parse_parms(int, char **, int,   /* parse command line       */
            struct cmd_parm *, char ***),
        read_disk(UINT, int, HUGE *),    /* read disk sectors        */
        get_bit(char *, UINT),           /* get bit from bit array   */
        control_break(void);             /* control break handler    */
UINT    walk_fat(UINT, int, int *);      /* find file's next cluster */
char    *pack_name(char *, char*),       /* fcb name to filename.ext */
        *read_label(void),               /* read drive label         */
        *translate_name(char *),         /* validate dir name        */
        *large_fmt(unsigned long);       /* format a large number    */
long    frag_check(char *, UINT, int);   /* file/dir frag'd check    */


/* *********************************************************************** *
 *       command line parms and switches                                   *
 * *********************************************************************** */

char    sw_verbose;                      /* switch parameters        */

struct  cmd_parm                         /* command line parm        */
    {
    char cp_ltr,                         /* switch letter            */
         cp_flag,                        /* entry type               */
         *cp_entry;                      /* pointer to data          */
    };

struct  cmd_parm parm_table[] =          /* CHKSTRUC cmd line parms  */
    {
    { 'V', 0, &sw_verbose },             /* V - verbose option       */
    };
                                         /* nbr of table entries     */
#define PARM_TABLE_CNT  sizeof(parm_table) / sizeof(struct cmd_parm)


/* *********************************************************************** *
 *       globals                                                           *
 * *********************************************************************** */

int     pos_found,                       /* number positionals found */
        init_drive,                      /* startup drive            */
        rc = 5,                          /* errorlevel return code    */
        secsize,                         /* sector size of drive      */
        percent_frag,                    /* percent fragmented        */
        frag_cnt,                        /* fragmented files          */
        unfrag_cnt,                      /* unfragmented files        */
        free_cnt,                        /* freespaces                */
        files_cnt,                       /* processed files           */
        dirs_cnt,                        /* processed directories     */
```

```
        repair;                                 /* bit mask for suggestions */
                                                /*  .... ...1 repair needed */
                                                /*  .... ..1. chkdsk /f     */
                                                /*  .... .1.. FILEnnnn.CHK  */
                                                /*  .... 1... defrag needed */

UINT    nclusters,                              /* number of clusters       */
        bad_cluster,                            /* bad cluster number       */
        max_cluster,                            /* max cluster number       */
        max_secs;                               /* largest read with int25  */

long    nsectors,                               /* number of sectors on drv */
        cluster_size,                           /* bytes per cluster        */
        avail_disk;                             /* available bytes on disk  */

char  **pos_parms,                              /* positional parms array   */
       *init_path,                              /* startup drive and path   */
        far  *old_dta,                          /* previous dta address     */
        huge *fat,                              /* address of FAT           */
       *fat_bits,                               /* FAT bit array            */
        fat_16,                                 /* 16 bit FAT entry flag    */
        drive[] = " :\\",                       /* drive and path to check  */
        drive_nbr,                              /* drive nbr (1 = A)        */
        sw_dos4;                                /* use dos 4 style int 25   */

struct  SREGS   s;                              /* segment registers        */
union   REGS    r;                              /* other registers          */


/* ********************************************************************* *
 *      messages and strings                                           *
 * ********************************************************************* */

char    copyright[]     = "CHKSTRUC 1.00 \xfe Copyright (c) 1992, "
                          "Bob Flanders and Michael Holmes\n"
                          "PC Magazine C Lab Notes \xfe "
                          "Check disk and directory structure\n\n",
        too_many[]      = "Too many parameters\n",
        bad_op[]        = "Invalid parameter %s\n",
        drive_error[]   = "Drive not ready\n",
        stop_here[]     = "\nStopping at user's request\n",
        bad_drive[]     = "Invalid drive specified\n",
        net_drive[]     = "Cannot check a network, remote, SUBST'd "
                          "or ASSIGN'd drive\n",
        no_mem[]        = "Not enough memory for processing\n",
        dos_error[]     = "Must run with DOS 2.0 or greater\n",

        fat_error[]     = "Error reading the File Allocation Table\n",
        boot_error[]    = "Error reading the Boot Record\n",
        missing_dots[]  = "is missing the . and/or .. files",
        bad_dir[]       = "Run aborted. Directories nested too deep in "
                          "..\n\t",
        serial_nbr[]    = "Serial: %04X-%04X",
        drive_info[]    = "          Drive %c: %s\n"
                          "          Disk Info: %lu Sectors, %u Clusters, "
                          "%lu Clustersize\n"
                          "          Capacity: %s, ",
        available[]     = "%s available\n",
        bad_nfat[]      = "    Fat Mismatch: FAT %d does not match the "
                          "first FAT ",
        bad_media[]     = "Media descriptor: FAT and boot record do not "
                          "match  ",
        frag_file[]     = " Fragmented File: %s  ",
        frag_dir[]      = "  Fragmented Dir: %s  ",
```

```
    free_areas[]    = "     Free Areas:  ",
    fat_checking[]  = "  Checking FATs:  ",
    struct_error[]  = "      Structure: %s %s  ",
    lost_cluster[]  = "    Lost Cluster: %u allocated but not part of "
                      "any file  ",
    chain_error[]   = "     Allocation: %s %s  ",
    leftovers[]     = " Recovery Files: CHKDSK recovery files found "
                      "in root directory  ",
    final_report[]  = "        Summary: %d files and %d directories "
                      "processed\n"
                      "                 %d unfragmented (%d%%), %d "
                      "fragmented (%d%%), %d free spaces\n",
    suggest_hdr[]   = "     Suggestion: ",
    suggestion[]    = "%.*s\n                    ",
    free_disp[]     = "%d  ",
    backspace[]     = "\b",
    same_line[]     = "\r",
    fats_ok[]       = "All FATs match the first FAT  ",
    sizing[]        = "directory and FAT sizes differ  ",
    null_line[]     = "",
    new_line[]      = "\n",
    return_line[]   = "\r",
    help[]          = "  Usage:  CHKSTRUC  [d:] [/V]\n"
                      "Options:   /V  enables verbose mode\n\n",
  *fat_err[]      = { "has an invalid cluster",
                      "is cross-linked",
                      "has a free cluster in the chain", "", "",
                      "has a bad cluster in the chain" },
   *requests[]    = { "No service needed\n",
                      "run a commercial disk repair program to fix "
                      "the disk structure. ",
                      "run CHKDSK supplied with DOS using the /F "
                      "parameter. ",
                      "check and delete any files named FILEnnnn.CHK "
                      "found in the root directory. ",
                      "use a disk defragmentation utility to "
                      "reorganize the disk space. " },
   *prefix[][4]   = {
                      { "", "", "", "" },
                      { "First, ", "Then, ", "", "" },
                      { "First, ", "Next, ", "Finally, ", "" },
                      { "First, ", "Then, ", "Next, ", "Finally, " }
                    };


/* ****************************************************************** *
 *       structures                                                  *
 * ****************************************************************** */

struct boot_rec                          /* boot record             */
    {
    char jmp[3],                         /* jump instruction        */
         oem[8];                         /* OEM name                */
    UINT bytes;                          /* bytes per sector        */
    char cluster;                        /* sectors per cluster     */
    UINT res_sectors;                    /* reserved sectors        */
    char fats;                           /* number of fats          */
    UINT roots,                          /* nbr of root dir entries */
         sectors;                        /* total sectors           */
    char media;                          /* media descriptor block  */
    UINT fatsize,                        /* sectors per fat         */
         tracksize,                      /* sectors per track       */
         heads;                          /* number of heads         */
    long hidden,                         /* hidden sectors          */
```

```
            sectors_32;                     /* sectors if above 32Mb    */
        } *BOOT;

struct dos4_i25                             /* dos 4.0 int 25 block      */
        {
        long sector;                        /* sector to read            */
        int  num_secs;                      /* number of sectors to read*/
        HUGE *read_addr;                    /* address of input area     */
        };

struct media_id                             /* media id block            */
        {
        int  info_level,                    /* information level         */
             serial1,                       /* serial number, part I     */
             serial2;                       /* ..part II                 */
        char vol_id[11],                    /* volume label              */
             file_sys[8];                   /* file system id            */
        };

struct mapped_dta                           /* mapped dta/dir entry      */
        {
        char dta_1[6],                      /* first part of fcb         */
             s_attrib,                      /* search attribute          */
             de_drive,                      /* drive                     */
             de_name[8],                    /* filename                  */
             de_ext[3],                     /* extension                 */
             de_attrib,                     /* directory attribute       */
             dta_2[10];                     /* more reserved space       */
        UINT de_time,                       /* directory time            */
             de_date,                       /* directory date            */
             de_cluster;                    /* first cluster             */
        long de_size;                       /* size of file              */
        char dta_3[88];                     /* reserved (to 128 bytes)   */
        } dir_entry;

struct   extended_fcb                       /* file control block        */
        {
        char    f_signature,                /* extended fcb signature    */
                f_extra[5],                 /* reserved                  */
                f_attrib,                   /* extended fcb attribute    */
                f_drive,                    /* drive                     */
                f_filename[8],              /* filename                  */
                f_ext[3];                   /* extension                 */
        UINT    block;                      /* block number              */
        long    filesize;                   /* file size                 */
        int     f_date,                     /* file date                 */
                f_time;                     /* ..and time                */
        char    f_system[8],                /* reserved area             */
                f_record;                   /* current record            */
        long    rnd_recno;                  /* random record number      */
        } ;


/* ******************************************************************** *
 *        main()                                                        *
 * ******************************************************************** */

void    main(int  ac,                       /* DOS cmd line token count  */
             char *av[])                    /* ..token strings           */
{
int     i;                                  /* loop counter, work        */
char    *p;                                 /* positional parm pointer   */
```

```
    printf(copyright);                          /* give copyright message   */

    ctrlbrk(control_break);                     /* set up ctrl break and    */
    _dos_setvect(0x24, critical_handler);       /* ..DOS critical handlers  */

    _dos_getdrive((UINT *) &init_drive);        /* get the default drive    */
    drive_nbr = init_drive;                      /* ..set up default drive   */
    *drive = init_drive + 'A' - 1;              /* ..nbr and ASCII string   */

    r.h.ah = 0x2f;                              /* ah = get dta address     */
    int86x(0x21, &r, &r, &s);                   /* issue DOS call           */
    old_dta = MK_FP(s.es, r.x.bx);              /* save old DTA segment     */

    r.h.ah = 0x1a;                              /* ah = set DTA             */
    s.ds = FP_SEG(&dir_entry);                  /* ds -> DTA segment        */
    r.x.dx = FP_OFF(&dir_entry);                /* ds:dx -> DTA             */
    int86x(0x21, &r, &r, &s);                   /* set up new DTA           */


    /* ******************** *
     * validate parameters  *
     * ******************** */

    if ((pos_found = parse_parms(ac, av,        /* parse switches and       */
            PARM_TABLE_CNT, parm_table,         /* ..positional parameters  */
            &pos_parms)) > 1)                   /* q. too may positionals?  */
        quit_with(0, too_many);                 /* a. yes .. give err/quit  */

    if (pos_found == 1)                         /* q. drive given?          */
        {
        p = *pos_parms;                         /* a. yes .. get pointer    */
        if ((strlen(p) == 2) && p[1] == ':')    /* q. valid size and shape? */
            *drive = *p;                        /* a. yes .. copy in drive  */
         else
            quit_with(0, bad_drive);            /* else .. give syntax err  */
        }

    drive[0] = toupper(drive[0]);               /* uppercase search drive   */
    drive_nbr = drive[0] - 'A' + 1;             /* get drive nbr from string*/
    _dos_setdrive(drive_nbr, (UINT *) &i);      /* set up target drive      */

    if ((init_path = getcwd(NULL, MAX_PATH))    /* q. get current path ok?  */
            == NULL)
        quit_with(0, drive_error);              /* a. no .. drive not ready */

    drive_check();                              /* check version and drive  */


    /* *************** *
     * process drive   *
     * *************** */

    get_fat();                                  /* read FAT into memory     */
    fat_check();                                /* check multiple FAT copies*/
    free_check();                               /* ..count freespaces       */
    chkdsk_files();                             /* ..and chkdsk leftovers   */
    dir_search(drive);                          /* search file chains       */
    unlinked_check();                           /* check unlinked clusters  */

    user_report(1);                             /* give final report ..     */
                                                /* ..then return to DOS     */
    }
```

```
/* ********************************************************************* *
 *       drive_check() -- check version and drive being local          *
 * ********************************************************************* */

void    drive_check(void)
{

if (_osmajor < 2)                       /* q. pre-DOS 2.00?         */
    quit_with(0, dos_error);            /* a. yes .. can't run it   */

if (strcmp(drive,                       /* q. real name different?  */
        translate_name(drive)))
        quit_with(0, net_drive);        /* a. yes .. error          */

if ((_osmajor == 3 && _osminor >= 1) || /* q. DOS 3.1 or higher?    */
        (_osmajor > 3))                 /* a. yes .. more checks     */
    {
    r.x.ax = 0x4409;                    /* ah = ioctl, local test   */
    r.h.bl = drive_nbr;                 /* bl = drive to test       */
    int86(0x21, &r, &r);                /* test drive               */

    if (r.x.cflag)                      /* q. bad drive?            */
        quit_with(0, bad_drive);        /* a. yes .. error          */

    if (r.x.dx & 0x9200)                /* q. network/remote/subst? */
        quit_with(0, net_drive);        /* a. yes .. error          */
    }

sw_dos4 |= (_osmajor >= 4) ||           /* use DOS v4 style i/o     */
        ((_osmajor == 3) &&             /* ..for DOS 3.31 and better*/
                (_osminor == 31));
}


/* ********************************************************************* *
 *       get_fat() -- read boot record and fat into memory             *
 * ********************************************************************* */

void    get_fat(void)
{

r.h.ah = 0x36;                          /* ah = get freespace       */
r.h.dl = drive_nbr;                     /* get drive                */
int86(0x21, &r, &r);                    /* r.x.cx = bytes/sector    */

BOOT = (struct boot_rec *)              /* get memory for boot rec  */
        cln_malloc(r.x.cx);

BOOT->bytes = r.x.cx;                   /* set up nbr bytes/sector  */
avail_disk = (long) r.x.bx;             /* ..nbr of avail clusters  */
max_secs = (UINT) ((65536L - 16) /      /* determine largest read   */
        BOOT->bytes);

if (read_disk(0L, 1, (HUGE *) BOOT))    /* q. read boot sector ok?  */
    quit_with(0, boot_error);           /* a. no .. give err msg    */

nsectors = (BOOT->sectors ?             /* compute ..               */
        (long) BOOT->sectors :          /* ..nbr of sectors on      */
        BOOT->sectors_32);              /* ..logical DOS drive      */
```

```
nclusters = (unsigned) ((long)((nsectors      /* ..nbr of DOS clusters  */
              - (BOOT->res_sectors
              + (BOOT->fatsize * BOOT->fats)
              + ((BOOT->roots * 32) / BOOT->bytes)))
              / BOOT->cluster));

fat_16 = nclusters > 4086;                     /* set if 16bit FAT table  */

max_cluster = nclusters + 2;                   /* ..max cluster number   */
bad_cluster = fat_16 ? 0xfff7 : 0xff7;         /* ..and the bad cluster nbr*/

cluster_size = BOOT->cluster * BOOT->bytes;    /* ..bytes per cluster    */
avail_disk *= cluster_size;                    /* ..available bytes      */

printf(drive_info, drive[0], read_label(),     /* give standard information*/
       nsectors, nclusters, cluster_size,      /* ..about logical volume  */
       large_fmt(nclusters * cluster_size));

printf(available, large_fmt(avail_disk));      /* ..and available space  */
fat = (HUGE *) cln_malloc((long)              /* get memory for a fat    */
         BOOT->fatsize * (long) BOOT->bytes);

fat_bits = (char *) cln_malloc((long)          /* ..and bit array        */
         (max_cluster + 7) / 8);

memset(fat_bits, 0, (max_cluster + 7) / 8);    /* ..initialize bit array  */

if (read_disk(BOOT->res_sectors,               /* q. read fat in?        */
         BOOT->fatsize, (char *) fat))
    quit_with(1, fat_error);                   /* a. no .. give error msg */

if (*fat != BOOT->media)                       /* q. valid fat?          */
    {
    keepalive(1);                              /* a. no .. clear k/a msg  */
    printf(bad_media);                         /* ..then give error message*/
    repair |= 1;                               /* ..and set up suggestion */
    }

}


/* ********************************************************************** *
 *       fat_check() -- check multiple FAT copies                         *
 * ********************************************************************** */

void    fat_check(void)
{
int     i, j, k,                               /* loop counters          */
        hdr_displayed = 0,                     /* verbose hdr displayed  */
        next_fat;                              /* next fat sector nbr    */
HUGE    *a_fat,                                /* alternate FAT pointers */
        huge *p;                               /* ..and work pointers    */

if (sw_verbose)                                /* q. tell where we're at? */
    {
    keepalive(1);                              /* a. yes .. clr keepalive */
    printf(fat_checking);                      /* ..and give new hdr msg  */
    hdr_displayed = 1;                         /* ..and set flag         */
    }

a_fat = (HUGE *) cln_malloc(BOOT->bytes);      /* get a sector buffer    */
```

```
    next_fat = BOOT->res_sectors;          /* ..and main FAT sector nbr*/

    for (i = 1; i < BOOT->fats; i++)       /* for each alternate FAT   */
        {
        next_fat += BOOT->fatsize;         /* get 1st sector number    */

        for (j = next_fat, k = BOOT->fatsize,  /* loop thru reading each */
                   p = fat; k;             /* ..sector and matching    */
                   k--, j++, p += BOOT->bytes) /* ..against primary FAT  */
            {
            if (read_disk(j, 1, a_fat))    /* q. read successful?      */
                quit_with(1, fat_error);   /* a. no .. quit w/err msg  */

            if (_fmemcmp(p, a_fat, BOOT->bytes))/* q. both sectors equal? */
                break;                     /* a. no .. exit loop       */

            keepalive(0);                  /* give a keepalive message */
            }

        if (k)                             /* q. both FATs equal?      */
            {                              /* a. no .. error detected  */
            if (hdr_displayed)             /* q. hdr been displayed?   */
                {
                printf(return_line);       /* a. yes .. over write hdr */
                hdr_displayed = 0;         /* ..and turn off flag      */
                }
             else
                keepalive(1);              /* else .. just next line   */

            printf(bad_nfat, i + 1);       /* give error message       */
            repair |= 1;                   /* ..and set up suggestions */
            }
        }

    farfree(a_fat);                        /* release sector buffer    */

    if (hdr_displayed)                     /* q. need to clean up hdr? */
        {
        fprintf(stderr, backspace);        /* a. yes .. fix up k/a msg */
        printf(fats_ok);                   /* ..put out all ok         */
        }

    }


/* ******************************************************************* *
 *      free_check() -- look for free spaces on the volume             *
 * ******************************************************************* */

void    free_check(void)
{
int     rc;                                /* work return code         */
UINT    i;                                 /* loop counter             */

    if (sw_verbose)                        /* q. tell user what's up?  */
        {
        keepalive(1);                      /* a. yes .. clr k/a msgs   */
        printf(free_areas);                /* ..then give hdr message  */
        }

    for(i = 2; i <= max_cluster; i++)      /* look for freespaces      */
```

```
        {
        keepalive(0);                           /* give keepalive message   */
        walk_fat(i, 0, &rc);                    /* get info on cluster      */

        if (rc == 2)                            /* q. free cluster?         */
            {
            free_cnt++;                         /* a. yes .. bump free count*/

            while (++i <= max_cluster)          /* find end of this space   */
                {
                keepalive(0);                   /* give keepalive message   */
                walk_fat(i, 0, &rc);            /* get info on this cluster */

                if (rc != 2)                    /* q. big free area?        */
                    break;                      /* a. no .. find next space */
                }
            }
        }

    if (sw_verbose)                             /* q. keeping user uptodate?*/
        {
        fprintf(stderr, backspace);             /* a. yes .. fix up k/a msg */
        printf(free_disp, free_cnt);            /* ..and give final stats   */
        }

    }


/* ******************************************************************** *
 *      chkdsk_files() -- check for chkdsk's FILEnnnn.CHK files         *
 * ******************************************************************** */

void    chkdsk_files(void)
{
char    *p;                                     /* string pointer           */
int     i;                                      /* loop counter             */
struct  find_t dos_entry;                       /* DOS directory entry      */
static
char    name[] = "\\FILE????.CHK";              /* chkdsk ambiguous filespec*/


for (rc = _dos_findfirst(name,                  /* find first and next file */
        _A_NORMAL, &dos_entry);                 /* ..'til a chkdsk recovery */
        NOT rc;)                                /* ..file found             */
    {
    for (i = 0, p = &dos_entry.name[4];         /* check for nnnn as last.. */
            isdigit(*p++) && i++ < 4;);         /* ..portion of filename    */

    if (i == 4)                                 /* q. valid chkdsk file?    */
        {
        keepalive(1);                           /* a. yes .. kill k/a msg   */
        printf(leftovers);                      /* ..and give error msg     */
        repair |= 4;                            /* ..set up suggestions     */
        break;                                  /* ..and exit loop          */
        }

    rc = _dos_findnext(&dos_entry);             /* set up to check next file*/

    }
}
```

```c
/* ********************************************************************* *
 *      dir_search() -- check a directory's files                        *
 * ********************************************************************* */
void    dir_search(char *base_dir)          /* base directory name      */
{
int     work_len,                           /* init length of work_dir  */
        dir_flag,                           /* directory entry flag     */
        dot_cnt = 0;                        /* dot files processed      */
char    *work_dir;                          /* work directory           */
struct  extended_fcb *find_work;            /* fcb work area            */
long    alloc_size;                         /* allocated cluster size   */
UINT    start_cluster;                      /* file/dir start cluster   */
struct  SREGS   s;                          /* segment registers        */
union   REGS    r;                          /* other registers          */


    work_dir = cln_malloc(                  /* get temporary memory for */
            MAX_PATH + 12 +                 /* ..full filespec          */
            sizeof(struct extended_fcb));   /* ..and the extended fcb   */

    find_work = (void *) &work_dir[MAX_PATH+12];/* ..and set up pointers */

    strcpy(work_dir, base_dir);             /* copy base directory      */

    if (strcmp(work_dir,                    /* q. JOIN'd?               */
            translate_name(work_dir)))
        {
        farfree(work_dir);                  /* a. yes .. release memory */
        return;                             /* ..and skip directory     */
        }

    chdir(base_dir);                        /* get to base directory    */

    if (strlen(base_dir) > 3)               /* q. need a trailing "\"?  */
        strcat(work_dir, "\\");             /* a. yes .. add trailing   */

    work_len = strlen(work_dir);            /* save initial length      */

    find_work->f_signature = 0xff;          /* extended fcb             */
    CLEAR(find_work->f_extra, 0);           /* set extra area           */
    CLEAR(find_work->f_filename, '?');      /* ..and filename           */
    CLEAR(find_work->f_ext, '?');           /* ..and extension          */
    find_work->f_drive = drive_nbr;         /* ..and drive number       */
    find_work->f_attrib = FILES;            /* set up attribute to find */
    r.h.ah = 0x11;                          /* ..and find first function*/

    s.ds = FP_SEG(find_work);               /* ds -> segment of fcb     */
    r.x.dx = FP_OFF(find_work);             /* ds:dx -> offset          */
    int86x(0x21, &r, &r, &s);               /* issue the dos call       */
    r.h.ah = 0x12;                          /* ..use findnext fnc later  */

    for(; NOT r.h.al;)                      /* look through current dir */
        {
        keepalive(0);                       /* give user warm fuzzies   */

        strcpy(&work_dir[work_len],         /* copy in directory        */
            pack_name(dir_entry.de_name,    /* ..and filename           */
            dir_entry.de_ext));

        if (strlen(work_dir) > MAX_PATH)    /* q. dir structure problem?*/
            {
            keepalive(1);                   /* a. yes .. kill k/a msgs   */
            printf(struct_error,            /* ..then give error msg    */
                bad_dir, work_dir);
```

```
        repair |= 1;                              /* ..set up for suggestion  */
        user_report(0);                           /* ..give summary and quit  */
        }

    if (dir_entry.de_name[0] == '.')              /* q. dot directory?        */
        {
        dot_cnt++;                                /* a. yes .. count it..     */
        int86x(0x21, &r, &r, &s);                 /* issue the dos call       */
        continue;                                 /* ..then to end of loop    */
        }

    start_cluster = dir_entry.de_cluster;         /* save starting cluster    */
    dir_flag = dir_entry.de_attrib &              /* ..and entry type         */
               _A_SUBDIR;

    if (dir_entry.de_attrib & _A_SUBDIR)          /* q. directory entry?      */
        dir_search(work_dir);                     /* a. yes .. call ourself   */

    alloc_size = frag_check(work_dir,             /* check for frag'd file..  */
            start_cluster, dir_flag);

    if (dir_flag)                                 /* q. directory entry?      */
        dirs_cnt++;                               /* a. yes .. tally dir's    */

     else
        {
        files_cnt++;                              /* count files processed    */

        if ((alloc_size -                         /* q. cluster size differs  */
                dir_entry.de_size ) >=            /* ..from directory entry   */
                cluster_size)                     /* ..size by > one cluster? */
            {
            keepalive(1);                         /* a. yes .. clear k/a msgs */
            printf(chain_error,                   /* ..then give error msg    */
                work_dir, sizing);
            repair |= 2;                          /* ..and set up suggestions */
            }
        }

    int86x(0x21, &r, &r, &s);                     /* issue findnext dos call  */

    }

if (work_len > 3 && dot_cnt != 2)                 /* q. dir have . and .. ?   */
    {
    keepalive(1);                                 /* a. no .. kill k/a msgs   */
    printf(struct_error,                          /* ..and give error message */
        base_dir, missing_dots);
    repair |= 1;                                  /* ..and set up suggestion  */
    }

farfree(work_dir);                                /* release temp memory      */

}


/* ********************************************************************** *
 *      unlinked_check() -- check for unlinked clusters                  *
 * ********************************************************************** */

void    unlinked_check(void)
{
int     rc;                                       /* error return code        */
```

```
UINT    i,                              /* loop counter              */
        lost_cnt = 0;                   /* lost cluster count        */


for (i = 2; i <= max_cluster; i++)      /* check thru entire FAT     */
    {
    keepalive(0);                       /* give the keepalive msg    */

    walk_fat(i, 0, &rc);                /* get info on this cluster  */

    if (rc == 0 || rc == 3 || rc == 4)  /* q. invalid or allocated?  */
        lost_cnt++;                     /* a. yes .. tally as lost   */
    }

if (lost_cnt)                           /* q. any lost clusters?     */
    {
    keepalive(1);                       /* a. yes .. clear k/a msgs  */
    printf(lost_cluster, lost_cnt);     /* ..then give bad news      */
    repair |= 2;                        /* ..and set up suggestion   */
    }

}


/* ********************************************************************** *
 *      frag_check() -- check for fragmented file                         *
 * ********************************************************************** */

long    frag_check(char *s,             /* file/directory name       */
                UINT start_cluster,     /* starting cluster number   */
                int  dflag)             /* directory flag            */
{
UINT    i,                              /* working cluster           */
        allocated,                      /* nbr of allocated bytes    */
        next_cluster;                   /* next cluster              */
int     flag = 0,                       /* flag for frag'd file      */
        rc;                             /* error return code         */


for (allocated = 0; start_cluster;)     /* walk down a file's FAT    */
    {
    allocated++;                        /* tally allocated clusters  */

    next_cluster = walk_fat(            /* check cluster chain and   */
            start_cluster, 1, &rc);     /* ..reset entries as we go  */

    if (rc <= 2 || rc == 5)             /* q. invalid or bad?        */
        {
        keepalive(1);                   /* a. yes .. kill k/a msg    */
        printf(chain_error, s, fat_err[rc]);/* ..and give error msg  */
        repair |= 2;                    /* ..set up suggestion       */
        break;                          /* ..go on to next file      */
        }

    if (rc == 4)                        /* q. end of chain?          */
        break;                          /* a. yes .. exit loop       */

    if ((start_cluster + 1) != next_cluster)/* q. non-contiguous area?  */
        {
        flag++;                         /* a. yes .. set frag flag   */

        if (next_cluster > start_cluster)   /* q. possibly bad cluster?  */
```

```
            {
            for (i = start_cluster + 1;     /* a. maybe .. check for .. */
                     i < next_cluster; i++) /* ..intervening bad ..     */
                {
                walk_fat(i, 0, &rc);        /* get info on cluster      */

                if (rc != 5)                /* q. bad cluster?          */
                    break;                  /* a. no .. exit loop       */
                }

            if (i == next_cluster)          /* q. was entire area bad?  */
                flag--;                     /* a. yes .. don't report   */
            }
        }

    start_cluster = next_cluster;           /* set up for next step     */

    }

if (flag)                                   /* q. fragmented file?      */
    {                                       /* a. yes .. process error  */
    if (sw_verbose)                         /* q. list frag'd files?    */
        {
        keepalive(1);                       /* a. yes .. 1st clear k/a  */
        printf(dflag ? frag_dir             /* ..then display frag'd    */
                     : frag_file, s);       /* ..file/directory name    */
        }

    frag_cnt++;                             /* accumulate frag'd count  */
    }

 else
    unfrag_cnt++;                           /* else total unfrag'd files*/

return(allocated * cluster_size);           /* return allocation size   */
}


/* ***************************************************************** *
 *      walk_fat() -- get next cluster in FAT chain                 *
 * ***************************************************************** */

UINT    walk_fat(UINT n,                    /* current cluster number   */
                int  flag,                  /* flag, 1=show processed   */
                int  *rc)                   /* error return code        */
                                            /*  0 = invalid cluster nbr */
                                            /*  1 = cross linked        */
                                            /*  2 = free                */
                                            /*  3 = allocated           */
                                            /*  4 = last in chain       */
                                            /*  5 = bad cluster         */
{
UINT    e,                                  /* entry number in FAT      */
        nc,                                 /* next cluster value       */
        huge *p;                            /* ptr for 16 bit FAT entry */

if (NOT (e = n) || (n > max_cluster))       /* q. invalid cluster nbr?  */
    {
    *rc = 0;                                /* a. yes .. set return code*/
    return(0);                              /* ..and return to caller   */
    }
```

```
    if (fat_16)                              /* q. 16 bit FAT entries?  */
        {
        p = (UINT huge *) &fat[0];           /* a. yes .. get FAT addr  */
        nc = p[e];                           /* retrieve next entry     */
        }

     else
        {
        e = ((n << 1) + n) >> 1;             /* cluster number * 1.5    */
        nc = *(UINT huge *) &fat[e];         /* get next cluster        */

        if (n & 1)                           /* q. need to do shift?    */
            nc >>= 4;                        /* a. yes .. shift by 4 bits*/
         else
            nc &= 0xfff;                     /* else .. strip upper bits */
        }
    if(get_bit(fat_bits, n))                 /* q. cross-linked?        */
        *rc = 1;                             /* a. yes .. mark w/error   */

     else if (nc == 1)                       /* q. invalid cluster?     */
        *rc = 0;                             /* a. yes .. show in rtn cd */

     else if (nc == 0)                       /* q. free cluster?        */
        *rc = 2;                             /* a. yes .. mark free      */

     else if (nc <= max_cluster)             /* q. allocated cluster?   */
        *rc = 3;                             /* a. yes .. show allocated */
     else if (nc == bad_cluster)             /* q. bad cluster?         */
        *rc = 5;                             /* a. yes .. show status    */

     else if (nc > bad_cluster)              /* q. EOF cluster?         */
        *rc = 4;                             /* else .. set up as EOF    */

     else                                    /* else ..                 */
        *rc = 0;                             /* ..cluster nbr is invalid */

    if (flag)                                /* q. need to flag entry?  */
        set_bit(fat_bits, n, 1);             /* a. yes .. set a bit      */

    return((*rc == 3) ? nc : 0);             /* return w/next cluster    */

    }


/* ******************************************************************* *
 *      get_bit() -- retrieve a bit from the bit array                 *
 * ******************************************************************* */

int     get_bit(char *array,                 /* bit array               */
                UINT element)                /* entry number            */
{
int     work;                                /* bits from array         */

work = array[element / 8];                   /* get a byte from the array*/
element %= 8;                                /* get bit number in byte   */

for (; element--; work >>= 1);               /* shift out unused bits    */

return(work & 0x01);                         /* return with requested bit*/

    }
```

```
/* ****************************************************************** *
 *      set_bit() -- set or clear a bit from the bit array          *
 * ****************************************************************** */

void    set_bit(char *array,            /* bit array               */
                UINT element,           /* entry number            */
                int  logical)           /* new logical bit value   */
{
int     i,                              /* loop counter            */
        mask = 1;                       /* mask for bit element     */


for (i = element % 8; i--; mask <<= 1);    /* get "or" mask        */

if (logical)                            /* q. turn bit on?         */
    array[element / 8] |= mask;         /* a. yes .. "or" it on    */

 else
    array[element / 8] &= NOT mask;     /* else .. "and" bit off   */

}



/* ****************************************************************** *
 *      pack_name() -- build a filename from an FCB                 *
 * ****************************************************************** */

char    *pack_name(char *filename,      /* name with trailing blks */
                   char *ext)           /* ..and extension         */
{
int     i;                              /* loop control            */
char    *p;                             /* work pointer            */
static
char    work[13];                       /* returned work area      */


p = work;                               /* initialize string pointer*/

for (i = 0; (i < 8) && (*filename != ' '); i++) /* move fname w/o blanks*/
    *p++ = *filename++;

if (*ext != ' ')                        /* q. extension blank?     */
    {
    *p++ = '.';                         /* a. no .. add the dot    */

    for (i = 0; (i < 3) && (*ext != ' '); i++)  /* add ext w/o blanks   */
        *p++ = *ext++;
    }

*p = 0;                                 /* terminate string w/null */

return(work);                           /* return string to caller */

}
```

```c
/* ********************************************************************** *
 *        read_label() -- get the volume's label, if available           *
 * ********************************************************************** */

char    *read_label(void)
{
char    *p, *q;                              /* work pointers           */
struct  find_t dir;                          /* directory entry         */
struct  media_id media;                      /* media id block          */
static
char    work[33] = { " :\\*.*" } ;           /* directory to check      */


work[0] = drive[0];                          /* set up for search string */

if (_osmajor == 2)                           /* q. DOS 2.x?              */
    return("");                              /* a. yes .. just return    */
if (_dos_findfirst(work, LABEL, &dir))       /* q. error on label get?   */
    work[0] = 0;                             /* a. yes .. then no label  */

  else
     {
     for(p = work, q = dir.name; *q; q++)    /* copy name w/o middle dot */
          if (*q != '.')                     /* q. is this char a dot?   */
              *p++ = *q;                      /* a. no .. copy it         */

     *p = 0;                                 /* make null terminated and */
     strcat(work, "  ");                     /* ..ready for serial number*/
     }


if (_osmajor >= 4)                           /* q. serial nbr available? */
     {
     media.info_level = 0;                   /* a. maybe .. set up call  */
     r.x.bx = drive_nbr;                     /* set up drive number..    */
     r.x.cx = 0x866;                         /* ..sub function code      */
     s.ds   = FP_SEG(&media);                /* ..work area segment      */
     r.x.dx = FP_OFF(&media);                /* ..and offset pointers    */
     r.x.ax = 0x440d;                        /* ..lastly function code   */
     int86x(0x21, &r, &r, &s);               /* issue dos call           */

     if (NOT r.x.cflag)                      /* q. complete ok?          */
         sprintf(&work[strlen(work)],        /* a. yes .. format into msg*/
            serial_nbr, media.serial2,
            media.serial1);
     }

return(work);                                /* ..return string          */

}



/* ********************************************************************** *
 *      quit_with() -- give an error message, then return to DOS          *
 * ********************************************************************** */

void    quit_with(int ka_flag,               /* give keepalive message   */
                char *msg)                   /* string to print          */
{
UINT    i;                                   /* work variable            */


if (ka_flag)                                 /* q. need to clean up?     */
```

```
        keepalive(1);                           /* a. yes .. clear k/a msg  */

    r.h.ah = 0x1a;                              /* ah = set DTA             */
    s.ds   = FP_SEG(&old_dta);                  /* ds -> DTA segment        */
    r.x.dx = FP_OFF(&old_dta);                  /* ds:dx -> DTA             */
    int86x(0x21, &r, &r, &s);                   /* restore old DTA          */

    _dos_setdrive(init_drive, &i);              /* reset the default drive  */

    if (init_path)                              /* q. valid path?           */
        chdir(init_path);                       /* a. yes .. then restore it*/

    printf(msg);                                /* give error message ..    */
    exit(rc);                                   /* ..and then quit          */

}


/* ***************************************************************** *
 *        keepalive() -- put out a keepalive blip to the user        *
 * ***************************************************************** */

void    keepalive(int flag)                     /* 0=put out next blip      */
                                                /* 1=clean up from k/a blip */
{
static
int     b_cnt = 0,                              /* blip counter             */
        b_call = 0,                             /* raw counter              */
        blip_freq = 25;                         /* frequency of keepalives  */
static
char    blips[] = "|/-\\",                      /* progress blips           */
        blip_fmt[]    = "\b%c",                 /* message format           */
        blip_clean[]  = "\b ";                  /* clean up message         */

    if (flag)                                   /* q. clean up call?        */
        {
        fprintf(stderr, blip_clean);            /* a. yes .. erase blip..   */
        printf(new_line);                       /* ..goto a new line        */
        b_call = 0;                             /* ..and reset counter      */
        }

     else
        if (NOT (b_call++ % blip_freq))         /* q. called enough times?  */
            fprintf(stderr, blip_fmt,           /* a. yes .. put next spoke */
                blips[b_cnt++ & 3]);            /* ..to simulate a wheel    */

}



/* ***************************************************************** *
 *                                                                   *
 *        parse_parms() -- parse command line parms                  *
 *                                                                   *
 *        returns: number of positional parms found                  *
 *                                                                   *
 * ***************************************************************** */

int     parse_parms(int  ac,                    /* argument count           */
                char *av[],                     /* command line arguments   */
                int  n,                         /* parse table entries      */
                struct cmd_parm *t,             /* cmd line parse table     */
                char ***parms_array)            /* positional parms array   */
```

```
{
int     i, j,                           /* loop counter              */
        parms_fnd = 0,                  /* positional parms found    */
        slash_fnd = 0;                  /* slash found in token      */
char    *p, *q,                         /* character pointer         */
        c;                              /* work character            */


*parms_array = (char **) cln_malloc(    /* set up for max nbr tokens*/
        sizeof(char *) * ac);

for (i = 1; i < ac; i++)                /* for each cmd line token   */
    {
    p = av[i];                          /* set up pointer to token   */

    while (*p)                          /* process token             */
        {
        if (*p == '/' || slash_fnd)     /* q. option available?      */
            {                           /* a. yes .. process switch  */
            if (NOT slash_fnd)          /* q. embedded slash?        */
                p++;                    /* a. no .. bump past slash   */

            c = toupper(*p);            /* get char and upcase it    */
            slash_fnd = 0;              /* reset switch              */

            if (c == '?')               /* q. help request?          */
                quit_with(0, help);     /* a. yes .. give help ..     */

            for (j = 0; j < n; j++)     /* check each table entry    */
                if (c == t[j].cp_ltr)   /* q. find match?            */
                    break;              /* a. yes .. exit loop       */

            if (j == n)                 /* q. no matches?            */
                {                       /* a. yes .. handle error    */
                if ((q = strchr(p, '/'))/* q. any more switches?     */
                        != 0)
                    *q = 0;             /* a. yes .. isolate bad one*/

                printf(bad_op, --p);    /* give error message        */
                quit_with(0, null_line);/* ..and exit w/errorlevel   */
                }

            if (t[j].cp_flag)           /* q. keyword parm w/data?   */
                {
                *(char **) t[j].cp_entry = ++p; /* a. yes .. save token */

                if (*(p += strcspn(p, "/")))/* q. any switches left?    */
                    {
                    *p++ = 0;           /* a. yes .. make a string   */
                    slash_fnd = 1;      /* ..show nxt char a switch   */
                    }
                }

            else
                {
                (*t[j].cp_entry)++;     /* show slash parm used      */
                p++;                    /* ..and point at next one   */
                }
            }
        else
            {
            (*parms_array)[parms_fnd++] = p;/* save positional string   */

            if (*(p += strcspn(p, "/")))    /* q. any switches left?     */
```

```
                {
                *p++ = 0;                          /* a. yes .. make a string  */
                slash_fnd = 1;                     /* ..show nxt char a switch */
                }
            }
        }

    }

*parms_array = (char **) farrealloc(           /* readjust array size      */
            *parms_array,                      /* ..for what was found     */
            sizeof(char *) * parms_fnd);

return(parms_fnd);                             /* rtn w/nbr of positionals */

}


/* *********************************************************************** *
 *      large_fmt() -- handle formatting of disk storage numbers         *
 * *********************************************************************** */

char    *large_fmt(unsigned long nbr)          /* number to be converted   */
{
int     g_flag = 0;                            /* gigabyte range flag      */
static
char    work[10];                              /* return string            */

if (nbr < 1000)                                /* q. less than 1k?         */
    sprintf(work, "%u bytes", nbr);            /* a. yes .. then use bytes */

 else
    {
    nbr /= 1000;                               /* make number in kilobytes */

    if (nbr < 1000)                            /* q. only in the kb range? */
        sprintf(work, "%ukb", nbr);            /* a. yes .. format as kb   */

      else
        {
        nbr /= 100;                            /* get mb or gb w/1 decimal */

        if (nbr > 10000)                       /* q. gigabyte range?       */
            {
            g_flag++;                          /* a. yes .. show as gb     */
            nbr /= 1000;                       /* ..and make in gigabytes  */
            }

        sprintf(work, "%lu.%lu%s",             /* format number            */
            nbr / 10, nbr % 10,
            g_flag ? "gb" : "mb");
        }
    }

return(work);                                  /* then give user the result*/

}
```

```
/* ********************************************************************** *
 *      cln_malloc() -- local malloc w/error handling                     *
 * ********************************************************************** */

void    *cln_malloc(long size)              /* amount of memory to get  */
{
void    *p;                                 /* temporary pointer        */

if (NOT (p = (void *) _fmalloc(size)))      /* q. enough memory?        */
    {
    printf(no_mem, size);                   /* a. no .. give error msg  */
    quit_with(1, null_line);                /* ..and quit               */
    }

return(p);                                  /* else .. return w/address */

}


/* ********************************************************************** *
 *      read_disk() -- absolute disk reads by sector                      *
 * ********************************************************************** */

int     read_disk(UINT start,               /* starting sector number   */
                  int  count,               /* count of sectors         */
                  HUGE *buffer)             /* disk buffer              */
{
UINT    read_secs;                          /* nbr sectors this read    */
struct  dos4_i25 d4_i25;                    /* dos 4.0 int 25 block     */

if (sw_dos4)                                /* dos version 4 interface? */
    {
    while (count)                           /* do until count expired   */
        {
        r.x.cx = -1;                        /* cx = 0xffff              */

        d4_i25.sector = start;              /* next sector number       */
        d4_i25.read_addr = buffer;          /* ..and disk buffer        */

        count -=                            /* size of next read ...    */
            (d4_i25.num_secs =              /* ..size of this read      */
                min(max_secs, count));      /* ..smaller of max, num    */

        start += d4_i25.num_secs;           /* next sector nbr          */
        buffer += (long) d4_i25.num_secs *  /* ..buffer address         */
                    BOOT->bytes;

        r.x.bx = FP_OFF(&d4_i25);           /* bx = offset of parm block*/
        s.ds   = FP_SEG(&d4_i25);           /* ds = segment of block    */
        r.h.al = drive_nbr - 1;             /* al = drive number        */

        int86x(0x25, &r, &r, &s);           /* read boot sector         */
        }
    }

  else
    {
    while (count)
        {
        read_secs = min(max_secs, count);   /* update remaining count   */
```

```
        r.x.cx = read_secs;                 /* cx = number of sectors  */
        r.x.dx = start;                      /* dx = starting sector    */
        r.x.bx = FP_OFF(buffer);             /* bx = offset of buffer   */
        s.ds   = FP_SEG(buffer);             /* ds = segment of buffer  */

        count -= read_secs;                  /* down count on sectors   */
        start += read_secs;                  /* upcount on sector nbr   */
        buffer += read_secs * BOOT->bytes;   /* ..and buffer address    */


        r.h.al = drive_nbr - 1;              /* al = drive number       */
        int86x(0x25, &r, &r, &s);            /* read boot sector        */
        }
    }


return(r.x.cflag);                          /* return TRUE for error   */

}



/* ****************************************************************** *
 *       translate_name() -- translate a DOS directory name         *
 * ****************************************************************** */

char    *translate_name(char *name)         /* name to translate       */
{
static
char    work[65];                           /* work/return area        */


if (_osmajor == 2)                          /* q. translate available? */
    return(name);                           /* a. no .. rtn with source */

r.h.ah = 0x60;                              /* ah = translate          */
r.x.si = FP_OFF(name);                      /* set ptr to input name   */
s.ds = FP_SEG(name);                        /* ..and segment           */
r.x.di = FP_OFF(work);                      /* set ptr to output area  */
s.es = FP_SEG(work);                        /* ..and segment           */
int86x(0x21, &r, &r, &s);                   /* translate the name      */

return(r.x.cflag ? NULL : work);            /* return workarea or null */

}




/* ****************************************************************** *
 *       user_report() -- give user final report                    *
 * ****************************************************************** */

void    user_report(int flag)               /* 0=partial report        */
                                            /* 1=full report           */
{
int     count = 0;                          /* options/work counter    */
char    **p,                                /* prefixes pointer        */
        *q,                                 /* work pointer            */
        *s;                                 /* string pointer          */


if (files_cnt + dirs_cnt)                   /* q. any files and dirs?  */
    percent_frag = (int) ((long)            /* a. yes .. compute the .. */
        (frag_cnt * 100L) /                 /* ..percentage fragmented */
        (files_cnt + dirs_cnt));            /* ..w/o getting div error */
```

```
if (NOT percent_frag && frag_cnt)      /* q. something frag'd?     */
    percent_frag = 1;                  /* a. yes .. show non-zero  */

if (percent_frag >= 10)                /* q. little fragmentation? */
    repair |= 8;                       /* a. yes .. set up for msg */

keepalive(1);                          /* clear keepalive msgs ..  */

if (flag)                              /* q. need a full report?   */
    printf(final_report,               /* a. yes .. give final     */
            files_cnt, dirs_cnt,       /* ..stats to the user      */
            unfrag_cnt, 100 - percent_frag,
            frag_cnt, percent_frag,
            free_cnt);

if (repair & 3)                        /* q. repair or chkdsk?     */
    count++;                           /* a. yes .. count as one   */

if (repair & 4)                        /* q. chkdsk files found?   */
    count++;                           /* a. yes .. then count one */

if (repair & 8)                        /* q. defrag'ing needed?    */
    count++;                           /* a. yes .. count as one   */

if (count == 0)                        /* q. everything ok?        */
    {
    rc = 0;                            /* a. yes .. set return code*/
    printf(suggest_hdr);               /* give header message      */
    quit_with(0, requests[0]);         /* ..and give ok msg & exit */
    }

s = cln_malloc(count * 80);            /* get string space         */
*s = 0;                                /* ..and make null string   */
p = &prefix[--count][0];               /* set prefixes for messages*/

if (repair & 1)                        /* q. structure repair?     */
    {
    strcat(s, *p++);                   /* a. yes .. copy in prefix */
    strcat(s, requests[1]);            /* ..and message text       */
    rc = 4;                            /* ..and set return code    */
    }

 else if (repair & 2)                  /* q. need to chkdsk?       */
    {
    strcat(s, *p++);                   /* a. yes .. copy in prefix */
    strcat(s, requests[2]);            /* ..and message text       */
    rc = 3;                            /* ..and set return code    */
    }

if (repair & 4)                        /* q. chkdsk files found?   */
    {
    strcat(s, *p++);                   /* a. yes .. copy in prefix */
    strcat(s, requests[3]);            /* ..message text           */
    rc = max(rc, 2);                   /* ..and set return code    */
    }

if (repair & 8)                        /* q. defrag'ing needed?    */
    {
    strcat(s, *p++);                   /* a. yes .. copy in prefix */
    strcat(s, requests[4]);            /* ..and message text       */
    rc = max(rc, 1);                   /* ..and set return code    */
    }

*s = toupper(*s);                      /* make sure we start w/cap */
```

```
    printf(suggest_hdr);                         /* give header message      */

    for (; (count = strlen(s)) > 1; s += count)  /* loop printing msg string */
        {
        count = min(count, 55);                  /* get a chunk of string    */

        for (q = &s[count]; count && *q != ' ';  /* backscan to find a blank */
                q--, count--)
            ;

        if (NOT count)                           /* q. last word?            */
            count = strlen(s);                   /* a. yes .. do remainder   */

        printf(suggestion, count, s);            /* put out a line of message*/
        }

    quit_with(0, return_line);                   /* finally, do exit process */

    }


/* ********************************************************************** *
 *      control_break() -- control break intercept routine              *
 * ********************************************************************** */

int     control_break(void)
{
UINT    i;                                       /* work parm for set drive  */

    _dos_setdrive(init_drive, &i);               /* reset the default drive  */

    if (init_path)                               /* q. valid path?           */
        chdir(init_path);                        /* a. yes .. then restore it*/

    printf(stop_here);                           /* give error message ..    */

    return(0);

    }


/* ********************************************************************** *
 *      critical_handler() -- DOS critical error handler                *
 * ********************************************************************** */

#pragma argsused                        /* hold unused argument messages    */
#pragma option -O2-b-e                   /* no global register allocation    */
                                         /* ..or dead code elimination       */

void    interrupt critical_handler(UINT bp,
            UINT di, UINT si, UINT ds, UINT es,
            UINT dx, UINT cx, UINT bx, UINT ax,
            UINT cs, UINT ip, UINT flags)
{

    if (ax & 0x800)                              /* q. fail allowed?         */
        ax = (ax & 0xff00) | 3;                  /* a. yes .. fail request   */
    else
        ax = (ax & 0xff00) | 2;                  /* else .. abort request    */

    }
```

9

MANAGING YOUR APPOINTMENTS WITH CAL

CAL displays an interactive calendar that lets you scroll through the days, weeks, and months.

Each day can have a short note attached, containing any information you care to enter.

Two basic functions provided by today's personal computers are storing information in files and maintaining the current date. Although it is easy to determine today's date, and a simple task to place information in a file, combining these functions (and more) to form a calendar management program is no simple matter. A calendar management program must be capable of date calculation, calendar navigation, and information storage and retrieval. CAL combines these function into a single, easy-to-use program. With CAL, you can easily navigate the dates on a calendar, as well as record notes that are associated with a given day.

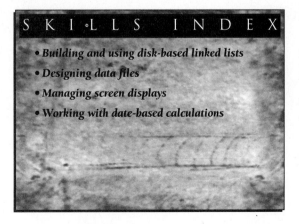

SKILLS INDEX

- *Building and using disk-based linked lists*
- *Designing data files*
- *Managing screen displays*
- *Working with date-based calculations*

■ USING CAL

To start CAL, simply enter the command CAL on DOS's command line. CAL supports no command line arguments, options, or switches, and if you add any to the command line, CAL ignores them.

As soon as you have entered the command, CAL displays its copyright notice for a moment, and then the calendar screen appears, with the current day (according to your system's date) highlighted. Figure 9.1 shows CAL's screen layout.

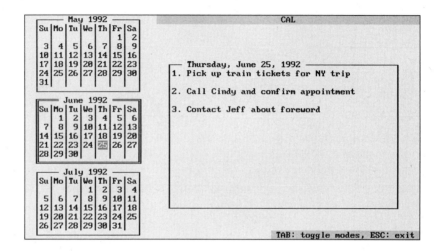

On the left side of the screen are three month calendars. The calendar in the center represents the current month, with the current day highlighted. Above and below are the previous and next months' calendars, respectively. On the right side of the screen is a box with a highlighted day and date at the top. The date corresponds to the highlighted day in the center calendar. This box contains any information that you have entered for the currently highlighted date.

Once CAL's screen is displayed, you have three options: Navigate through days on the calendars, add or modify a note for a specific day, or return to DOS.

- ### Navigating CAL's Screen

You can move through the dates on CAL's calendars by day, week, or month. Movement through the days is accomplished with the Left Arrow and Right Arrow keys. To move to the previous day, press Left Arrow; to move to the next day, press Right Arrow. Similarly, you can move backward a week at a time by pressing Up Arrow, and forward a week at a time by pressing Down Arrow. The Page Up and Page Down keys move backward and forward a month at a time, respectively. As you move through the months, CAL tries to keep you on the same day of the month. If, however, you are at the end of a month when you move to a shorter month, CAL will highlight the last day of the new month.

■ Recording a Note

Using the text box on the right side of the screen, you can attach any information you wish to the date currently highlighted. To use the text box, highlight a date in any of the calendars, and press the Tab key. CAL then places the cursor in the text box.

Once in the text box, you may use any of the following keys:

- Character keys to enter text

- Arrow keys to move around within the text box

- Enter key to move to the start of the next line

- Backspace key to delete the preceding character

- Tab key to return to the calendar

Entering text in the text box overwrites any text already in the corresponding positions; there is no insert mode. Also, each time you press Backspace, all the text on the following lines is shifted one character to the left and wrapped onto preceding lines. As you type (or use the arrow keys) and reach the rightmost column, the cursor automatically moves to the beginning of the subsequent line when you type the next character. If the cursor is on the last position within the box, it automatically wraps to the first position when you type the next character.

To return to calendar navigation after you finish typing in the box, press the Tab key again. When you do, CAL updates the calendar file with the new information you placed in the text box.

At any time, you may press the Escape key to return to DOS. If you press Esc when in the text box, the current information in the text box is written to the calendar file before the program returns to DOS.

■ Setting Up to Use CAL

When you invoke CAL, it looks in the current directory to find the file CAL.DAT. If the file is not there, CAL looks in all of the directories named in the PATH environment variable. If CAL exhausts PATH's directories without finding CAL.DAT, the program creates CAL.DAT in the current directory.

After running CAL for the first time, you can move the CAL.DAT file to a directory named on the PATH environment variable. From then on, whenever you invoke CAL, it will find CAL.DAT (as long as you don't remove the directory from the PATH statement).

■ INSIDE CAL

CAL is a complicated program that fulfills two primary requirements: calendar navigation and date file management. To accomplish this, CAL's functions fall into three general categories: date calculation, screen management, and file management. As we'll see, CAL ties all of this together in a few high-level routines.

■ CAL's Startup

When you run CAL, it starts by displaying its copyright notice and calling initialization(). The initialization() routine sets up CAL's environment by first setting the control break and DOS critical error handler vectors. Next, initialization() gets information about the current screen mode, sets the screen attributes based on that mode, and allocates memory for the various data file records in CAL.DAT.

Then, initialization() opens CAL.DAT by calling find_file(). The find_file() routine attempts to open CAL.DAT in the current directory. If the file is there, find_file() returns to initialization(). Otherwise, find_file() retrieves the value assigned to the PATH environment variable, and enters a loop, checking for CAL.DAT in each directory specified by the PATH variable. If find_file() finds CAL.DAT, the file is opened and the first record, known as the super-record, is read into memory. If CAL.DAT is not found, initialization() creates the file in the current directory, and initializes the file by writing the super-record. The super-record will be explained later in the chapter.

Setting up the screen is the initialization() routine's last function. Two routines, set_up_screen() and draw_box(), are invoked to display CAL's initial screen format. The set_up_screen() function prepares the screen by setting the display attributes, clearing the screen, and displaying the header and footer lines. The draw_box() routine displays the empty text box on the right side of the screen. Although draw_box() does place the lines for the text box on the screen, the date is not added at the top of the text box until later in the program. Once draw_box() finishes, initialization() returns to main().

■ CAL Starts Running

Immediately upon completion of initialization(), the main() routine calls keyboard_loop(), in which CAL intercepts keystrokes and calls the associated routines. The keyboard_loop() function first calls get_today(), which retrieves the current day and displays the three month calendars, including any note for the current day from CAL.DAT. To do this, get_today() calls _dos_getdate().

Before studying CAL's display management, you'll want to first understand how CAL works with dates, and the file structure of CAL.DAT.

■ Date Calculations

Date calculations are often frustrating and confusing. It may be easy to answer the question "What was the date exactly two months ago today?" but it requires some thought to answer "How many days ago was that?" Similarly, you can easily respond to "What is the name of the day that occurred exactly two weeks ago today?" but "What was the name of the day that occurred on this date last month?" probably sends you scrambling for a calendar.

The varying lengths of months and years confuse the issue of date calculation. CAL solves this problem by working with dates in two formats: the Gregorian date (day, month, and year); and the number of days since a *base date*, represented as a number of days since March 1, 1 B.C., with a base date of zero representing that date.

At the center of the date calculations are two routines: greg2base() and base2greg(). The greg2base() routine translates a Gregorian date into a base date. The base2greg() routine accepts a base date value and translates it into a day, month, year, and day of week. Before examining base2greg()'s formula, let's look at the rules for a leap year.

Generally, a leap year is a year that is evenly divisible by four. The exceptions to this rule are years when the century changes. Although it is evenly divisible by four, the year of a century change is only a leap year when it is evenly divisible by 400. So the years 1600 and 2000 are leap years, but the years 1700, 1800, and 1900 are not.

We know exactly how many days are in each year. We also know that a combination century change/leap year leap year only occurs every 400 years. Thus we can calculate the number of days in a 400-year period like this:

```
leap_yrs = (400 / 4) - 3;              /* 97 leap years in 400 years */
non_leaps = 400 - leap_yrs;            /* 303 non-leap yrs in 400 yrs*/
days = (non_leaps * 365) + (leap_yrs * 366);  /* days in 400 years        */
                                       /* = 146,097 days per 400 yrs */
```

When it knows this value (146,097), base2greg() can use a base date to calculate the century, and the year within the century—finally yielding the absolute year (such as 1992).

Two other numbers used by base2greg() are 1,461 (the number of days in a four-year period) and 153 (the number of days in a five-month period). Using these values, and the remainder of days left from calculating the year, base2greg() derives the month and day.

As mentioned earlier, the base date zero refers to March 1, 1 B.C. When March 1 is used (instead of January 1) as the first day of a year, the leap date (February 29) always occurs at the end of each leap year. In CAL, March 1 is always the "first" day of the year (for calculation purposes), and the beginning of all subsequent months after March is a fixed number of days from March 1.

■ **Note.** *If you start with the assumption that the year begins in March, and you count any five-month period in which the entire five months are contained in a single March-to-February year, all possible combinations but the last, which includes February, contain exactly 153 days. Try it... it's true!*

All of CAL's calendar navigation occurs by calculating and translating base dates. Using the base date format provides a clear advantage: Moving through the calendar requires simply adding or subtracting the number of days to or from the base date. Once the new base date is calculated, it can easily be returned to Gregorian date with base2greg().

■ **GETTING CAL'S FIRST DATE**

After get_today() retrieves the current date, it calls display_day() to display the appropriate months and note. Since display_day() requires a base date, get_today() calls greg2base(), which passes the current date converted to base date. The display_day() routine performs three calls: base2greg() to calculate the current Gregorian date, display_note() to show the note associated with the current date, and display_calendar() to display the three month calendars.

■ ## The Structure of CAL.DAT

Most C compilers do not provide any tools (such as btree, ISAM, and so on) for advanced organization of data within files. All reasonable C compilers do, however, provide direct access into disk files. This being the case, CAL organizes the records in CAL.DAT as a series of linked lists, and accesses them by seeking directly to records and reading the information. The technique used in arranging CAL.DAT's contents is a *sparse array*. In a sparse array, space is only allocated for items that are in use. Figure 9.2 is a graphic layout of CAL.DAT's internal format.

CAL.DAT contains five types of records: the super-record, year records, month records, day records, and deleted records. All of these records start with two fields: a 16-bit length field and a single-byte identification field. The length field records how long the record is; the identification field indicates the type of record.

FIGURE 9.2

*CAL.DAT's
internal
structure*

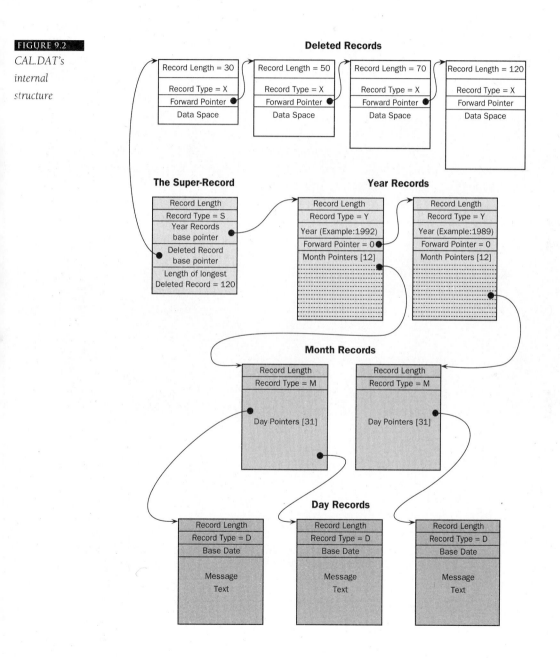

The *super-record* serves as a base pointer for two chains of records: the year records and the deleted records. The super-record also retains the length of the largest deleted record. When CAL needs to allocate another day record, it can check the length in the super-record before searching, in vain, for a deleted record of sufficient length.

The *year records* are placed on the year record chain, with the record representing the highest year at the head of the chain and the following years in descending order. Each year record contains the year represented, a pointer to the next year record, and 12 pointers to month records. If any of the month pointers contain a zero, no month record has been allocated for that month and year. Finally, if the year record's forward pointer is zero, it is the last record in the chain. (In an alternate algorithm, the month records could have been chained to the year records, but CAL would have had to perform as many as 12 seeks and reads to retrieve the December record. To avoid this, it made sense to sacrifice some disk space for retrieval speed.)

A *month record* consists of 31 pointers to day records. Each pointer can contain the offset of the associated day record. (In this case, too, an alternative algorithm could have chained the day records to the month records, but this would require as many as 31 seeks and reads to retrieve a particular day's record. As before, retrieval speed wins out over disk space conservation.)

This entire record structure exists to support the *day records*. The day records contain a base date representing the date for that record, and a note field associated with that date. Though all the other records have a fixed length, the day records are never shorter than eight bytes, and are as long as necessary to contain all the day record text. CAL derives the length of the text in the day record from the record length field in the header.

Note that, beyond storing the date of the record, CAL does not use the base date field in day records. This field is provided so you can write a file-recovery-and-reorganize utility, as mentioned in the suggested enhancements at the end of the chapter.

Finally, *deleted records* are day records that have been completely erased by the user. Whenever a new record is added to the file (or an existing record is lengthened), CAL first searches the deleted records for a record large enough to hold the newly entered data. If no suitable record is found, CAL allocates a new one. Although it may seem excessive to place deleted records in length order on the deleted chain, it facilitates the use of a best-fit algorithm for reusing records. Since CAL retrieves records in length order, the first record with enough space is used.

■ CAL's File Interface Routines

At the lowest level, CAL has five routines that directly read and write to CAL.DAT: cal_read(), cal_read_x(), cal_write(), cal_write_x(), and new_rec().

The cal_read() routine seeks to the requested offset in the file, and reads the two-byte length from the file. Using that length, cal_read() reads the remainder of the record into memory. When CAL needs to read either the super-record, a year record, a month record, or a day record into memory, it uses cal_read() to do so. When reading deleted records, CAL uses cal_read_x(). This routine only retrieves and reads the first seven bytes of a deleted record (the balance of the deleted record is of no interest).

The cal_write() and cal_write_x() routines write active and deleted records, respectively, to CAL.DAT. Like cal_read_x(), cal_write_x() only writes the first seven bytes of a deleted record to the file.

The new_rec() routine seeks to the end of CAL.DAT and allocates a new record by writing it to the file. The offset of the new record within the file is returned by new_rec() to its caller.

■ Working with CAL.DAT's Records

At the next level, CAL provides a set of routines to work with specific record types: find_year(), find_month(), find_day(), allocate_note(), delete_note(), and chain_note().

The find_year() routine searches CAL.DAT for a year record. If the requested year record is not found, find_year() creates one. In either case, the buffer allocated by initialization() for a year record is eventually filled in by find_year().

Similarly, find_month() retrieves or allocates a month record. The find_month() routine assumes that the associated year record is already in memory, and uses the pointers in that year record. If find_month() allocates a new month record, it rewrites the year record after filling in the pointer to the new month record.

The find_day() routine retrieves the day record associated with the highlighted day on the calendar. When called, find_day() first verifies that the proper year and month records are in memory, and retrieves them if necessary. If either the year or month record does not exist, the day record cannot exist either, and is therefore not retrieved. If, however, the year and month records are found, find_day() checks the pointer to the day record. If the pointer is not zero, the day record is read into memory.

The allocate_note() routine checks the deleted record list to see if it contains a record large enough to hold the current day record. If it does, the routine searches the deleted list for a record of suitable length, and removes it from the deleted chain. If no suitable record exists, the routine simply seeks to the end of the file and writes out the day record, effectively creating a new day record.

The delete_note() routine moves an active day record to the deleted record list. In order to delete a day record, delete_note() first verifies that some deleted records already exist. If not, this deleted record is chained as the first. Otherwise, delete_note() reads the list of deleted records and inserts the newly deleted record at the appropriate place on the list.

Finally, the chain_note() routine chains the current day record to the current month record. In the case of a deleted record, chain_note() replaces the pointer in the month record with a zero.

■ The High-Level Interface

The whole structure of CAL.DAT exists to facilitate the quick retrieval of day records. The year and month records simply serve as indices to the day records. Ultimately, CAL only cares about two functions: reading and writing day records.

The read_note() and write_note() routines perform these important functions for CAL. The read_note() routine sets an indicator showing that no day record is in memory, fills the buffer with blanks, and calls find_day() to retrieve the record associated with the day highlighted on the calendar. After retrieving the record, read_note() ensures that the note field terminates with a null character.

The complexity of write_note() more than compensates for the simplicity of read_note(). The write_note() routine creates, updates, or deletes records in CAL.DAT. There are four situations write_note() must handle: deleting an existing record, creating a new record, updating an existing record, and replacing a short record.

Two conditions must be met before write_note() deletes a record. The contents of the text box must be blank, and a day record must exist for the highlighted date. If both of these conditions are true, write_note() places the day record on the deleted chain by calling delete_note(), and resets the associated pointer in the month record.

When the text box is not empty, write_note() looks for a day record for the highlighted date. If there isn't one, write_note() allocates one by calling allocate_note().

When the text box is not empty *and* a day record does exist, write_note() verifies that the existing record is large enough to contain the text. If the record is large enough, write_note() updates the existing record. Otherwise, the existing record is moved to the chain of deleted records and a larger record is allocated to hold the text.

■ Displaying and Working with Calendars

Knowing the internals of CAL's date calculation routines and file manipulation routines, we can now tie all this together with the display management and user interface routines.

The main interface routine for display management is display_day(). As mentioned earlier, display_day() accepts a base date representing the day to be displayed. After calling base2greg() to convert the base date to its Gregorian equivalent, display_date() calls display_note(). A fairly simple routine, display_note() places the current day and date at the top of the text box, retrieves the day record for the highlighted date, and displays the data found in the record. After display_note() completes, display_day() calls display_calendars() to format and display the three calendars on the left side of the screen.

■ **Displaying the Calendars**

When working with a full-screen, formatted display, it is important that the screen not be unnecessarily updated. Redrawing the entire screen every time an update is made to the screen data can lead to a sluggish program with long response times. CAL avoids unnecessary screen redraws by calculating a key based on year and month. Only if the key changes between calls to the display_calendars() routine will all three calendars be redrawn. The middle calendar, however, is redrawn every time the day changes.

All calendar updates are performed by display_one_calendar(), which positions the cursor, calculates the first starting day, and actually draws the calendar. When display_one_calendar() encounters the date requested by the user, it highlights that entry.

As CAL runs, notice that the lower two calendars shift positions as you move through the months. CAL does this so that there will always be enough space on the screen for three calendars. In order to have three fixed calendars in the format used by CAL, 27 screen lines are required. The date line, day line, and bottom line account for 3 lines per calendar, or 9 total lines. And because any given month may use up to 6 week lines (or 18 lines for three months), that amount of space must be reserved for a fixed display. Since the display is usually 25 lines long, that is not enough room to display three fixed length calendars. To accommodate this shortfall, CAL adjusts the length of the calendars dynamically as the months change. Even in the worst-case scenario—July (31 days), August (31 days), and September (30 days), when July starts on a Saturday—the calendar takes a maximum of 25 lines to display.

■ **CAL's User Interface**

All of CAL's interactive functions are controlled by two routines: keyboard_loop() when the user is moving through calendars, and edit_text() when the user is editing a day record.

When called, keyboard_loop() first calls get_today() to display the initial calendars and day record, and then enters a for loop that accepts keystrokes. Because so much of the work is handled in lower-level routines, keyboard_loop() merely has to recalculate the base date and call display_day() to handle movement around the calendar.

The exception to this is when the Page Up or Page Down key is pressed. In these cases, keyboard_loop() modifies the current month and calls validate_date(). If the modified month or day falls outside of the valid range, validate_date() makes an appropriate adjustment. For example, if the highlighted date is January 15, 1992, and you press Page Up (to go to the previous month), the month value will change to zero. The validate_date() routine will recognize the invalid month, change it to a 12 (December), and decrement the year.

Similarly, if the day becomes invalid for the month selected, validate_date() sets it to an acceptable value. For example, if the highlighted day is March 31, 1992, and you press Page Down (to go to the next month), validate_date() will know that April 31 is an invalid date, and adjust the day back to April 30. Once validate_date() finishes adjusting the date, keyboard_loop() calls display_day() as usual.

■ Editing the Day Record

When you press the Tab key, CAL changes to edit mode, allowing you to edit the current day record. When Tab is pressed, keyboard_loop() calls edit_text(). The edit_text() routine defines the limit of the screen by calling C's window() routine. Next, edit_text() places the cursor on the first position within that window, and enters a loop waiting for keystrokes.

As edit_text() receives keystrokes, it performs the requested function. Most of the code in edit_text() is self-explanatory, but there is one small and interesting routine: validate_cursor(). This routine checks the new coordinates set for the cursor. If either the row or column is out of range, validate_cursor() modifies the offending coordinate, placing the cursor back inside the box. The modified coordinate causes the cursor to move to the top of the box when the cursor reaches the bottom, or move to the next line when the cursor reaches the end of the previous line, or restart on line 1 when the cursor reaches the end of the last line. In short, validate_cursor() guarantees that the cursor stays in the text box.

When you press either Esc or Tab, edit_text() writes the day record (if it's not blank) to the file. In response to Esc, edit_text() returns to DOS. With Tab, edit_text() returns to keyboard_loop() so you can move to a different date.

- **Shutdown**

  When you press Esc to exit from CAL, the close_down() routine is invoked. This routine clears the screen and closes the CAL.DAT file. Finally, CAL prints an exit message and returns to DOS.

- # SUMMARY

  CAL combines display management, file processing, and date calculation into a single program. Although these functions are used cooperatively here, they are each sufficiently self-contained to allow movement to and use in other programs. Here are some enhancements you may want to try and add to CAL:

  - Allow the entry of a date, letting the user move directly to a day without displaying all of the intervening months.

  - Using CAL as the basis, write a program to purge inactive day, month, and year records from the file. Write another program that will recover a file after a chain pointer has been corrupted.

  - Add code to allow the use of the Insert and Delete keys when the user edits a day record.

CAL 1.00

```
/* ********************************************************************* *

   CAL 1.00, Copyright (c) 1992, Michael Holmes and Bob Flanders
   PC Magazine C Lab Notes, Calendar program

 * ********************************************************************* *

   This code for Borland C++ version 3.0. (MSC version on diskette)

        Compile with:  BCC -O2 -ms cal.c

   To compile for Microsoft C, you need to change the following:
        - screen scrolling routines, insline() and delline()
        - screen color setting routines, textcolor() and textbackground()
        - logical screen definition routine, window()
        - change control break handling for ctrlbrk() and control_break()
        - change #pragma as necessary

 * ********************************************************************* */


#pragma  pack(1)                               /* pack to byte alignment    */
#include <stdio.h>                             /* standard i/o library      */
#include <io.h>                                /* i/o routine headers       */
#include <stdlib.h>                            /* ANSI compatibility        */
#include <dos.h>                               /* DOS rtn definitions       */
#include <stdarg.h>                            /* argument functions        */
#include <malloc.h>                            /* memory declarations       */
#include <string.h>                            /* string functions          */
#include <conio.h>                             /* console i/o routines      */


                                               /* shorthands                */
#define NOT          !                         /* logical not               */
#define CLEAR(x)     memset(x, 0, sizeof(x))   /* clear field to nulls      */
#define LAST(x)      x[strlen(x) - 1]          /* get last char in string   */
#define LEN(x)       sizeof(struct x)          /* structure size            */
#define READ(x, y)   cal_read(x,  (void *) y)  /* read record from database*/
#define WRITE(x, y)  cal_write(x, (void *) y)  /* ..and write a record      */
#define UINT         unsigned int              /* unsigned integer type     */
#define MAX_PATH     79                        /* max path length           */
#define B_WIDTH      20                        /* calendar box width        */
#define B_XPOS       3                         /* ..and starting x position*/
#define DRAW(x)      cprintf("%c", x)          /* line draw one character   */
#define BAR          "\xb3"                    /* vertical bar character    */
#define CAL_DAT      "CAL.DAT"                 /* data file name            */


                                               /* key definitions           */
#define UP           0x100 + '\x48'            /* up key                    */
#define DOWN         0x100 + '\x50'            /* down key                  */
#define LEFT         0x100 + '\x4b'            /* left arrow key            */
#define RIGHT        0x100 + '\x4d'            /* right arrow key           */
#define CR           '\r'                      /* carriage return           */
#define ESC          '\x1b'                    /* escape key                */
#define BACKSPACE    '\b'                      /* backspace key             */
```

```
#define TAB          '\t'                    /* tab key                   */
#define PAGE_UP      0x100 + '\x49'          /* page up key               */
#define PAGE_DOWN    0x100 + '\x51'          /* page down key             */


/* ********************************************************************* *
 *        routine definitions                                          *
 * ********************************************************************* */

void    quit_with(char *, ...),             /* quit with error message   */
        initialization(void),               /* screen and file set up    */
        keyboard_loop(void),                /* main keyboard loop        */
        get_today(void),                    /* display today's calendar  */
        display_day(long),                  /* display cal for jul date  */
        display_calendars(void),            /* ..full calendars          */
        display_one_calendar(enum box_types,/* ..one calendar block      */
            int, int, int, int),
        display_note(void),                 /* ..note record for date    */
        read_note(void),                    /* read current day's note   */
        write_note(void),                   /* ..then write note         */
        allocate_note(void),                /* allocate a day's note     */
        delete_note(void),                  /* ..or delete one           */
        chain_note(void),                   /* update pointers to record*/
        set_up_screen(void),                /* init screen environment   */
        close_down(void),                   /* close down full screen    */
        color_set(enum select_types),       /* select color palette      */
        draw_box(struct box_coordinates *), /* draw a box                */
       *rec_malloc(int, char),              /* allocate memory           */
        cal_read(long, void *),             /* read a database record    */
        cal_read_x(long),                   /* ..or a deleted record     */
        cal_write(long, void *),            /* write a database record   */
        cal_write_x(long),                  /* ..or a deleted record     */
        find_year(void),                    /* find the year record      */
        find_month(void),                   /* ..and the month record    */
        find_day(void),                     /* ..and the day record      */
        validate_cursor(int *, int *),      /* validate cursor location  */
        validate_date(int *, int *, int *), /* validate/fix up date      */
        interrupt critical_handler(UINT,    /* critical error handler    */
            UINT, UINT, UINT, UINT, UINT,
            UINT, UINT, UINT, UINT, UINT,
            UINT);

int     edit_text(void),                    /* edit text window          */
        trim(char *),                       /* trim extra blanks         */
        leap_year(int),                     /* leap year test            */
        base2greg(long n,                   /* base date to gregorian    */
            int *, int *, int *, int *),
        control_break(void),                /* control break handler     */
        get_key(void);                      /* get any type of key       */

long    new_rec(void *z),                   /* write a new record        */
        greg2base(int, int, int);           /* gregorian to base date    */

FILE    *find_file(char *, char *);         /* find and open a file      */


/* ********************************************************************* *
 *        globals                                                      *
 * ********************************************************************* */

int     rc = 1,                             /* errorlevel return code    */
        full_screen,                        /* full screen mode active   */
        text_fg = WHITE,                    /* default foreground color  */
        text_bg = BLUE,                     /* ..background color         */
```

```
        hdr_fg = YELLOW,                /* header foreground color  */
        hdr_bg = CYAN,                  /* ..background color       */
        max_lines,                      /* screen size              */
        month, day, year,               /* current date             */
        dow,                            /* day of week, 0=Sunday    */
        last_display_y,                 /* row of curr month display*/
        note_line,                      /* length of one text line  */
        note_lines,                     /* ..lines in text box      */
        note_max,                       /* ..total field length     */
        rec_length;                     /* data record length       */

char    *note;                          /* text box field string    */

long    b_day,                          /* current date's base day  */
        last_display,                   /* last calendar displayed  */
        year_offset,                    /* year record offset       */
        month_offset,                   /* ..month record offset    */
        day_offset;                     /* ..day record offset      */

FILE    *fi;                            /* calendar file            */

extern
int     _wscroll = 0;                   /* disable screen scrolling */


/* ********************************************************************** *
 *      structures                                                       *
 * ********************************************************************** */

enum    box_types                       /* line drawing box types   */
        {
        single_line,                    /* single line box          */
        double_line;                    /* double line box          */
        };

enum    select_types                    /* display line types       */
        {
        selected,                       /* highlighted line         */
        unselected,                     /* normal display line      */
        border                          /* border lines             */
        };

struct  header                          /* standard record header   */
        {
        int     len;                    /* record length            */
        char    id;                     /* record identifier        */
        };

struct  super_rec                       /* super record             */
        {
        struct  header s_hdr;           /* record header            */
        long    s_year,                 /* year link field          */
                s_delete;               /* delete link field        */
        int     s_max_del;              /* max len on delete chain  */
        } *super_r;                     /* working record buffer    */

struct  year_rec                        /* year record              */
        {
        struct  header y_hdr;           /* record header            */
        int     y_year;                 /* year number              */
        long    y_fwd,                  /* next year record link    */
                y_months[12];           /* links to month records   */
        } *year_r;                      /* working record buffer    */
```

```
struct  month_rec                             /* month record            */
    {
    struct  header m_hdr;                     /* record header           */
    long    m_day[31];                        /* links to day records    */
    } *month_r;                               /* working record pointer  */

struct  day_rec                               /* day record              */
    {
    struct  header d_hdr;                     /* record header           */
    long    d_bday;                           /* day in base day format  */
    char    d_note[1];                        /* text field              */
    } *day_r;                                 /* working record pointer  */

struct  delete_rec                            /* delete record           */
    {
    struct  header x_hdr;                     /* record header           */
    long    x_fwd;                            /* link to next delete rec */
    } *delete_r;                              /* working record pointer  */

struct  box_characters                        /* box drawing characters  */
    {
    char ul_char,                             /* upper left corner       */
         ur_char,                             /* upper right corner      */
         ll_char,                             /* lower left corner       */
         lr_char,                             /* lower right corner      */
         top_char,                            /* horizontal line         */
         side_char;                           /* vertical line           */
    } box_chars[2] =
        {
        { '\xda', '\xbf', '\xc0', '\xd9',     /* single line box         */
          '\xc4', '\xb3'},
        { '\xc9', '\xbb', '\xc8', '\xbc',     /* double line box         */
          '\xcd', '\xba'}
        };

struct  box_coordinates                       /* box locations and type  */
    {
    char  upper_x, upper_y,                   /* upper left corner       */
          lower_x, lower_y;                   /* lower right corner      */
    enum  box_types box_type;                 /* box type                */
    } text_box =                              /* text box definition     */
        {
        30, 6, 76, 22, single_line
        };

char    day_table[2][12] =                    /* days per month          */
    {
    { 31, 28, 31, 30, 31, 30, 31, 31, 30, 31, 30, 31 }, /* non-leap year*/
    { 31, 29, 31, 30, 31, 30, 31, 31, 30, 31, 30, 31 }  /* leap year    */
    };

char    *month_table[12] =                    /* month's names           */
    { "January",    "February",    "March",
      "April",      "May",         "June",
      "July",       "August",      "September",
      "October",    "November",    "December"
    };

char    *days_table[12] =                     /* day's names             */
    { "Sunday",     "Monday",      "Tuesday",
      "Wednesday",  "Thursday",    "Friday",
      "Saturday"
    };
```

```c
/* ********************************************************************* *
 *      messages and strings                                           *
 * ********************************************************************* */

char    copyright[]     = "CAL 1.00 \xfe Copyright (c) 1992, "
                          "Michael Holmes and Bob Flanders\n"
                          "PC Magazine C Lab Notes \xfe "
                          "Calendar program\n\n",
        bell[]          = "\a",
        bad_width[]     = "Screen must be at least 80 columns wide\n",
        no_memory[]     = "Insufficient memory to continue processing\n",
        create_error[] = "Could not create calendar file\n",
        read_error[]    = "Error reading from calendar file\n",
        write_error[]   = "Error writing to calendar file\n",
        stop_here[]     = "\nStopping at user's request\n",
        day_header[]    = " %s, %s %d, %d",
        header[]        = "%25.25sCAL%25.25s",
        footer[]        = " TAB: toggle modes, ESC: exit ",
        day_headings[] = "%cSu" BAR "Mo" BAR "Tu" BAR "We" BAR "Th" BAR
                          "Fr" BAR "Sa%c",
        done[]          = "CAL completed normally\n";

/* ********************************************************************* *
 *      main()                                                         *
 * ********************************************************************* */

void    main(void)
{

printf(copyright);                          /* display copyright msg   */
initialization();                           /* handle initialization   */

keyboard_loop();                            /* process keyboard commands*/
close_down();                               /* clean up screen and file */

rc = 0;                                     /* clear errorlevel and    */
quit_with(done);                            /* ..return to DOS         */

}

/* ********************************************************************* *
 *      initialization() -- screen and file setup                      *
 * ********************************************************************* */

void    initialization(void)
{
struct  text_info screen;                   /* screen info structure   */

ctrlbrk(control_break);                     /* set up ctrl break handler*/
_dos_setvect(0x24, critical_handler);       /* ..DOS critical handlers  */

gettextinfo(&screen);                       /* get current screen info */
max_lines = screen.screenheight;            /* save maximum lines on scr*/

if (screen.screenwidth < 80)                /* q. less than 80 columns? */
    quit_with(bad_width);                   /* a. yes .. give error/quit*/

if (screen.currmode == BW80 ||              /* q. black and white mode..*/
         screen.currmode == MONO)           /* ..or monochrome mode?    */
```

```
         {
         text_bg = hdr_bg = BLACK;                  /* a. yes .. set up mono..  */
         text_fg = hdr_fg = WHITE;                  /* ..palette for text/hdrs  */
         }

    note_line = (text_box.lower_x -                 /* determine max line..     */
                 text_box.upper_x - 1) ;            /* ..length in text box     */

    note_lines = (text_box.lower_y -                /* determine the number..   */
                  text_box.upper_y - 1) ;           /* ..of lines in text box   */

    note_max = note_line * note_lines;              /* max note length          */

    super_r = rec_malloc(LEN(super_rec), 'S');      /* allocate for super record*/
    year_r = rec_malloc(LEN(year_rec), 'Y');        /* ..year record            */
    month_r = rec_malloc(LEN(month_rec), 'M');      /* ..month record           */
    day_r = rec_malloc(LEN(day_rec) +               /* ..day record             */
                 note_max, 'D');
    delete_r = rec_malloc(LEN(delete_rec), 'X');    /* ..and a delete record    */

    note = day_r->d_note;                           /* set up ptr to note field */

    if (NOT (fi = find_file(CAL_DAT, "r+b")))       /* q. find calendar file?   */
         {                                          /* a. no .. create one      */
         if (NOT (fi = fopen(CAL_DAT, "w+b")))      /* q. create new file ok?   */
             quit_with(create_error, CAL_DAT);      /* a. no .. give error/quit */
          else
             WRITE(0L, super_r);                    /* else .. write super rec  */
         }
     else
         READ(0L, super_r);                         /* else .. read super record*/

    set_up_screen();                                /* set up screen colors     */
    draw_box(&text_box);                            /* draw text box            */

    }



/* ****************************************************************** *
 *       keyboard_loop() -- handle calendar display and movement    *
 * ****************************************************************** */

void    keyboard_loop(void)
{

    get_today();                                    /* display calendar and text*/

    while (1)                                       /* loop 'til user quits     */
         {
         switch (get_key())                         /* handle waiting character */
              {
              case 0:                               /* no key available         */
                  continue;                         /* ..then try again         */

              case UP:                              /* up key                   */
                  display_day(b_day -= 7);          /* ..goto previous week     */
                  break;                            /* ..then wait for next key */

              case DOWN:                            /* down key                 */
                  display_day(b_day += 7);          /* ..goto next week         */
                  break;                            /* ..then wait for next key */
```

```
        case LEFT:                          /* left key              */
            display_day(--b_day);           /* ..goto previous day   */
            break;                          /* ..then wait for next key */

        case RIGHT:                         /* right key             */
            display_day(++b_day);           /* ..goto next day       */
            break;                          /* ..then wait for next key */

        case PAGE_UP:                       /* page up arrow         */
            month--;                        /* ..goto previous month */
            validate_date(&month,           /* validate date         */
                    &day, &year);
            display_day(b_day =             /* display new calendars */
                    greg2base(month,        /* ..by finding a new..  */
                            day, year));    /* ..base date           */
            break;                          /* ..then wait for next key */

        case PAGE_DOWN:                     /* page down arrow       */
            month++;                        /* ..goto next month     */
            validate_date(&month,           /* validate date         */
                    &day, &year);
            display_day(b_day =             /* display new calendars */
                    greg2base(month,        /* ..by finding a new..  */
                            day, year));    /* ..base date           */
            break;                          /* ..then wait for next key */

        case TAB:                           /* tab key               */
            if (edit_text())                /* q. edit and exit?     */
                return;                     /* a. yes .. return to DOS */
            break;                          /* else .. just wait for key*/

        case ESC:                           /* escape key            */
            return;                         /* ..exit gracefully     */

        default:                            /* error case            */
            printf(bell);                   /* ..just ring bell      */
        }
    }
}


/* ********************************************************************* *
 *      get_today() -- read and display today's calendar               *
 * ********************************************************************* */

void    get_today(void)
{
struct  dosdate_t today;                    /* DOS date structure    */


_dos_getdate(&today);                       /* get current date      */
month = (int) today.month;                  /* fill in global variables */
day = (int) today.day;                      /* ..like month, day, and.. */
year = today.year;                          /* ..year                */

display_day(b_day = greg2base(month,        /* display today's calendars*/
        day, year));                        /* ..and any note records */

}
```

```
/* ****************************************************************** *
 *         display_day() -- display a day on the calendar           *
 * ****************************************************************** */

void    display_day(long base_day)
{

base2greg(base_day, &month, &day,          /* get gregorian date      */
          &year, &dow);

display_note();                            /* display a note record   */
display_calendars();                       /* ..and calendar boxes    */

}



/* ****************************************************************** *
 *         display_note() -- display note record                    *
 * ****************************************************************** */

void    display_note(void)
{
int     i;                                 /* work variable           */
char    h_work[60];                        /* window heading work area */

                                           /* display date heading    */
i = text_box.lower_x - text_box.upper_x - 1;/* length of window top side*/
h_work[i] = 0;                             /* null terminate buffer   */
memset(h_work,                             /* preformat to border char */
          box_chars[text_box.box_type].top_char, i);
sprintf(&h_work[2], day_header,            /* format a date string .. */
          days_table[dow],                 /* ..with day of week      */
          month_table[month - 1], day,     /* ..and month, day ..     */
          year);                           /* ..and year              */
h_work[strlen(h_work)] = ' ';              /* fix up heading          */

gotoxy(text_box.upper_x + 1,               /* locate on top border    */
          text_box.upper_y);
cprintf(h_work);                           /* ..and display date string*/

window(text_box.upper_x + 1,               /* define text window      */
          text_box.upper_y + 1,
          text_box.lower_x - 1,
          text_box.lower_y);
gotoxy(1, 1);                              /* locate at top of window  */
read_note();                               /* read day's note from file*/
cprintf("%s", note);                       /* ..and display in window  */
window(1, 1, 80, max_lines);               /* ..redefine full screen  */

}



/* ****************************************************************** *
 *         display_calendars() -- display full calendars            *
 * ****************************************************************** */

void    display_calendars(void)
{
int     m, d, y,                           /* working dates           */
        d_first;                           /* day of week of the first */
long    current_display;                   /* current display request  */
```

```
d_first = (((dow - day + 1) % 7) + 7) % 7;    /* day of week of the first */
current_display = year * 12 + month;          /* key is year and month    */

if (last_display != current_display)          /* q. need to redraw?       */
    {                                         /* a. yes .. new months     */
    gotoxy(B_XPOS, 1);                        /* set up cursor position   */
    m = month - 1;                            /* get to previous month    */
    d = 1;                                    /* ..on the first           */
    y = year;                                 /* ..of this year           */

    validate_date(&m, &d, &y);                /* check for valid date     */

    d = (((d_first -                          /* day of week of the first */
          day_table[leap_year(y)][m - 1])     /* ..in the previous month  */
         % 7) + 7) % 7;

    display_one_calendar(single_line,         /* display previous month.. */
        m, 0, y, d);                          /* ..calendar block         */

    gotoxy(B_XPOS, wherey() + 1);             /* goto next screen line..  */
    last_display_y = wherey();                /* ..and save last position */
    }
 else
    gotoxy(B_XPOS, last_display_y);           /* goto upper left position */

display_one_calendar(double_line,             /* display current month..  */
        month, day, year, d_first);           /* ..in middle calendar blk */

if (last_display != current_display)          /* q. redrawing calendars?  */
    {
    last_display = current_display;           /* a. yes .. note month & yr*/
    m = month + 1;                            /* get to next month        */
    d = 1;                                    /* ..on the first           */
    y = year;                                 /* ..of this year           */

    validate_date(&m, &d, &y);                /* check for valid date     */

    d = (((d_first +                          /* day of week of the first */
          day_table[leap_year(year)][month - 1])  /* of the next month*/
         % 7) + 7) % 7;

    gotoxy(B_XPOS, wherey() + 1);             /* goto next screen line..  */
    display_one_calendar(single_line,         /* ..and display next month */
        m, 0, y, d);

    while (wherey() < 25)                      /* loop thru remaining lines*/
        {
        gotoxy(B_XPOS, wherey() + 1);         /* ..goto next line         */
        cprintf("%22.22s", "");               /* ..and clear that line    */
        }
    }
}


/* ****************************************************************** *
 *       display_one_calendar() -- display one calendar              *
 * ****************************************************************** */

void    display_one_calendar(enum box_types bt, /* box drawing type      */
                        int month,      /* month to display           */
                        int day,        /* day to highlight if not 0*/
                        int year,       /* year of month              */
```

```
                                    int d_first)     /* day of week 1st falls on */
{
int     i, j,                                       /* loop control              */
        x, y,                                       /* calendar base location    */
        d,                                          /* day in month              */
        d_max;                                      /* max day in month          */
char    buf[25],                                    /* month heading string      */
        *mn;                                        /* work pointer              */
struct  box_characters *b;                          /* box drawing characters    */


mn = month_table[month - 1];                        /* month name                */
b = &box_chars[bt];                                 /* point to box characters   */

x = wherex();                                       /* base x location..         */
y = wherey() + 2;                                   /* ..and base y location     */

d = 1 - d_first;                                    /* day of first sq in month  */
d_max = day_table[leap_year(year)]                  /* last day in month         */
        [month - 1];

buf[0] = b->ul_char;                                /* start with corner..       */
memset(&buf[1], b->top_char, B_WIDTH);              /* ..clear to line character */
buf[B_WIDTH + 1] = b->ur_char;                      /* ..end with corner         */
buf[B_WIDTH + 2] = 0;                               /* ..then terminate string   */

sprintf(&buf[(B_WIDTH - strlen(mn) - 5) / 2],       /* format the month/year     */
        " %s %d", mn, year);                        /* ..into the middle         */
buf[strlen(buf)] = ' ';                             /* ..of the string           */
cprintf(buf);                                       /* ..then put it out         */

gotoxy(x, y - 1);                                   /* get to day headings area  */
cprintf(day_headings,                               /* ..and put out headings    */
        b->side_char, b->side_char);                /* ..for the days of week    */

for (i = 0; d <= d_max; i++)                        /* for each week in month..  */
    {
    gotoxy(x, y + i);                               /* set up at start of week   */
    cprintf("%c", b->side_char);                    /* put out box edge..        */

    for (j = 0; j < 7; j++, d++)                    /* for each day in week..    */

        {
        if (day && d == day)                        /* q. special day?           */
            {
            color_set(selected);                    /* a. yes .. special colors  */
            cprintf("%2d", d);                      /* ..to display the day      */
            color_set(unselected);                  /* ..then back to normal     */
            }
        else
            {
            if (d < 1 || d > d_max)                 /* q. day in this month?     */
                cprintf("  ");                      /* a. no .. put out blanks    */
            else
                cprintf("%2d", d);                  /* else .. format day        */
            }

        if (j != 6)                                 /* q. at end of week?        */
            cprintf("\xb3");                        /* a. no .. put out divider  */
        }

    cprintf("%c", b->side_char);                    /* put out other box edge..  */
    }
```

```c
buf[0] = b->ll_char;                    /* start with corner..        */
memset(&buf[1], b->top_char, B_WIDTH);  /* ..clear to line character*/
buf[B_WIDTH + 1] = b->lr_char;          /* ..end with corner          */
buf[B_WIDTH + 2] = 0;                    /* ..then terminate string    */

gotoxy(x, y + i);                       /* set up at start of line    */
cprintf(buf);                           /* ..and put out box bottom   */

}


/* ********************************************************************* *
 *       edit_text() -- edit text window                               *
 * ********************************************************************* */

int     edit_text(void)
{
int     x, y,                           /* current positioning        */
        key;                            /* key character              */
char    *p;                             /* character work pointer      */

window(text_box.upper_x + 1,            /* define text window          */
        text_box.upper_y + 1,
        text_box.lower_x - 1,
        text_box.lower_y);

gotoxy(x = 1, y = 1);                   /* locate at top of window    */

while (1)                               /* loop 'til user quits       */
    {
    switch (key = get_key())            /* handle waiting character   */
        {
        case 0:                         /* no key available           */
            continue;                   /* ..then try again           */

        case LEFT:                      /* left key                   */
            x--;                        /* move left one space        */
            break;                      /* ..then set up cursor       */

        case RIGHT:                     /* right key                  */
            x++;                        /* move right one space       */
            break;                      /* ..then set up cursor       */

        case UP:                        /* up key                     */
            y--;                        /* move up one line           */
            break;                      /* ..then set up cursor       */

        case DOWN:                      /* down key                   */
            y++;                        /* move down one line         */
            break;                      /* ..then set up cursor       */

        case TAB:                       /* tab key                    */
            write_note();               /* write note back to file    */
            window(1, 1, 80, max_lines);/* ..redefine window..        */
            return(0);                  /* ..and goto calendar mode   */

        case CR:                        /* carriage return            */
            x = 1;                      /* start from left margin..   */
            y++;                        /* ..on the next line         */
            break;                      /* ..then set up cursor       */

        case ESC:                       /* escape key                 */
            write_note();               /* write note back to file    */
```

```
            return(1);                          /* ..exit back to DOS      */

        case BACKSPACE:                          /* backspace               */
            if (x == 1 && y == 1)                /* q. at top of window?    */
                {
                printf(bell);                    /* a. yes .. give warning  */
                break;                           /* ..and wait for another.. */
                }

            x--;                                 /* move left one character  */
            validate_cursor(&x, &y);             /* verify cursor parameters */

            strcpy(p = &note[(y - 1) *           /* copy from next position  */
                    note_line + x - 1],          /* ..to current position    */
                    &note[(y - 1) *
                    note_line + x]);

            note[note_max - 1] = ' ';            /* put a blank at very end  */

            gotoxy(x, y);                        /* locate cursor in window  */
            cprintf("%s", p);                    /* display to end of window */
            break;                               /* ..and wait for next key  */

        default:                                 /* error case               */
            if (key & 0xff00 ||                  /* q. function key..        */
                    key < ' ')                   /* ..or less than a blank?  */
                {
                printf(bell);                    /* a. yes .. just ring bell */
                break;                           /* ..and get next key       */
                }

            note[(y - 1) * note_line +           /* save character in string */
                    x - 1] = (char) key;
            cprintf("%c", key);                  /* ..and display in field   */

            x++;                                 /* move right one space..   */
            break;                               /* ..then get next key      */
        }

    validate_cursor(&x, &y);                     /* check cursor..           */
    gotoxy(x, y);                                /* ..then go there          */

    }
}


/* ********************************************************************* *
 *      read_note() -- read text note for current day                  *
 * ********************************************************************* */

void    read_note(void)
{

day_offset = 0L;                                 /* show record not found    */
memset(note, ' ', note_max);                     /* clear buffer to blanks   */

find_day();                                      /* try to find a day record */

note[strlen(note)] = ' ';                        /* open up string to..      */
note[note_max] = '\0';                           /* ..the end of the window  */

}
```

```
/* ******************************************************************* *
 *      write_note() -- write text note for current day              *
 * ******************************************************************* */

void    write_note(void)
{
int     rec_len;                            /* record length          */

if (NOT (rec_len = trim(note)))             /* q. trim'd string empty? */
    {                                       /* a. yes .. delete record */
    if (day_offset)                         /* q. record in database?  */
        {
        delete_note();                      /* a. yes .. delete it and..*/
        day_offset = 0L;                    /* ..clear record offset and*/
        chain_note();                       /* ..update year/month recs */
        }

    return;                                 /* ..finally return        */
    }

rec_len += LEN(day_rec);                     /* complete record size   */
day_r->d_bday = b_day;                      /* ..and stow base day     */

if (NOT day_offset)                         /* q. new record needed?   */
    {                                       /* a. yes .. build new one */
    day_r->d_hdr.len = rec_len;             /* save size in record     */
    allocate_note();                        /* ..allocate file space   */
    }
 else
    {
    if (rec_len > day_r->d_hdr.len)         /* q. old record too small? */
        {
        delete_note();                      /* a. yes .. delete old    */
        day_r->d_hdr.len = rec_len;         /* save size in record     */
        allocate_note();                    /* ..and get a new record  */
        }
     else
        WRITE(day_offset, day_r);           /* update record in file   */
    }

chain_note();                               /* update year & month ptrs */

}


/* ******************************************************************* *
 *      cal_read() -- read a database record                         *
 * ******************************************************************* */

void    cal_read(long offset,                /* file offset            */
                void *r)                    /* record                  */
{
int     rl;                                 /* remaining length to read */

fseek(fi, offset, SEEK_SET);                /* seek to requested place  */

if (fread(r, 2, 1, fi) != 1)                /* q. read record length?  */
    quit_with(read_error);                  /* a. no .. give error/quit */
```

```
    rl = *(int *) r - 2;                        /* get remaining length    */
    r = (char *) r + 2;                         /* point at next portion.. */

    if (fread(r, rl, 1, fi) != 1)               /* q. read remaining record?*/
        quit_with(read_error);                  /* a. no .. give error/quit */

    }


/* ******************************************************************** *
 *      cal_read_x() -- read a deleted record from the database         *
 * ******************************************************************** */

void    cal_read_x(long offset)                 /* file offset             */
{


    fseek(fi, offset, SEEK_SET);                /* seek to requested place */

    if (NOT (fread((void *) delete_r,           /* q. read anything..      */
            LEN(delete_rec), 1, fi)))           /* ..interesting?          */
        quit_with(read_error);                  /* a. no .. give error/quit */

    }



/* ******************************************************************** *
 *      cal_write() -- write a database record                          *
 * ******************************************************************** */

void    cal_write(long offset,                  /* file offset             */
                void *r)                        /* record buffer           */
{

    fseek(fi, offset, SEEK_SET);                /* seek to requested place */

    if (fwrite(r, ((struct header *) r)->len,   /* q. write successful..   */
            1, fi) != 1)                        /* ..for whole record?     */
        quit_with(write_error);                 /* a. no .. give error/quit */

    }



/* ******************************************************************** *
 *      cal_write_x() -- write a deleted record to the database         *
 * ******************************************************************** */

void    cal_write_x(long offset)                /* file offset             */
{


    fseek(fi, offset, SEEK_SET);                /* seek to requested place */

    if (NOT (fwrite((void *) delete_r,          /* q. write go ok?         */
            LEN(delete_rec), 1, fi)))           /* a. no .. give error/quit */
        quit_with(read_error);

    }
```

```
/* ********************************************************************* *
 *         chain_note() -- check links thru database for current day     *
 * ********************************************************************* */

void    chain_note(void)
{

find_year();                                /* find/alloc the year rec  */
find_month();                               /* ..and the month record   */

if (month_r->m_day[day - 1] != day_offset)  /* q. month points to us?   */
    {
    month_r->m_day[day - 1] = day_offset;   /* a. no .. but, now it does*/
    WRITE(month_offset, month_r);           /* ..then write it back ..   */
    }
}


/* ********************************************************************* *
 *       find_year() -- find or allocate a year record                   *
 * ********************************************************************* */

void    find_year(void)
{
long    p = 0,                              /* offset of prev year rec  */
        y;                                  /* offset of year record    */

if (year == year_r->y_year)                 /* q. right year in memory? */
    return;                                 /* a. yes .. rtn to caller  */

month_offset = 0;                           /* show new month rec needed*/

if ((y = super_r->s_year) != 0)             /* q. first record?          */
    {
    for (; y; p = y, y = year_r->y_fwd)     /* walk down year chain..    */
        {                                   /* ..highest years first     */
        READ(y, year_r);                    /* get a year record         */

        if (year_r->y_year == year)         /* q. current year?          */
            return;                         /* a. yes .. rtn to caller   */

        if (year > year_r->y_year)          /* q. need new record here?  */
            {                               /* a. yes .. insert one      */
            year_r->y_year = year;          /* save current year         */
            year_r->y_fwd = y;              /* ..next record pointer     */
            CLEAR(year_r->y_months);        /* clear month array         */
            year_offset = new_rec(year_r);  /* ..and allocate a record   */

            if (NOT p)                      /* q. new first record?      */
                {                           /* a. yes .. build a one     */
                super_r->s_year =           /* save new record address..*/
                        year_offset;        /* ..in super record         */
                WRITE(0L, super_r);         /* ..and update super record*/
                }
            else
                {
                READ(p, year_r);            /* read previous record      */
                year_r->y_fwd = year_offset;/* previous record points    */
                WRITE(p, year_r);           /* write prev record back    */

                READ(year_offset, year_r);  /* ..reread current record   */
```

```
                }
            return;                             /* return, we're done here  */
                }
            }
        }

    year_r->y_year = year;                      /* save current year        */
    year_r->y_fwd = y;                          /* ..next record pointer    */
    CLEAR(year_r->y_months);                    /* clear month array        */
    year_offset = new_rec(year_r);              /* ..and allocate a record  */

    if (p)                                      /* q. previous record avail?*/
        {                                       /* a. yes .. chain it to us */
        READ(p, year_r);                        /* read in old last record  */
        year_r->y_fwd = year_offset;            /* previous record points   */
        WRITE(p, year_r);                       /* write prev record back   */

        READ(year_offset, year_r);              /* ..reread current record  */
        }
    else
        {
        super_r->s_year = year_offset;          /* else .. set up super rec */
        WRITE(0L, super_r);                     /* ..and update database    */
        }
    }


/* ********************************************************************* *
 *      find_month() -- find or allocate a month record                *
 * ********************************************************************* */

void    find_month(void)
{
long    m;                                      /* offset of month record   */

if ((m = year_r->y_months[month - 1]) != 0      /* q. month offset valid..  */
            && m == month_offset)               /* ..and in memory?         */
        return;                                 /* a. yes .. just return    */

if (m)                                          /* q. record available?     */
    {                                           /* a. yes .. read it in      */
    READ(m, month_r);                           /* ..save month's offset    */
    month_offset = m;                           /* ..save month's offset    */
    month_r->m_day[day - 1] = day_offset;       /* store in day's offset    */
    WRITE(m, month_r);                          /* rewrite month record     */
    }
else
    {
    CLEAR(month_r->m_day);                      /* clear day array          */
    month_r->m_day[day - 1] = day_offset;       /* store in day's offset    */
    month_offset =                              /* save record offset ..    */
            year_r->y_months[month - 1] =       /* ..and in year record     */
            new_rec(month_r);                   /* ..for new record         */
    WRITE(year_offset, year_r);                 /* update year record       */
    }
}
```

```
/* ********************************************************************* *
 *        find_day() -- find a day record                               *
 * ********************************************************************* */

void    find_day(void)
{
long    r;                                  /* record address            */

if (year != year_r->y_year)                 /* q. right year in memory? */
    {                                       /* a. no .. find year rec    */
    r = (year < year_r->y_year) ?           /* choose a starting point   */
            year_r->y_fwd : super_r->s_year;/* ..for the year rec search*/

    year_offset = 0;                        /* clear year record offset */

    if (NOT r)                              /* q. year unavailable?     */
        {                                   /* a. yes .. clean up by..  */
        month_offset = day_offset = Ø;      /* ..clearing record offsets*/
        return;                             /* ..and returning to caller*/
        }

    for (; r; r = year_r->y_fwd)            /* walk down year chain..    */
        {
        READ(r, year_r);                    /* read a year record        */

        if (year == year_r->y_year)         /* q. find year record?      */
            {
            year_offset = r;                /* a. yes .. save offset     */
            break;                          /* ..and exit loop           */
            }
          else if (year < year_r->y_year)   /* q. needed year unavail?   */
            {                               /* a. yes .. clean up by..   */
            month_offset = day_offset = 0;  /* ..clearing record offsets*/
            return;                         /* ..and returning to caller*/
            }
        }
    }

if ((r = year_r->y_months[month - 1]) != 0) /* q. month rec available?   */
    {                                       /* a. yes .. check further   */
    if (r != month_offset)                  /* q. already in memory?     */
        {
        READ(r, month_r);                   /* a. no .. read month rec   */
        month_offset = r;                   /* ..and save record offset */
        }

    if ((r = month_r->m_day[day - 1]) != 0) /* q. day record available? */
        {                                   /* a. yes .. check some more*/
        if (r != day_offset)                /* q. already have this one?*/
            {
            READ(r, day_r);                 /* a. no .. read day record */
            day_offset = r;                 /* ..and save record offset */
            }
        }
      else
        day_offset = 0;                     /* clear day record offset   */
    }
  else
    month_offset = day_offset = 0;          /* clear record offsets      */
}
```

```
/* ********************************************************************* *
 *        new_rec() -- write a new record                                *
 * ********************************************************************* */
long     new_rec(void *z)                       /* record to write         */
{
long     record_start;                          /* starting offset of record*/

fseek(fi, 0L, SEEK_END);                        /* position at end of file  */
record_start = ftell(fi);                       /* save record's seek offset*/
WRITE(record_start, z);                         /* write the new record     */
return(record_start);                           /* ..and return its offset  */

}



/* ********************************************************************* *
 *      allocate_note() -- allocate and write a day record to database   *
 * ********************************************************************* */
void     allocate_note(void)
{
int      ll = 0;                                /* last and largest found   */
long     d,                                     /* delete chain pointer     */
         p = 0;                                 /* previous record offset   */

if (super_r->s_max_del >= day_r->d_hdr.len)     /* q. any big deletes?      */
    {                                           /* a. yes .. find one       */
    for (d = super_r->s_delete; d;              /* walk delete chain to find*/
            p = d, d = delete_r->x_fwd,         /* ..a big enough record    */
            ll = delete_r->x_hdr.len)
        {
        cal_read_x(d);                          /* get a deleted record     */

        if (delete_r->x_hdr.len >=              /* q. was this record big.. */
                day_r->d_hdr.len)               /* ..enough to handle it?   */
            break;                              /* a. yes .. exit loop      */
        }

    day_offset = d;                             /* save new record's offset */
    day_r->d_hdr.len = delete_r->x_hdr.len;     /* ..and length             */

    if (p)                                      /* q. previous record avail?*/
        {                                       /* a. yes .. unchain record */
        d = delete_r->x_fwd;                    /* ..and prev's new fwd ptr */
        cal_read_x(p);                          /* read in previous delete  */
        delete_r->x_fwd = d;                    /* ..and store new fwd link */
        cal_write_x(p);                         /* ..then write back        */
        }
      else
        {
        super_r->s_delete = delete_r->x_fwd;/* make next record be head */
        WRITE(0L, super_r);                     /* ..and rewrite super rec  */
        }

    if (NOT delete_r->x_fwd)                     /* q. just used the biggest?*/
        {
        super_r->s_max_del = ll;                /* a. yes .. save largest   */
        WRITE(0L, super_r);                     /* ..and rewrite super rec  */
        }
    }
else
```

```
    }
    {
    fseek(fi, 0L, SEEK_END);              /* position at end of file  */
    day_offset = ftell(fi);               /* save record's seek offset*/
    }

WRITE(day_offset, day_r);                 /* write record to database */


}


/* *********************************************************************** *
 *      delete_note() -- delete text note for current day                 *
 * *********************************************************************** */

void    delete_note(void)
{
long    d,                                /* delete chain pointer       */
        p = 0;                            /* previous record offset     */

if (super_r->s_delete)                    /* q. any previous deletes? */
    {                                     /* a. yes .. insert by size */
    for (d = super_r->s_delete; d;        /* walk delete chain to find*/
            p = d, d = delete_r->x_fwd)   /* ..the right place in list*/
        {
        cal_read_x(d);                    /* get a deleted record     */

        if (delete_r->x_hdr.len <         /* q. should a new record.. */
                day_r->d_hdr.len)         /* ..be inserted?           */
            {                             /* a. yes .. insert one here*/
            if (NOT p)                    /* q. new first record?     */
                {
                delete_r->x_fwd = d;      /* a. yes .. new rec points */
                                          /* ..at old first record    */
                delete_r->x_hdr.len =     /* set up new record's ..    */
                        day_r->d_hdr.len; /* ..length in delete record*/
                cal_write_x(day_offset);  /* ..then write to database  */

                super_r->s_delete =       /* set up super record..     */
                        day_offset;       /* ..with new record         */
                WRITE(0L, super_r);       /* ..and update database      */
                }
            else
                {
                delete_r->x_hdr.len =     /* set up new record's ..    */
                        day_r->d_hdr.len; /* ..length in delete record*/
                delete_r->x_fwd = d;      /* set up next pointer link  */
                cal_write_x(day_offset);  /* ..then write to database  */

                cal_read_x(p);            /* read previous record      */
                delete_r->x_fwd =         /* previous record points    */
                        day_offset;       /* ..to the new record       */
                cal_write_x(p);           /* write prev record back     */
                }

            return;                       /* ..and return, we're done */
            }
        }
    }

delete_r->x_hdr.len =                     /* set up new record's ..    */
        super_r->s_max_del =              /* ..and super record's      */
        day_r->d_hdr.len;                 /* ..length of delete        */
```

```
    delete_r->x_fwd = 0L;                       /* ..show end of chain        */
    cal_write_x(day_offset);                    /* ..and write to database    */

    if (p)                                      /* q. previous record avail?*/
        {                                       /* a. yes .. chain it to us  */
        cal_read_x(p);                          /* read in old last record   */
        delete_r->x_fwd = day_offset;           /* set up next pointer        */
        cal_write_x(p);                         /* ..and rewrite to file      */
        }
    else
        super_r->s_delete = day_offset;         /* chain from super record    */

    WRITE(0L, super_r);                         /* update super record        */

    }




/* ********************************************************************** *
 *         draw_box() -- draw a box                                       *
 * ********************************************************************** */

void    draw_box(struct box_coordinates *p) /* box location and type      */
{
int     i;                                      /* loop control               */
struct  box_characters *b;                      /* box characters             */


b = &box_chars[p->box_type];                    /* get line drawing group     */

                                                /* draw top of box            */
gotoxy(p->upper_x, p->upper_y);                 /* goto upper left corner     */
DRAW(b->ul_char);                               /* put out first corner       */

for (i = p->upper_x + 1;                        /* build top of box..         */
        i < p->lower_x; i++)
    DRAW(b->top_char);                          /* ..with horizontals         */

DRAW(b->ur_char);                               /* ..and upper right corner   */

                                                /* draw bottom of box         */
gotoxy(p->upper_x, p->lower_y);                 /* goto lower left corner     */
DRAW(b->ll_char);                               /* put out bottom corner      */

for (i = p->upper_x + 1;                        /* build bottom of box        */
        i < p->lower_x; i++)
    DRAW(b->top_char);                          /* ..with horizontals         */

DRAW(b->lr_char);                               /* ..and lower right corner   */

                                                /* draw left side of box      */
for (i = p->upper_y + 1;                        /* put out side characters    */
        i < p->lower_y; i++)
    {
    gotoxy(p->upper_x, i);                      /* jump to a place on the..   */
    DRAW(b->side_char);                         /* ..line and draw a chunk    */
    }

                                                /* draw right side of box     */
for (i = p->upper_y + 1;                        /* put out side characters    */
        i < p->lower_y; i++)
    {
    gotoxy(p->lower_x, i);                      /* jump to a place on the..   */
```

```
            DRAW(b->side_char);                         /* ..right side and draw     */
        }
    }




    /* ****************************************************************** *
     *      set_up_screen() -- set up screen, headers and footers        *
     * ****************************************************************** */

    void    set_up_screen(void)
    {

    full_screen = 1;                                    /* set up full screen flag   */

    window(1, 1, 80, max_lines);                        /* define window coordinates*/
    color_set(unselected);                              /* set up standard colors    */
    clrscr();                                           /* clear screen              */

    color_set(border);                                  /* set up border colors      */
    gotoxy(28, 1);                                      /* position at top right     */
    cprintf(header, "", "");                            /* ..display header          */

    gotoxy(82 - sizeof(footer), max_lines);             /* position at bottom right  */
    cprintf(footer);                                    /* ..and display footer      */

    _wscroll = 1;                                       /* enable text scrolling     */
    color_set(unselected);                              /* set up standard colors    */

    }




    /* ****************************************************************** *
     *      color_set() -- select current foreground and background colors *
     * ****************************************************************** */

    void    color_set(enum select_types s_flag)  /* selected/unselected       */
    {


    switch (s_flag)                                     /* based on flag ..          */
        {
        case selected:                                  /* selected line             */
            textcolor(text_bg);                         /* set up the inverted..     */
            textbackground(text_fg);                    /* ..color scheme            */
            break;                                      /* ..then continue           */

        case unselected:                                /* unselected line           */
            textcolor(text_fg);                         /* set up the normal..       */
            textbackground(text_bg);                    /* ..color scheme            */
            break;                                      /* ..then continue           */

        case border:                                    /* border lines              */
            textcolor(hdr_fg);                          /* set up the border..       */
            textbackground(hdr_bg);                     /* ..color scheme            */
            break;                                      /* ..then continue           */
        }

    }
```

```
/* ********************************************************************** *
 *          close_down() -- close windows and quit to DOS               *
 * ********************************************************************** */
void    close_down(void)
{

window(1, 1, 80, max_lines);            /* define full screen window*/
color_set(unselected);                  /* set up normal colors     */
clrscr();                               /* clear screen             */
full_screen = 0;                        /* ..and full screen flag   */
printf(copyright);                      /* redisplay program banner */

if (fi)                                 /* q. data file open?       */
    fclose(fi);                         /* a. yes .. close file     */

}



/* ********************************************************************** *
 *          trim() -- trim trailing blanks from a string                *
 * ********************************************************************** */
int     trim(char *s)                   /* source and target string */
{
int     i;                              /* string length            */

i = strlen(s);                          /* get current length       */
s = &s[i - 1];                          /* ..and last char of string*/

for (; i; s--, i--)                     /* do until string exhausted*/
    if (*s != ' ')                      /* q. find a nonblank?      */
        {
        *++s = '\0';                    /* a. yes .. put in new null*/
        break;                          /* ..and exit loop          */
        }

return(i);                              /* return with new length   */

}



/* ********************************************************************** *
 *          get_key() -- get a key (including function keys)            *
 * ********************************************************************** */
int     get_key(void)
{
int     k = 0;                          /* local key variable       */

if (kbhit())                            /* q. key available?        */
    {                                   /* a. yes .. process it      */
    if (NOT (k = getch()))              /* q. function key?          */
        k = 0x100 + getch();            /* a. yes .. special key     */
    }

return(k);                              /* return w/key if available*/

}
```

```
/* ****************************************************************** *
 *        greg2base() -- convert from month/day/year to base date    *
 * ****************************************************************** */

long    greg2base(int month,                /* month               */
                  int day,                  /* day                 */
                  int year)                 /* year                */
{


if (month > 2)                              /* q. past Feb?        */
    month -= 3;                             /* a. yes .. fix base month */

 else                                                                
    {
    month += 9;                             /* Jan & Feb goto the end.. */
    year -= 1;                              /* ..of the previous year   */
    }
return(((146097L * (year / 100)) / 4) +     /* days thru to this century*/
       ((1461L * (year % 100)) / 4) +       /* ..and days this century  */
       ((153 * month + 2) / 5) +            /* ..days thru this month   */
       day);                                /* ..days this month        */


}


/* ****************************************************************** *
 *        base2greg() -- convert from base date to month/day/year    *
 * ****************************************************************** */

int     base2greg(long  n,                  /* base date           */
                  int   *m,                 /* month..             */
                  int   *d,                 /* ..day               */
                  int   *y,                 /* ..year with century */
                  int   *dow)               /* day of week, 0=Sunday */
{
long    dd;                                 /* work variable       */
int     doy,                                /* day of year         */
        f;                                  /* leap year flag      */


*dow = (int) ((n - 5) % 7);                 /* compute day of week     */

*y = (UINT) ((4 * n - 1) / 146097L);        /* get century number      */
n = 4 * n - 1 - (146097L * *y);             /* ..remove that many days */
dd = n / 4;                                 /* get to the year         */
n = (4 * dd + 3) / 1461;                    /* ..within the century    */
*y = (UINT) (100 * *y + n);                 /* ..then year with century */
dd = 4 * dd + 3 - 1461 * n;                 /* get to days within 4 yrs */
f = ((dd % 4) == 3) ? 1 : 0;                /* set leap year flag      */
dd = (dd + 4) / 4;                          /* get days within base yr */
*m = (int) ((5 * dd - 3) / 153);            /* get month               */
doy = (int) (dd + 59 + f);                  /* get day in calendar year */
dd = 5 * dd - 3 - (153 * *m);               /* get to the day ..       */
*d = (int) ((dd + 5) / 5);                  /* ..within the month      */

if( *m < 10)                                /* q. need to adjust month? */
    *m += 3;                                /* a. yes .. normalize nbr  */

 else
```

```
         {
         *m -= 9;                                /* adjust for March base    */
         (*y)++;                                 /* ..date and fix year too  */
         doy %= (365 + f);                       /* ..and day in year        */
         }

     return(doy);                                /* and return w/day of year */

     }


/* ************************************************************************** *
 *       validate_date() -- validate/fix up date                            *
 * ************************************************************************** */

void    validate_date(int *month,               /* month from 0 to 13       */
                      int *day,                  /* day from 1 to 31         */
                      int *year)                 /* year                     */
{

if (*month == 0)                                 /* q. before January?       */
      {                                          /* a. yes .. backup into Dec*/
      *month = 12;                               /* set up in December       */
      (*year)--;                                 /* ..in previous year       */
      }
 else if (*month == 13)                          /* q. after December?       */
      {                                          /* a. yes .. move up to Jan */
      *month = 1;                                /* set up in January        */
      (*year)++;                                 /* ..in the next year       */
      }

*day = min(*day,                                 /* check for valid day      */
          day_table[leap_year(*year)][*month - 1]);

}



/* ************************************************************************** *
 *       leap_year() -- test for a leap year                                *
 * ************************************************************************** */

int     leap_year(int year)                      /* year to check            */
{

return(((year % 4 == 0) &&                       /* if divisible by 4..      */
        (year % 100 != 0) ||                     /* ..and not by 100..       */
        (year % 400 == 0)) ? 1 : 0);             /* ..or divisible by 400..  */
                                                 /* then return 1 else 0     */

}


/* ************************************************************************** *
 *       rec_malloc() -- allocate memory, handling error conditions         *
 * ************************************************************************** */

void    *rec_malloc(int n,                       /* amt of memory to malloc  */
                    char c)                      /* id field character       */
{
struct  header *p;                               /* any type of record ptr   */

if (NOT (p = (struct header *) malloc(n)))       /* q. memory available?     */
```

```
        quit_with(no_memory);                /* a. no .. give error/quit */

memset((char *) p, 0, n);                    /* clear block to nulls     */
p->len = n;                                  /* set up length of record  */
p->id = c;                                   /* ..and id field           */

return((void *) p);                          /* return to caller w/addr  */

}


/* **************************************************************** *
 *      validate_cursor() -- check if valid cursor position         *
 * **************************************************************** */

void    validate_cursor(int *x,              /* new x location ..        */
                        int *y)              /* ..and new y location     */
{

if (*x == 0)                                 /* q. at left border?       */
    {
    *x = note_line;                          /* a. yes .. goto right side*/
    (*y)--;                                  /* ..then fake an up key     */
    }

if (*y == 0)                                 /* q. at top border?        */
    *y = note_lines;                         /* a. yes .. goto bottom    */

if (*x > note_line)                          /* q. at right border?      */
    {
    *x = 1;                                  /* a. yes .. goto left side */
    (*y)++;                                  /* ..and fake a down key     */
    }

if (*y > note_lines)                         /* q. at bottom border?     */
    *y = 1;                                  /* a. yes .. goto top       */

}


/* **************************************************************** *
 *      find_file() -- find and open a file                         *
 * **************************************************************** */

FILE    *find_file(char *s,                  /* file name to find        */
                char *mode)                  /* mode to open file in     */
{
char    *path, *m_path,                      /* path environment string  */
        buf[MAX_PATH];                       /* path/filename buffer     */
FILE    *fi = 0;                             /* input file handle        */

if ((fi = fopen(s, mode)) != 0)              /* q. find file?            */
    return(fi);                              /* a. yes .. return w/handle*/

if (NOT (m_path = getenv("PATH")))           /* q. find path variable    */
    return(0);                               /* a. no .. return w/o file */

path = m_path = strdup(m_path);              /* get a copy of the string */

for (; (path = strtok(path, ";")) != 0;      /* using each path segment..*/
```

```
            path = 0)                        /* ..of the path variable   */
        {
        sprintf(buf, "%s%s%s", path,         /* build a filename from     */
                LAST(path) == '\\' ? "" : "\\",  /* ..each path subdirectory */
                s);                          /* ..and base filename       */

        if ((fi = fopen(buf, mode)) != 0)    /* q. find file?             */
            break;                           /* a. yes .. exit loop       */
        }
    free(m_path);                            /* free copy of path string  */
    return(fi);                              /* finally return w/handle   */

    }


/* ********************************************************************** *
 *      quit_with() -- give an error message, then return to DOS        *
 * ********************************************************************** */

void    quit_with(char *msg, ...)            /* string to print           */
{
va_list list;                                /* variable list             */

if (full_screen)                             /* q. full screen mode?      */
    close_down();                            /* a. yes .. clear screen    */

va_start(list, msg);                         /* set up variable list      */
vprintf(msg, list);                          /* give error message ..     */
exit(rc);                                    /* ..and then quit           */

}


/* ********************************************************************** *
 *      control_break() -- control break intercept routine              *
 * ********************************************************************** */

int     control_break(void)
{


quit_with(stop_here);                        /* give error msg and quit   */
return(0);                                   /* ..and abort processing    */

}


/* ********************************************************************** *
 *      critical_handler() -- DOS critical error handler                *
 * ********************************************************************** */

#pragma argsused                             /* hold unused argument messages */
#pragma option -O2-b-e                       /* no global register allocation */
                                             /* ..or dead code elimination    */

void    interrupt critical_handler(UINT bp,
            UINT di, UINT si, UINT ds, UINT es,
            UINT dx, UINT cx, UINT bx, UINT ax,
            UINT cs, UINT ip, UINT flags)
```

```
{

if (ax & 0x800)                    /* q. fail allowed?        */
    ax = (ax & 0xff00) | 3;        /* a. yes .. fail request  */
else
    ax = (ax & 0xff00) | 2;        /* else .. abort request   */

}
```

APPENDIX

THE ACCOMPANYING DISK

At the back of the book, you will find a 360k, 5¹/₄-inch floppy disk that contains two files: CLABNOTE.EXE and INSTALL.EXE. CLABNOTE.EXE is a self-extracting .ZIP file containing the source and executable files for all of the utilities presented in this book. If you are not familiar with using a self-extracting .ZIP file, INSTALL.EXE is an interactive program that lets you select where the source and executable files are installed.

If you want to exchange the 5¹/₄-inch disk for a 3¹/₂-inch disk, see the disk exchange offer at the back of the book.

■ INSTALLING THE DISK

INSTALL is very easy to use. To start INSTALL, simply place the disk in a drive, and type the command ***d*:INSTALL** on the command line, where *d* represents the letter of the drive containing the disk. INSTALL does not accept any command line arguments, and if you enter any on the command line, INSTALL ignores them.

Once started, INSTALL displays the screen shown in Figure A.1. As shown, there are two fields that you may modify—source and destination. In the source field, you must enter the letter of the drive containing the CLABNOTE.EXE program. If you are running DOS version 3.0 or higher, the source field will be initialized to the drive from which you executed INSTALL.

In the destination field, enter the destination directory for the executable and source files. INSTALL always starts with the destination field set to C:\CLABNOTE. If you enter a directory that does not exist, INSTALL will create it for you, even if multiple levels of directories must be created. For example, if you enter C:\ZDP\CLABNOTE in the destination field, and the directory ZDP does not already exist, INSTALL will create both the ZDP and the CLABNOTE directories.

```
INSTALL 1.00 ■ Copyright (c) 1992, Bob Flanders and Michael Holmes
PC Magazine C Lab Notes ■ Install program


        INSTALL expands and places the contents of the PC Magazine C Lab
        Notes diskette into the destination directory of your choice.
        You should fill in the source with the drive containing the
        diskette from the book.  The destination should be a drive and
        directory where the source and executables will be stored.




              Source: ▯
         Destination: C:\CLABNOTE




                                              ESC: exit  F10: install
```

Since it is likely that INSTALL knows which drive is the source, INSTALL starts by placing the cursor on the first character of the destination field. (Any characters you enter overwrite any characters already in the field. Although the Delete and Insert keys are not honored by INSTALL, you can delete characters by using the Backspace key.) At this point, you have several options: You can move within the field, move between fields, modify a field, start the installation, or exit without installing.

The Left Arrow and Right Arrow keys move the cursor within the current field. When you reach the rightmost position within that field, the cursor will not move beyond that position.

There are several ways to move between fields. You can press the Up Arrow, Down Arrow, Tab, or Enter key. In every case, INSTALL moves the cursor to the first position of the other field.

To start the actual install, press F10. INSTALL starts by determining if the requested destination directory exists, creating it if necessary. Then INSTALL invokes the CLABNOTE.EXE program to install the executable files in the destination directory. CLABNOTE also creates two subdirectories beneath the destination directory: BC and MSC. The BC directory contains the Borland C++ 3.0 compatible source (as well as two additional files, described below); the MSC directory contains the Microsoft C/C++ 7.0 compatible source. (The executable files were compiled from the Borland C++ source.)

■ COMPILING THE PROGRAMS

In each of the source subdirectories, you will find a file called COMPILE.BAT. To compile a program, simply type

```
COMPILE program-name
```

on the command line, substituting *program-name* with the name of the program to compile. For example, to compile SYNC, you would type COMPILE SYNC. The COMPILE.BAT file selects the appropriate command line options based on the *program-name* argument you enter.

■ THE ADDITIONAL FILES IN THE BC DIRECTORY

In the BC directory, you will also find the two source files, INSTALL.C and DUMPCAL.C.

INSTALL.C contains the source code for the INSTALL program presented in this appendix.

DUMPCAL.C is a debug program that we developed when writing CAL (Chapter 9). DUMPCAL displays the data found in the CAL.DAT file. Like CAL, DUMPCAL looks for CAL.DAT in the current directory; if it is not found there, DUMPCAL looks in the directories named in the DOS PATH environment variable. The executable file for DUMPCAL is also provided. Should you decide to modify the CAL program, you may find DUMPCAL helpful when deciphering CAL.DAT's contents.

INDEX

Numbers in boldface type indicate figures or tables.

■ TO RECEIVE 3½-INCH DISK(S)

The Ziff-Davis Press software contained on the $5\frac{1}{4}$-inch disk(s) included with this book is also available in $3\frac{1}{2}$-inch (720k) format. If you would like to receive the software in the $3\frac{1}{2}$-inch format, please return the $5\frac{1}{4}$-inch disk(s) with your name and address to:

Disk Exchange
Ziff-Davis Press
5903 Christie Avenue
Emeryville, CA 94608